The Gay, Lesbian, and Bisexual
Students' Guide to Colleges,
Universities, and Graduate Schools

The
Gay, Lesbian, and Bisexual
STUDENTS' GUIDE
to Colleges, Universities,
and Graduate Schools

Jan-Mitchell Sherrill and
Craig A. Hardesty

New York University Press • New York and London

NEW YORK UNIVERSITY PRESS
New York and London

Library of Congress Cataloging-in-Publication Data
Sherrill, Jan-Mitchell.
  The gay, lesbian, and bisexual students' guide to colleges,
universities, and graduate schools / Jan-Mitchell Sherrill
and Craig A. Hardesty.
       p. cm.
    ISBN 0-8147-7984-0 (alk. paper)—ISBN 0-8147-7985-9
(pbk.: alk. paper)
    1. Homosexuality and education—United States.
2. Universities and colleges—Sociological aspects—United
States. 3. Gays—Education (Higher)—United States.
4. Lesbians—Education (Higher)—United States.
5. Bisexuals—Education (Higher)—United States.
I. Hardesty, Craig A. II. Title.
LC192.6.S54 1994
378.1'982664—dc20   93–35460
                              CIP

New York University Press books are printed on acid-free paper,
and their binding materials are chosen for strength and durability.

Manufactured in the United States of America

10   9   8   7   6   5   4   3   2   1

Book design by Kathleen Szawiola

The publication of this book has been made possible in part by a grant from
A Different Light Foundation.

For Violet Sherrill, whose love and support have been wonderful gifts.

—J.M.S

For Karen Glidewell, who simply knows.

—C.A.H

Contents

Preface

The study that has generated this *Guide* has been two years in the making. Many of the problems we encountered in the undertaking of such work we anticipated: How would we actually find the students who could, in fact, evaluate their campuses? How could we convince any publisher that a market for this kind of information exists?

The National Gay and Lesbian Task Force provided mailing labels for those student groups registered with the Task Force, and we are especially grateful to Kevin Berrill for his help in that regard. Unfortunately, even the Task Force's access is limited to those groups who have been lucky enough to be *connected,* plugged in to mainstream political activism. Not all groups, by any means, enjoy that vital linkage.

Because we were committed to reflecting accurately what the students told us, some of the information may seem, at times, contradictory. How could students who wouldn't choose the same college again recommend it to others? How can students who describe their school police as supportive still not feel safe on campus? Are these, at face value, conflicting responses real discrepancies?

The short answer is, no, they're not.

College and university police forces often face difficult problems on the campuses they serve. When crime occurs, they are blamed for ineffectively protecting their constituents; when no crime is reported, the common belief is that police are either "burying" the statistics or making it difficult for victims to come forward. Lesbian, gay, and bisexual students rarely report their victimization (Ehrlich 1992). Too often, when they have, either nothing is done, or, because reporting their victimization may stigmatize or force them to reveal themselves, they have been or have felt to have been revictimized.

Feeling supported by the campus police, then, is a separate issue from a gay, lesbian, or bisexual student's safety on campus. Moreover, training to sensitize police to all minority concerns, particularly those relating to sexual orientation, are still new. We can only hope that, in subsequent editions of this *Guide,* students will feel and experience a different reality.

Bisexual, lesbian, and gay students, as we stated earlier, recommend their schools for a variety of reasons. We were told again and again that, though their individual experiences may have been difficult, a larger population of openly gay, lesbian, and bisexual students on campus might help to change the predominant culture: as more "strength in numbers" than "misery loves company." We want to believe that there is something hopeful in the number of students who recommend their schools even though their choices to attend, had they known then what they now know, would have been different. It may suggest optimism in some otherwise bleak scenarios.

Nevertheless, one cannot read these responses without remembering that lesbian, gay, and bisexual students, in most ways, reflect the contradictions, uncertainties, and obliviousness of any traditionally student-aged group. These responses are, therefore, based on both individual as well as group concerns.

The student response to our request for information and evaluation was, in itself, a study in the variety of gay, lesbian, and bisexual people. We were constantly thanked, lectured to, and criticized for our undertaking. Our language was alternately questioned and applauded, and we found ourselves moved, humbled, and often irritated by our respondents.

What we learned was far more than what these numbers tell. What is politically correct and what is accurate don't always seem to coincide, and we are still hopeful that the one simple "thank you" from a lesbian cross-dresser equals the several sneering responses from some of the students at a large and prestigious, politically correct (self-described) campus who responded to that question with "Who cares? We don't want them anyway!" Some students took time to write out their life stories for us; some students wrote back refusing to answer demographic questions because our language was "politically oppressive." We are sure of two things. The lesbian, gay, and bisexual political leadership in this country speaks with many, many voices, and developing a rigid standard of acceptability that would blend or sometimes silence those voices is dangerous, contemptible, and most important, wrong-headed. "Right-speak" and "Right-think," while often trumpeting inclusiveness, in fact drown out, through their own clamor, the variety that makes us who we are.

The second thing about which we are certain is that we would not trade this experience for anything, and we look upon this *Guide* as a beginning. To succeed at doing what this *Guide* sets out to do, we need to reach more students at more schools. We invite alumni, current students, administrators, and faculty to help us do that by writing to us with their evaluations. Help us enlarge this *Guide* with your ideas, program descriptions, and thoughts.

We also urge any lesbian, gay, or bisexual student who is applying for admission to or considering enrolling in any undergraduate, graduate, or professional school program not listed here to use the questionnaire upon which this *Guide* is based to survey administrators before deciding ultimately where to send those tuition dollars. If they don't know the answers, ask them to find out, or ask for the address of the gay, lesbian, or bisexual student groups on campus. If there isn't a group, the question may be moot, but any information at all may help the decision-making process.

Finally, we would like to thank those friends and colleagues who have helped, in some measure, to bring this information to you: Norman Laurila, our friend, agent, and benefactor; Niko Pfund, our editor who needed no convincing that such a guide had an important market; David Bergman, poet and scholar, who encouraged the work; the George Washington University Dean of Students Office: Linda Donnels, Barbara Framer, Kevin McAnally, Kitty Boney, Stacey Chatman, Christy Willis, and especially Dan Serviss, all of whom generously supported this work; Patricia Frawley, who volunteered her weekends at home to help; Professor Guy Wolf, who personally delivered surveys to Hawaii; and finally, to the Towson State University Diverse Sexual Orientation Collective, which inspired the work.

The Gay, Lesbian, and Bisexual Students' Guide to Colleges, Universities, and Graduate Schools

I

Gay and Lesbian 101: Who Am I and Who Cares?

An instructor of a course, "Gay Themes in Modern Literature," told us about a question he was asked on his first day in class:

"How are we going to know the people in these books are gay?"

"I'm not sure I fully understand your question," the teacher responded.

"I mean, are they going to *do* things?"

The student's question was sincere, and for the instructor the need for such a course was dramatically demonstrated in a funny but no less poignant way. It may make us all begin to think about just how polarized our society is, with respect to gay/lesbian/bisexual people versus the heterosexual majority. In some important ways, everything an openly lesbian, bisexual, or gay person does—not only with whom they sleep—becomes a political act: simply by being who they are, they affect the attitude of the larger, heterosexual world. Education should be a means of bridging that gap, shouldn't it?

"Coming Out 101," a video produced by the Campus Violence Prevention Center that looks at some of the coming-out experiences of college students on campus, begins with a highly stylized scene in an American college classroom. The students take a "quiz" on what they're learning: in this case, the punchlines to vicious, homophobic jokes. The curious students begin asking questions about famous people, "Oscar Wilde, was he gay?" to which the teacher responds—all the while leering—"No, he was just a bit overly aesthetic." There is self-congratulation in the instructor's leer; there is, unquestionably, an open contempt for that portion of Oscar Wilde which may or may not have most informed his art. But, given the utter contempt with which the instructor responds, it's a cinch that won't be a topic for spirited discussion in his class.

As has been the case throughout the history of education, a discussion of a person's sexual orientation will simply not occur. And if it is somehow brought up, it will be ignored, derided, or patronizingly explained away as not germane to the rigors of academic discourse. For though it pretends to a kind of monastic objectivity, education, while it purports to search for Truth and Enlightenment, is, after all, no different from the entertainment industry in how it reflects contemporary values.

After a hysteria during the 1970s about openly gay, lesbian, or bisexual teachers "converting" or "recruiting" American children to a deviant "life-style," American education had seemed to settle into a silence about lesbian, bisexual, and gay people's contribution to the treasure pile of knowledge. Most recently, however, new debate over curricula has been generated by those who support "family" or "traditional" values, a curriculum that seems primarily concerned with excluding any mention of gay, lesbian, or bisexual orientation. In Colorado, Oregon, and in at least twelve other states, legislation is being prepared, debated, or has passed that would, in varying degrees, further alienate the nonheterosexual minority. In New York City, the school board has challenged the superintendent for his proposed inclusive curriculum. Rather than lead the way, American education seems to prefer the fuguelike state of "no answer" to any real questioning or examination of a "distasteful" subject.

Of course, "no answer" is, in fact, quite a loud answer, and gay, lesbian, and bisexual students are hearing it clearly. African Americans, other ethnic minorities, Native Americans, and women have, historically, also been the blank entries in the table of contents of the American educational canon. Multiculturalism—though the term has become, like "politically correct," a war totem for right-wing extremists—has altered some curricula, challenged the history texts, and started to allow all people to learn how their individual culture and shaping experiences inform and create the total American experience.

Well, actually, not everyone; there remains the big silence, and the invisibility of the gay, lesbian, and bisexual minority. The educational establishment, whose enlightenment allows for a reinterpretation of history with respect to ethnic and racial minorities, can only go so far. Enlightenment has very distinct limits. Again, in "Coming Out 101," a straight white male says to a gay African-American male, "It's bad enough you're black, you have to be gay, too?" It might actually be funny, sort of like the whine of a 1970s sit-com character, if the results of refusing to teach or even acknowledge the cultural contributions of lesbians, bisexuals, and gay men were not so tragic.

Conservative estimates put the number of gay and lesbian teen suicide at 1,500 each year. *Pediatrics* magazine says 30 percent of gay and lesbian youth attempt suicide near the age of 15, and a 1989 study found that suicide is the leading cause of death among lesbian, gay, and bisexual teenagers in America. Is it stretching a point, therefore, to see American education as contributing to the bad self-images young gay, lesbian, and bisexual people have of themselves? If that's too strong an indictment, then let's say the educational establishment does nothing to dispel the bad self-image. The truth is it does nothing; it gives no answer. And, in case you've forgotten, we'll say it again: no answer *is* an answer.

In a discussion for this book with the dean of the College of Liberal Arts at a mid-sized public university about whether or not lesbian and gay contributions were part of the curriculum, she said she couldn't imagine, for instance, teaching a class on Walt Whitman's poetry without talking about Whitman's homosexuality. In an informal poll we conducted of the American Literature survey-course instructors who teach the course at that university and under that dean, not one of them mentions in class the fact that Whitman was gay. What's going on? Was the dean lying? Well, yes and no. In the interest of scholarship, she couldn't imagine the class taught without all the relevant and important facts brought out about the poet. But she has actually never asked about what is taught with respect to Whitman's or Wilde's, or Melville's, or Marlowe's, or Cather's, or Emily Dickinson's, or Millay's sexual orientation. It's the lie of omission: no one asks.

Debate rages on in the public sector regarding the appropriateness, advisability, possibly even the danger of introducing discussion of homosexuality to impressionable children in the elementary, middle, or high schools. We are, after all, a country that still bans books from curricula and from school libraries. With that fact in mind, it is interesting to note that Barry M. Dank, in his work, *Coming Out in the Gay World*, surveyed men of whom 15 percent came to a realization of their gayness through reading. As David Bergman points out in *Gaiety Transfigured*, given how little, overall, Americans read and how marginal access has been to literature dealing with the subject, the figure seems of almost heroic proportion. Perhaps the precollege student population will remain woefully uninformed. Those educators who might seek to include sexual orientation as part of what a child learns about as acceptable or even as a healthy difference continue to lose the argument. Gay, lesbian, and bisexual children, as well as heterosexual children, whose adult world is still the only world, will not learn to perceive sexual difference as anything more than alien, forbidding; at worst, as dangerous. "Homosexual children," as David Bergman has said, "conceive their sexual selves in isolation," and the educational establishment helps to maintain that isolation.

But what about college? This is a world that, like it or not, offers initiation in endless variety. Students are challenged both intellectually and socially almost on a daily basis. As a colleague recently commented about how differently students perceive themselves in changing from high school to college, "In high school even the virgins weren't virgins; in college, even the non-virgins are."

Socially, students are encountering differences beyond what an 18-year-old could ever imagine. For some, college is the first time students may personally meet other students who are African-American or who are in any way ethnically or racially different from themselves. And these "different" students may feel and act just as entitled as white students. In college, too, heterosexual students may meet openly gay, lesbian, and bisexual students. It is entirely possible that at no other time in their lives may as many different kinds of people interact socially.

Coming face to face with "otherness" is, at least, a risky proposition. For gay, lesbian, and bisexual people, it has been truly dangerous. For when one is not taught how to accommodate difference, the clash of cultures can be emotionally if not physically violent. The National Institute Against Prejudice and Violence concludes that 20 percent of minority students experience some form of ethnoviolent attack during an academic year. A quarter of those students are multiple victims. The Campus Violence Prevention Center has shown in study after study that the college campus tends to reflect the values, and, to a large degree, the violence of the parent society. One in three college students will be the victim of a crime during his/her college experience (Bausell, Maloy, Sherrill 1990). A 1990 survey of 128 four-year colleges and universities, conducted by *USA Today* and People for the American Way, shows that, of the colleges reporting acts of intolerance on their campuses, sexual orientation, more than race or ethnicity, accounted for the intolerance.

The majority of gay, lesbian, and bisexual students indicate that they were self-acknowledged before college. Whether this is revisionist history or not is open to speculation. Regardless, a sizable minority come out while they are college students. These students describe themselves as socially active: they date mostly other students on campus. Over one third of these students live on campus in residence halls. Not only may heterosexual students encounter gay, lesbian, or bisexual students for the first time, but they may be their roommates and they may meet their friends and dates. For most students this is a far greater degree of sophistication than their parents may have. How do they cope? What resources are available to help them cope? How do they learn to respect these differences? The American Council on Education's recent data on entering college freshmen indicate that a little more than half supported laws prohibiting homosexual relations (Astin et al. 1987). As recently as the late 1980s most Americans have come to believe that it is socially acceptable to use violence to achieve certain goals or as a response to insult (*Washington Post*/ABC News Poll 1986). With this kind of societal context, it's hard to imagine how students can learn to respect anyone who is different from themselves.

In fact, there is increasing evidence that fear-engendered violence—that which would seek to suppress expression of difference—may receive tacit approval by merely governmental consideration of antigay/lesbian legislation. The National Gay and Lesbian Task Force reports a 350 percent increase in Colorado of hate crimes against gays and lesbians just since the passage of Question Two; and in Oregon, where a similar, yet more repressive initiative was defeated, hate crimes against gays and lesbians increased 500 percent before November. (Since that time, and the initiative's defeat, hate crimes have already decreased by half.) Among the reasons cited for continuing the ban against gays and lesbians in the armed services is that officials expect increased violence against homosexual-identified service people should the ban be lifted. A lie is often a stubborn, insistent thing protected and cherished, while the truth, as has always been the case, can be dangerous.

We don't know a great deal about the treatment of lesbians, bisexuals, and gay men who are in military service, simply because to identify oneself had generally meant one was almost immediately discharged. Should one have been unfortunate enough to be "unofficially found out," the harassment that may have followed would, more than likely, go unreported. The United States military, much like college campuses, reflects the values, energies, and dangers of American society. Violent homophobia, sexual harassment, and blackmail thrive there, countenanced and supported by silence and dishonesty.

For lesbian, bisexual, and gay people, being outside the cultural mainstream, particularly when a cultural pluralism may otherwise begin to dominate, is highly frustrating. A strange pecking order, almost Orwellian in scope, is established. Which harassed minority is most entitled to reparation, and by what measure is it decided? Size, length of torment, depth of suffering, rate of victimization? And who is the accountant of everything that the disenfranchised don't have?

We must look again to the education system, that great objectifier of that which is most subjective about who we are. Does education change the prevailing values or merely transmit them? If we believe that the college experience provides education of the whole person, isn't what we offer students socially, within the context of the college/institutional community, important? Might not that cocurricular life, particularly if it acts as a catalyst for the changing of values, ultimately affect a corresponding change in curriculum?

If there is not a moral imperative that schools, with their services and curricula, begin to reflect the complete spectrum of diversity on their campuses, perhaps lesbian, bisexual, and gay students should begin, with their dollars, to demand change.

If the American Psychological Association is correct, one in six college students is lesbian, gay, or bisexual. It therefore makes good sense for colleges and universities to respond to this very sizable market. Respondents to our survey, as a group, were largely students with combined SAT scores of 1100 and above, and most had overall GPAs of 3.0 or higher on a 4-point scale.

But a significant percentage of respondents reported dropping out of college or transferring, earlier in their college careers, because of issues surrounding coming out on campus and subsequent victimization or harassment. Only half the respondents said their institutions included sexual orientation as part of their nondiscrimination statements, and only 29 percent of respondents reported that their schools had any kind of campus committee to examine lesbian, bisexual, and gay issues. Less than half report specific or inclusive curricula. On the other hand, 67 percent of the students said that their school's position on lesbian, gay, and bisexual students was negative or noncommittal, and if we compare the respondents' reportage of victimization, we see that something is seriously wrong.

As we examine the perceptions of gay, lesbian, and bisexual students, we begin to see that the support that's there comes from the students themselves, for each other. They look for help from faculty and staff and get very little. They see themselves reflected almost nowhere. They will not see themselves on television, in movies, or in print advertising. And they will not see themselves nor learn about themselves in almost any context within the educational system. They do not exist.

But of course they do. Gay, lesbian, and bisexual people, as stated earlier, are a large market, a large consumer of higher education; and they are eager to put their educational dollars into institutions that treat them as a significant part of American culture, that acknowledge their very rich differences and their similarities to the majority. Forty percent of respondents say that, had information such as is contained in this guide been available to them, their choices of where to attend college would have been different. For the average, midsized institution of 10,000 students, we're describing a potential loss of 640 students, or nearly 7 percent of the student body as a whole. Not many institutions could sustain such a sizable decline in enrollment.

Maybe the information our respondents have provided is what some refer to, in the vernacular, as a "wake-up call" for American colleges and universities. It is our fervent hope that administrators, all decision makers on college campuses, can see the positive aspects to acknowledging and supporting gay, lesbian, and bisexual students. It does not require additional staff, but sensitive staff; not necessarily new or different programming, but programming that is truly inclusive. Finally, the most supportive gestures—statements from college presidents that show support for lesbian, gay, and bisexual students who may have been victimized, either individually or as a group, campus police who are trained to respond quickly and professionally to hate/bias crimes, and faculty who acknowledge the contributions of lesbian, bisexual, and gay scholars, scientists, writers, artists, heads of state, and philosophers—actually provide the moral leadership most of us expect from our educational institutions. Moral leadership is still, after all, best taught by example.

BIBLIOGRAPHY

Astin, Alexander W., et al. *The American Freshman: National Norms for Fall 1987.* Los Angeles: Higher Education Research Institute, University of California, 1987.

Bausell, C., C. Maloy, and J. Sherrill. "The Linkages among Campus Crime, Alcohol, and Other Drugs." Paper presented at the Fifth National Conference on Campus Violence, Baltimore, February 5, 1991.

Ehrlich, Howard J. "Campus Ethnoviolence: A Research Review." Paper presented at the American Sociological Association, Cincinnati, August 1991.

Washington Post/ABC News Poll. "An Eye for an Eye." *Washington Post Weekly Edition,* September 22, 1986.

II

The Gay, Lesbian, and Bisexual Student Profile

This book gives voice to the largest number of lesbian, gay, and bisexual students ever studied: six thousand gay, lesbian, and bisexual students at six hundred colleges and universities throughout the United States. Students were surveyed anonymously through mailings to the lesbian, gay, and bisexual student groups on college campuses. It is the first major study of its kind.

Evaluations of 189 colleges and universities were made by 1,464 students. The school and student sample represented every state, both co-educational and single-sex schools, public and private institutions. *Evaluations and perceptions are solely those of the survey population.*

The average age of the respondent was 23 years old, with the overall age range being 17–47. Thirty-nine percent were female, 61 percent male. The respondents were white (82%), Asian (6%), African American (5%), Hispanic (3.5%), Native American (2.5%), and other (1%). Sixty-one percent reported combined SAT scores of 1100 or higher, and 72 percent have overall grade point averages of 3.0 or higher (using a 4-point scale). Eleven percent were freshmen, 19 percent were sophomores, 22 percent were juniors, 28 percent were seniors, and 20 percent were graduate and professional (mostly law) school students.

A large majority described themselves as openly gay, lesbian, or bisexual on their campuses. Those who were not open on their campuses chose not to reveal themselves because of fear of reprisal; a very small number identified themselves as members of ROTC, and therefore felt constrained about revealing their sexual orientation.

Most said they were open to their families and friends, with a small minority describing themselves as largely closeted.

The majority of students who responded to the survey lived off campus, but almost as many lived in campus residence halls. Some lived off campus with their partners, and slightly fewer lived with their families. A very small minority resided in fraternity or sorority housing.

Fewer than one tenth described themselves as belonging to Greek-letter organizations, and even fewer indicated that they were currently members of athletic teams. Fewer than one hundred volunteered the information that they had been members of athletic teams, but had left their teams around the time they came out. The numbers of men and women athletes were almost even; fraternity members outnumbered sorority members almost two to one.

A majority said that they were self-acknowledged gays, lesbians, and bisexuals prior to college—a larger percentage of men than women. While nearly one-third say that their sexual orientation influenced the decision as to which college or graduate/professional school to attend, 40 percent said that their choices would have been different had information on the climate for bisexuals, lesbians, and gays at the particular institution been available.

A small minority identified themselves as cross-dressers (more women than men), and a few more identified themselves as being into leather (again, more women than men). A little more of the respondents date other students, with nearly half of them indicating that their dating activity takes place on the campus. Almost one third of the students responding to the survey say that their partners attend the same school and that they met him or her there.

Because the amount of victimization of gay, lesbian, and bisexual students is quite large, it is not surprising that 40 percent indicated that they do not feel completely safe on their campuses, with 57 percent saying that their schools do nothing in response to hate crimes occurring on their campuses. Forty percent feel that the campus police or security force are not supportive of gay, lesbian, and bisexual students, and overwhelmingly, most students believe homophobia to be a serious problem at their schools.

Most lesbian, gay, and bisexual students, from our survey, live openly off campus and are most likely to be out to their families and friends. They date other students, with the dating activity occurring on campus. They say they have been self-acknowledged gays or lesbians since high school.

They know the obvious dangers associated with being openly gay on campus, having either experienced some form of harassment (often threatened, beaten, called names or harassed in other ways), or they know someone or have witnessed other gay, lesbian, or bisexual students' victimization, including physical assault. Still, these students feel relatively safe on their campuses. But their view, like most of their lesbian, gay, and bisexual friends' views, have become somewhat cynical with respect to safety as a publicly gay lesbian or bisexual person. One student summed up what was largely the prevailing attitude this way: "I want other students to leave me alone, and I know I should be able to expect that, but it just isn't the case; so, I try not to go too many places by myself, and even if it makes me angry when some people say things to me or call me names, I try not to answer. I don't want to get beaten up."

They have taught themselves about themselves as gay, lesbian, or bisexual people, reading both fiction and history, and seeing as many films as there are, but they know that many of the representations they see, especially in movies or on television, don't accurately portray them: "We're either dying of AIDS, we're psychotic, or we're these asexual beings with no personal lives."

In most ways, they are very similar to all other American college students with notable exceptions: higher SATs, higher GPAs, nearly three times as likely to be victimized while a student and on campus, and two to three times more likely to have attempted suicide.

They feel informed about the AIDS crisis in America and have been educated about safer sex practices. They are more likely to have been tested for HIV than are their non-gay, non-lesbian, non-bisexual student counterparts.

They also stand a very good chance of dropping out of school for one semester or longer. Nearly one in three lesbian, bisexual, or gay students will leave school sometime during their undergraduate careers. Of that number, one third will do so because of coming-out issues and victimization subsequent to coming out. One student summed up his experience relative to "surviving" coming out on campus this way:

When I came out during my sophomore year, both my roommates moved out, so I had to move out of residence because I couldn't afford a single room unless I told my parents, which I wasn't willing to do yet. Somebody magic-markered 'AIDS CARRIER' on my room door, twice. As it turned out, my parents found out anyway because somebody from school—I never knew who it was—wrote them some anonymous letters. They got upset and wouldn't pay for school anymore. I finally got back after a semester working as a waiter to support myself and pay rent. Now I'm finishing up as a part-time student, but it's been tough. I don't owe anybody anything, though.

Even with these experiences, most lesbian, gay, and bisexual students would recommend their schools to other gay, lesbian, and bisexual students, but not always because they see their particular institutions as hospitable to them. Many felt that more gay, lesbian, and bisexual students would help to sensitize their campuses; some felt that no American college campus really wanted, welcomed, or supported gay students so that their school was really no worse than any other. The cynicism of some of these students is quite deep.

Gay, lesbian, and bisexual students obviously face more obstacles than do their heterosexual peers, and yet they persevere. With more hospitable campus climates, with strategies aimed at attracting and retaining gay students, colleges and universities may bolster otherwise dwindling enrollments.

III

College Guide

Questionnaires were sent to schools whose lesbian, bisexual, and gay student groups appeared on mailing lists for the National Gay and Lesbian Task Force. Mailings represented every state, both coeducational and single-sex schools, public and private institutions.

It is important to note that the authors have not, themselves, evaluated the schools but merely present the evaluations by gay, lesbian, and bisexual students of their own campus climates. It is also important, however, that, especially with respect to programs that might be aimed at this specific population, these students' knowledge of programming efforts may help determine how effective these efforts have been. While students, in general, may be passive recipients of education, targeted populations within the larger whole are usually sensitive to projects created on their behalf.

Alfred University • *Alfred, New York*

Students define Alfred University's position on gay, lesbian, and bisexual issues somewhere between negative and noncommittal. Although the university does not have a committee on gay, lesbian, and bisexual issues, sexual orientation is included in its affirmative action policy. However, counseling services are not available for gay, lesbian, and bisexual students. Students do not know if housing for cohabitating couples is available. According to the students, the municipality in which the university is located has a civil rights law that includes sexual orientation.

Unanimously, students believe that homophobia is a serious problem on the campus. Half of those responding report being victims of verbal abuse and harassment. Moreover, all of the students have knowledge of hate crimes committed on the campus, including assault.

Although the university maintains hate-crime statistics, none of the students believe that Alfred takes action in response to hate crimes. Students are divided concerning the security force's support. Most of the time, however, students do feel safe on the campus as gays, lesbians, and bisexuals.

Gay, lesbian, and bisexual students between the ages of 20–21 responded to the survey. Students are juniors and seniors with SAT scores of 1100 or higher and grade point averages of 3.5 or higher. Students have majors in the liberal arts.

All of the students are openly gay on the campus as well as to their parents and families. All are considered out-of-state students and live both in residence halls and in off-campus apartments. Half of the students responding came out before attending college, and none said that being gay, lesbian, or bisexual affected their choosing Alfred. Furthermore, if information on the climate for gay, lesbian, and bisexuals at Alfred been available, the respondents' choices would not have been different.

The respondents are involved in the gay, lesbian, and bisexual student group, which has an average membership of 12 students and sponsors speakers, safe-sex education, and Pride and National Coming Out Day activities. The group receives no funding from the student government. In addition, students are active in other organizations such as the radio station, literary magazine, the political science club, and the student senate. The students date other Alfred students and state that most of their dating activity takes place on the campus.

All of the students view substance abuse as the largest problem at Alfred, with the lack of role models following second.

Although gay men's and lesbians' cultural contributions are not a

part of regular courses, the university does offer courses on gay, lesbian, and bisexual issues in history and art. The university provides free, confidential HIV testing, but no counseling for those who are HIV+ or have AIDS, nor does it provide condoms. Both the Health Center and the student group provide safe-sex education.

Half of the respondents recommend Alfred University to other gay, lesbian, and bisexual students.

American University • *Washington, D.C.*

Students define American's position on gay, lesbian, and bisexual issues as noncommittal. Although the university does not have a committee on gay, lesbian, and bisexual issues, sexual orientation is included in its affirmative action policy. In addition, counseling services are available for gay, lesbian, and bisexual students. Students do not know if housing for cohabitating couples is available. According to the students, the municipality in which the university is located does have a civil rights law that includes sexual orientation.

Unanimously, students believe that homophobia is a serious problem on the campus. Most of those responding report being victims of verbal abuse. Moreover, all of the students have knowledge of hate crimes committed on the campus. The student group maintains hate-crime statistics.

All of the students believe that American takes action in response to hate crimes and agree that the university's security force is supportive. Consequently, all of the students feel safe on the campus as gays, lesbians, and bisexuals.

Gay, lesbian, and bisexual students between the ages of 23–31 responded to the survey. Students are juniors, seniors, and graduate student with SAT scores of 900 or higher and grade point averages of 3.0 or higher (graduate students have GPAs of 3.5 or higher). Students have majors in the liberal arts.

All of the students are openly gay on the campus and most are out to their parents and families. All are considered out-of-state students and live off campus, some with their families in the Maryland and Virginia suburbs. The majority of the students responding came out before attending college, and none said that being gay, lesbian, or bisexual affected their choosing American. However, if information on the climate for gays, lesbians, and bisexuals at American had been available, half of the respondents would have chosen to go elsewhere.

The respondents are involved in the gay, lesbian, and bisexual student group, which has an average membership of 25 students and sponsors dances, speakers, safe-sex education, and Pride and National Coming Out Day activities. The group receives funding from the student government. The students date other American students and state that their dating activity takes place on the campus. Off campus, students congregate in bars.

All of the students view coming out as the largest problem at American, with the lack of role models and student organization following second.

Although gay men's and lesbians' cultural contributions are not a part of regular courses, the university does offer courses on gay, lesbian, and bisexual issues in anthropology. The university does not provide free, anonymous HIV testing, counseling for those who are HIV+ or have AIDS, or condoms free of charge. Both the Health Center and the student group provide safe-sex education.

All of the respondents recommend American to other gay, lesbian, and bisexual students, with few reservations.

American University, Washington College of Law •
Washington, D.C.

Students define American's position on gay, lesbian, and bisexual issues as proactive. Although the university does not have a committee on gay, lesbian, and bisexual issues, sexual orientation is included in its affirmative action policy. In addition, counseling services are available for gay, lesbian, and bisexual students. Students do not know if housing for cohabitating couples is available. According to the students, the municipality in which the university is located has a civil rights law that includes sexual orientation.

Unanimously, students believe that homophobia is not a serious problem on the campus. None of those responding report being victims of hate crimes. However, all of the students have knowledge of hate crimes committed on the campus. Students do not know who, if anyone, maintains hate-crime statistics.

All of the students believe that American takes action in response to hate crimes and agree that the university's security force is supportive. Consequently, all of the students feel safe on the campus as gays, lesbians, and bisexuals.

Gay, lesbian, and bisexual students between the ages of 26–45 responded to the survey. Students are graduates with SAT scores of 1100 or higher and grade point averages of 3.5 or higher. Students are all Juris Doctor candidates.

All of the students are openly gay on the campus as well as to their parents and families. None are considered out-of-state students and all live off campus, some with life partners. All of the students responding came out before attending college, and none said that being gay, lesbian, or bisexual affected their choosing American. Furthermore, if information on the climate for gay, lesbian, and bisexuals at American had been available, the respondents' choices would not have been different.

The respondents are involved in the gay, lesbian, and bisexual student group, which has an average membership of 14 students and sponsors speakers, safe-sex education, and Pride and National Coming Out Day activities. The group receives funding from the student government. In addition, students are active in various law associations. The students tend not to date other American students.

All of the students view the lack of role models as the largest problem at American.

Although gay men's and lesbians' cultural contributions are not a part of regular courses, the university does offer courses on gay, lesbian, and bisexual issues in English and law. The university does not provide free, anonymous HIV testing, but counseling is available for those who are HIV+ or have AIDS. Students do not know if condoms are provided. Both the Health Center and the student group provide safe-sex education.

All of the respondents recommend American's law school to other gay, lesbian, and bisexual students.

Arizona State University • *Tempe, Arizona*

Students define Arizona State's position on gay, lesbian, and bisexual issues as noncommittal. Although the university does not have a committee on gay, lesbian, and bisexual issues, sexual orientation is included in its affirmative action policy. In addition, counseling services are available for gay, lesbian, and bisexual students. Students do not know if housing for cohabitating couples is available. According to the students, the municipality in which the university is located does not have a civil rights law that includes sexual orientation.

Unanimously, students believe that homophobia is a serious problem on the campus. Those responding report being victims of verbal abuse. Moreover, all of the students have knowledge of hate crimes committed on the campus. Students do not know who, if anyone, maintains hate-crime statistics.

Additionally, none of the students knows how Arizona State reacts to hate crimes. All, however, agree that the university's security force is supportive, and all of the students feel safe on the campus as gays, lesbians, and bisexuals.

Gay, lesbian, and bisexual students between the ages of 19–21 responded to the survey. Students are sophomores, juniors, and seniors with grade point averages of 2.5 or higher. Students have majors in the liberal arts.

All of the students are openly gay on the campus but are not out to their parents and families. None are considered out-of-state students and all live in off-campus apartments and houses. None of the students responding came out before attending college; consequently, none said that being gay, lesbian, or bisexual affected their choosing Arizona State. Furthermore, if information on the climate for gays, lesbians, and bisexuals at Arizona State had been available, the respondents' choices would not have been different.

The respondents are involved in the gay, lesbian, and bisexual student group, which has an average membership of 20–50 students and sponsors speakers, safe-sex education, and Pride and National Coming Out Day activities. The group receives funding from the student government. In addition, students are active in Amnesty International. The students date other Arizona State students and indicate that their dating activity takes place off campus, where they congregate in bars and coffeehouses.

All of the students view coming out as the largest problem at Arizona State; the lack of role models and alcohol abuse following second.

Gay men's and lesbians' cultural contributions are not a part of regular courses, nor does the university offer courses on gay, lesbian, and bisexual issues. The university provides free, confidential HIV testing and counseling for those who are HIV+ or have AIDS. Students do not know if condoms are provided. Both the Health Center and the student group provide safe-sex education.

All of the respondents recommend Arizona State to other gay, lesbian, and bisexual students.

Bard College • *Annandale-on-Hudson, New York*

Students define Bard's position on gay, lesbian, and bisexual issues as proactive. Although the college does not have a committee on gay, lesbian, and bisexual issues, sexual orientation is included in its affirmative action statement, and counseling services are provided for gay, lesbian, and bisexual students. Students do not know if housing for cohabitating couples is available. According to the students, the municipality in which the college is located does not have a civil rights law that includes sexual orientation.

Eighty percent of the students do not believe that homophobia is a serious problem on the campus. Forty percent of those responding report being victims of verbal abuse. Sixty percent of the students have knowledge of hate crimes committed on the campus, including assault. The college and the student group maintain hate-crime statistics.

All of the students believe that Bard takes action in response to these incidents. The majority of the respondents state that they feel supported by the college's security force. All of the students feel safe on the campus as gays, lesbians, and bisexuals.

Gay, lesbian, and bisexual students between the ages of 18–22 responded to the survey. Students are freshmen, sophomores, juniors, seniors, and graduate students with SAT scores of 1100 or higher and grade point averages of 3.0 and higher. Students have majors in literature, gender studies, social science, art history, film, history, engineering, and political science.

The majority of the students surveyed are openly gay on the campus; those who are not cite fear of reprisal as the primary reason. All of the students, though, are out to their parents and families. Half are considered out-of-state students and all live in residence halls. Eighty percent of the students responding came out before attending college, and said that being gay, lesbian, or bisexual affected their choosing Bard. However, if information on the climate for gays, lesbians, and bisexuals at Bard had been available, 20 percent of the respondents would have chosen to go elsewhere.

The respondents are involved in the gay, lesbian, and bisexual student group, which has an average membership of 15 students and sponsors dances, speakers, safe-sex education, and Pride and National Coming Out Day activities. The group receives funding from the student government. Two percent of the respondents are cross-dressers. In addition, students are active in other organizations such as the literary magazine and athletics. The students date other Bard students and state that their dating activity takes place on the Bard campus. Off campus, students congregate in bars and at the community center.

All of the students view coming out as the largest problem at Bard, with the lack of role models and student organization following second.

Gay men's and lesbians' cultural contributions are a part of some regular courses. The college also offers courses on gay, lesbian, and bisexual issues in history, English, education, the social sciences, and women's studies. Although the college does not provide free, anonymous HIV testing, counseling is available for those who are HIV+ or have AIDS. Twenty percent state that condoms are available free of charge. Both the Health Center and the student group provide safe-sex education.

All of the respondents recommend Bard to other gay, lesbian, and bisexual students.

Barnard College • *New York, New York*

Students define Barnard's position on gay, lesbian, and bisexual issues as noncommittal. Although the college does not have a committee on gay, lesbian, and bisexual issues, sexual orientation is included in its affirmative action policy. Counseling services are not available for gay, lesbian, and bisexual students. Students do not know if housing for cohabiting couples is available. According to the students, the municipality in which the college is located has a civil rights law that includes sexual orientation.

Unanimously, students believe that homophobia is a serious problem on the campus. Two-thirds of those responding report being victims of harassment and verbal abuse. Moreover, all of the students have knowledge of hate crimes committed on the campus, including assault. Students do not know who, if anyone, maintains hate-crime statistics.

All of the students believe that Barnard takes action in response to hate crimes and agree that the college's security force is supportive. Students feel marginally safe on the campus as gays, lesbians, and bisexuals.

Gay, lesbian, and bisexual students between the ages of 19–21 responded to the survey. Students are sophomores, juniors, and seniors with SAT scores of 1100 or higher and grade point averages of 3.0 or higher. Students have majors in the liberal arts.

All of the students are openly gay on the campus as well as to their parents and families. All are considered out-of-state students and live in residence halls. Two thirds of the students responding came out before attending college, and said that being gay, lesbian, or bisexual affected their choosing Barnard. Furthermore, if information on the climate for gay, lesbian, and bisexuals at Barnard had been available, the respondents' choices would not have been different.

The respondents are involved in the gay, lesbian, and bisexual student group, which has an average membership of 200 students and sponsors dances, speakers, safe-sex education, and Pride and National Coming Out Day activities. The group receives funding from the student government. The students date other Barnard students and state that their dating activity takes place on the campus. Off campus, students congregate in bars and private homes and apartments.

All of the students view coming out as the largest problem at Barnard, with the lack of role models and alcohol abuse following second.

Although gay men's and lesbians' cultural contributions are not a part of regular courses, the college does offer courses on gay, lesbian, and bisexual issues in women's studies and in history. Students do not know if the college provides free, anonymous HIV testing, counseling for those who are HIV+ or have AIDS, or condoms free of charge. The student group provides safe-sex education.

All of the respondents recommend Barnard to other gay, lesbian, and bisexual students.

Baruch College of the City University of New York •
New York, New York

Students define Baruch's position on gay, lesbian, and bisexual issues as proactive. The college has a committee on gay, lesbian, and bisexual issues, and sexual orientation is included in the college's affirmative action policy. In addition, counseling services are available for gay, lesbian, and bisexual students. Housing for cohabitating couples is not available. According to the students, the municipality in which the college is located has a civil rights law that includes sexual orientation.

Unanimously, students believe that homophobia is a serious problem on the campus. Those responding report being victims of hate mail and harassment. Moreover, all of the students have knowledge of hate crimes committed on the campus, including assault. Students do not know who, if anyone, maintains hate-crime statistics.

All of the students believe that Baruch does nothing in response to hate crimes. All, however, agree strongly that the college's security force is supportive. All of the students feel relatively safe on the campus as gays, lesbians, and bisexuals.

Gay, lesbian, and bisexual students between the ages of 21–23 responded to the survey. Students are juniors and seniors with SAT scores of 900 or higher and grade point averages of 3.0 or higher. Students have majors in the liberal arts and business administration.

All of the students are openly gay on the campus as well as to their parents and families. None are considered out-of-state students and all live off campus, some with life partners. All of the students responding came out before attending college and said that being gay, lesbian, or bisexual affected their choosing Baruch. However, if information on the climate for gays, lesbians, and bisexuals had been available, all of the respondents would have chosen to go elsewhere.

The respondents are involved in the gay, lesbian, and bisexual student group, which has an average membership of 30 students and

sponsors dances, speakers, safe-sex education, and Pride and National Coming Out Day activities. The group receives funding from the student government. The students tend not to date other Baruch students. Off campus, students congregate in bars and clubs.

All of the students view coming out as the largest problem AT Baruch with the lack of role models following second.

Gay men's and lesbians' cultural contributions are a part of regular courses. The college also offers courses on gay, lesbian, and bisexual issues in English and history. Students do not know if the college provides free, anonymous HIV testing or counseling for those who are HIV+ or have AIDS. Condoms, however, are available free of charge. Both the Health Center and the student group provide safe-sex education.

All of the respondents recommend Baruch to other gay, lesbian, and bisexual students.

Bates College • *Lewiston, Maine*

Students define Bates's position on gay, lesbian, and bisexual issues somewhere between proactive and noncommittal. Although the college does not have a committee on gay, lesbian, and bisexual issues, sexual orientation is included in its affirmative action policy. In addition, counseling services are available for gay, lesbian, and bisexual students. Housing for cohabitating couples is not available. According to the students, the municipality in which the college is located does not have a civil rights law that includes sexual orientation.

Unanimously, students believe strongly that homophobia is a serious problem on the campus. Those responding report being victims of harassment. Moreover, all of the students have knowledge of hate crimes committed on the campus, including assault. Both the college and the student group maintain hate-crime statistics.

All of the students believe that Bates takes action in response to hate crimes and agree that the college's security force is supportive. However, only half of the students feel safe on the campus as gays, lesbians, and bisexuals.

Gay, lesbian, and bisexual students between the ages of 20–22 responded to the survey. Students are juniors and seniors with SAT scores of 1100 or higher and grade point averages of 2.5 or higher. Students have majors in theater, English, and cultural studies.

Most of the students are openly gay on the campus as well as to their parents and families. Those who are not cite the knowledge of others' bad experiences as the primary reason. All are considered out-of-state students and live both in residence halls and in off-campus houses and apartments. None of the students responding came out before attending college, and none said that being gay, lesbian, or bisexual affected their choosing Bates. However, if information on the climate for gays, lesbians, and bisexuals at Bates had been available, half of the respondents would have chosen to go elsewhere.

The respondents are involved in the gay, lesbian, and bisexual student group, which has an average membership of 10–12 students and sponsors dances, speakers, safe-sex education, and Pride and National Coming Out Day activities. The group receives funding from the student government. In addition, students are active in the school literary magazine and the environmental coalition. The students tend not to date other Bates students.

All of the students view coming out as the largest problem at Bates, with the lack of role models and substance abuse following second.

Although gay men's and lesbians' cultural contributions are not a part of regular courses, the college does offer courses on gay, lesbian, and bisexual issues in art, women's studies, and political science. The college does not provide free, anonymous HIV testing or counseling for those who are HIV+ or have AIDS. Condoms are provided free of charge. Both the Health Center and the student group provide safe-sex education.

All of the respondents recommend Bates, with some reservation, to other gay, lesbian, and bisexual students, "if they're strong, confident, brave."

Berklee College of Music • *Boston, Massachusetts*

Students define Berklee's position on gay, lesbian, and bisexual issues as noncommittal. The college does not have a committee on gay, lesbian, and bisexual issues, and sexual orientation is not included in its affirmative action policy. However, counseling services are available for gay, lesbian, and bisexual students. Housing for cohabitating couples is not available. According to the students, the municipality in which the college is located has a civil rights law that includes sexual orientation.

Unanimously, students believe strongly that homophobia is a serious problem on the campus. None of those responding report being victims of hate crimes. However, all of the students have knowledge of hate crimes committed on the campus. Students do not know who, if anyone, maintains hate-crime statistics.

Students do not know how Berklee reacts to hate crimes. All, however, agree that the College's security force is not supportive. Yet all of the students feel safe on the campus as gays, lesbians, and bisexuals.

Gay, lesbian, and bisexual students between the ages of 19–21 responded to the survey. Students are sophomores and juniors with SAT scores of 1100 or higher and grade point averages of 3.5 or higher. Students have majors in performance.

All of the students are openly gay on the campus and most are out to their parents and families. All are considered out-of-state students and live in off-campus houses and apartments. All of the students responding came out before attending college, and none said that being gay, lesbian, or bisexual affected their choosing Berklee. Furthermore, if information on the climate for gays, lesbians, and bisexuals had been available, the respondents' choices would not have been different.

The respondents are involved in the gay, lesbian, and bisexual student group, which has an average membership of 20 students. The group receives no funding from the student government. In addition, students are active in the international club. The students date other Berklee students and state that some of their dating activity takes place on the campus. Off campus, students congregate in bars.

All of the students view coming out as the largest problem at Berklee, with the lack of role models and student organization following second.

Gay men's and lesbians' cultural contributions are not a part of regular courses, nor does the college offer courses on gay, lesbian, and bisexual issues. Counseling is available for those who are HIV+

or have AIDS. The college does not have a Health Center for testing and condom distribution. The student group provides safe-sex education.

None of the respondents recommends Berklee to other gay, lesbian, and bisexual students, although they do admit that there aren't many other choices for such a unique education.

Boston University • *Boston, Massachusetts*

Students define BU's position on gay, lesbian, and bisexual issues as noncommittal. The university does not have a committee on gay, lesbian, and bisexual issues, sexual orientation is not included in its affirmative action statement, and housing for cohabitating couples is not available. Counseling services, however, are available for gay, lesbian, and bisexual students. According to the students, the municipality in which the university is located has a civil rights law that includes sexual orientation.

Unanimously, undergraduate students believe that homophobia is a serious problem on the campus. Those responding report being victims of verbal abuse, harassment, and vandalism. Moreover, all of the students have knowledge of hate crimes committed on the campus, with the exception of assault. Both the university and the student group maintain hate-crime statistics.

All of the students believe that BU takes action in response to hate crimes, and all feel supported by the university's security force. Consequently, students feel relatively safe on the campus as gays, lesbians, and bisexuals.

Gay, lesbian, and bisexual students between the ages of 21–28 responded to the survey. Students are seniors and graduate students with SAT scores of 1100 or higher and grade point averages of 3.5 and higher. Students have majors in the liberal arts.

All of the students surveyed are openly gay on the campus but not to their parents and families. All are considered out-of-state students and live both in off-campus houses and apartments and in residence halls (undergraduates). None of the students responding came out before attending college, and only graduate students said that being gay, lesbian, or bisexual affected their choosing BU. However, if information on the climate for gays, lesbians, and bisexuals had been available, the respondents' choices would not have been different.

The respondents are involved in the gay, lesbian, and bisexual student group, which has an average membership of 50 students and sponsors dances, speakers, safe-sex education, and Pride and National Coming Out Day activities. In addition, some of the students are active in student government. Some of the students state that they date other BU students and that their dating activity takes place on the BU campus. Off campus, students congregate in bars.

All of the students view alcohol abuse as the largest problem at BU, with coming out and the lack of role models following second. Gay men's and lesbians' cultural contributions are a part of some undergraduate courses, but the university does not offer courses on gay, lesbian, and bisexual issues. The university does not provide free, anonymous HIV testing, condoms, or counseling for those who are HIV+ or have AIDS. The student group provides safe-sex education.

All of the respondents recommend BU to other gay, lesbian, and bisexual students.

Boston University, School of Law • *Boston, Massachusetts*

Eighty percent of the students define BU's position on gay, lesbian, and bisexual issues as negative. The university has a committee on gay, lesbian, and bisexual issues, and sexual orientation is included in the university's affirmative action policy. In addition, counseling services are available for gay, lesbian, and bisexual students. Housing for cohabiting couples is not available. According to the students, the municipality in which the university is located has a civil rights law that includes sexual orientation.

Sixty percent of the students believe that homophobia is a serious problem on the campus. Those responding report being victims of verbal abuse. Moreover, 80 percent of the students have knowledge of hate crimes committed on the campus. Students do not know who, if anyone, maintains hate-crime statistics.

Students believe that BU does nothing in response to hate crimes, or they don't know how the administration reacts. The majority of students agree that the university's security force is not supportive. Yet 80 percent of the students feel safe on the campus as gays, lesbians, and bisexuals.

Gay, lesbian, and bisexual students between the ages of 23–28 responded to the survey. Students are Juris Doctor candidates with SAT scores of 1100 or higher and grade point averages of 2.5 or higher.

Eighty percent of the students are openly gay on the campus. Those who are not cite fear of reprisal as the primary reason. Forty percent are out to their parents and families. All are considered out-of-state students and most students live off campus, but some live in residence halls. All of the students responding came out before attending college, and 80 percent said that being gay, lesbian, or bisexual affected their choosing BU. Furthermore, if information on the climate for gays, lesbians, and bisexuals had been available, 60 percent of the respondents would have made a different choice.

The respondents are involved in the gay, lesbian, and bisexual student group, which has an average membership of 18–30 students and sponsors dances, speakers, safe-sex education, and Pride and National Coming Out Day activities. The group receives funding from the student government. In addition, students are active in the various law student associations. Very few of the students date other BU students and state that their dating activity takes place on the campus. Off campus, students congregate in bars and at the community center.

All of the students view the lack of role models as the largest problem at BU, with coming out and the lack of student organization following second.

Although gay men's and lesbians' cultural contributions are not a part of regular courses, the university does offer courses on gay, lesbian, and bisexual issues in law. Students do not know if the university provides free, anonymous HIV testing, counseling for those who are HIV+ or have AIDS, or condoms. Both the Health Center and the student group provide safe-sex education.

Forty percent of the respondents recommend BU Law School to other gay, lesbian, and bisexual students.

Bowling Green State University • *Bowling Green, Ohio*

Students define Bowling Green's position on gay, lesbian, and bisexual issues as negative. The university does not have a committee on gay, lesbian, and bisexual issues, sexual orientation is not included in its affirmative action statement, and counseling services are not available for gay, lesbian, and bisexual students. Students do not know if housing for cohabiting couples is available. According to the students, the municipality in which the university is located does not have a civil rights law that includes sexual orientation.

Unanimously, students believe strongly that homophobia is a serious problem on the campus. Those responding report being victims of hate mail and harassment. Moreover, all of the students have knowledge of hate crimes committed on the campus, including assault. Students do not know who, if anyone, maintains hate-crime statistics.

Students do not know how Bowling Green reacts to hate crimes, but none feel supported by the university's security force. Yet most students feel safe on the campus as gays, lesbians, and bisexuals.

Gay, lesbian, and bisexual students between the ages of 20–22 responded to the survey. Students are juniors, seniors, and graduate students with SAT scores of 900 or higher and grade point averages of 3.5 and higher. Students have majors in the liberal arts.

None of the students surveyed are openly gay on the campus but are out to some family members. Most are considered out-of-state students and all live in residence halls. None of the students responding came out before attending college, and none said that being gay, lesbian, or bisexual affected their choosing Bowling Green. However, if information on the climate for gays, lesbians, and bisexuals at Bowling Green had been available, all of the respondents would have chosen to go elsewhere.

The respondents are involved in the gay, lesbian, and bisexual student group, which has an average membership of 10–15 students and sponsors safe-sex education. The group receives funding from the student government. Students tend not to date other Bowling Green students. Off campus, students congregate in bars.

All of the students view the lack of role models as the largest problem at Bowling Green, with the lack of student organization and coming out following second.

Gay men's and lesbians' cultural contributions are not a part of regular courses, nor does the university offer courses on gay, lesbian, and bisexual issues. Students do not know if the university provides free, anonymous HIV testing or counseling for those who are HIV+ or have AIDS. Condoms are not provided. Both the Health Center and the student group provide safe-sex education.

None of the respondents recommend Bowling Green to other gay, lesbian, and bisexual students.

Brandeis University • *Waltham, Massachusetts*

One third of the students surveyed define Brandeis's position on gay, lesbian, and bisexual issues as proactive, the remaining students do not know the administration's position. The university has a committee on gay, lesbian, and bisexual issues, sexual orientation is included in the university's affirmative action statement, and counseling services are available for gay, lesbian, and bisexual students. A minority of students say that housing for cohabitating couples is available. According to the students, the municipality in which the university is located has a civil rights law that includes sexual orientation.

A little more than two-thirds of the students do not believe that homophobia is a serious problem on the campus. Most of those responding report being victims of verbal abuse and vandalism. Moreover, all of the students have knowledge of hate crimes committed on the campus. Students do not know who, if anyone, maintains hate-crime statistics.

One third of the students believe that Brandeis takes action in response to hate crimes; the remaining students do not know how the administration reacts. Two thirds feel supported by the university's security force. All of the students feel safe on the campus as gays, lesbians, and bisexuals.

Gay, lesbian, and bisexual students between the ages of 18–20 responded to the survey. Students are freshmen and juniors with SAT scores of 1100 or higher and grade point averages of 3.0 and higher. Students have majors in computer science, politics and the history of thought, and chemistry.

All of the students surveyed are openly gay on the campus as well as to their parents and families. Two thirds are considered out-of-state students and all live in residence halls. Two thirds of the students responding came out before attending college, and none said that being gay, lesbian, or bisexual affected their choosing Brandeis. Furthermore, if information on the climate for gays, lesbians, and bisexuals at Brandeis had been available, the respondents' choices would not have been different.

The respondents are involved in the gay, lesbian, and bisexual student group, which has an average membership of 20–30 students and sponsors dances, speakers, safe-sex education, and Pride and National Coming Out Day activities. The group also receives funding from the student government. In addition, students are active on various academic committees. One-third of the students date other Brandeis students and state that their dating activity takes place on the campus. Off campus, students congregate in bars and at the community center.

All of the students view coming out as the largest problem at Brandeis, with the lack of student organization and role models following second.

Gay men's and lesbians' cultural contributions are a part of some regular courses, and the university also offers courses on gay, lesbian, and bisexual issues in English, history, women's studies, and the social sciences. The university does not provide free, anonymous HIV testing, counseling for those who are HIV+ or have AIDS, or condoms. Both the Health Center and the student group provide safe-sex education.

All of the respondents recommend Brandeis to other gay, lesbian, and bisexual students.

Bridgewater State College • *Bridgewater, Massachusetts*

Students define Bridgewater State's position on gay, lesbian, and bisexual issues as proactive. The college has a committee on gay, lesbian, and bisexual issues, and sexual orientation is included in the college's affirmative action policy. Students do not know if counseling services are available for gay, lesbian, and bisexual students or if housing is available for cohabitating couples. According to the students, the municipality in which the college is located has a civil rights law that includes sexual orientation.

Unanimously, students believe strongly that homophobia is a serious problem on the campus. Those responding report being victims of verbal abuse, harassment, hate mail, and vandalism. Moreover, all of the students have knowledge of hate crimes committed on the campus, including assault. The college maintains hate-crime statistics.

Most of students believe that Bridgewater State takes action in response to hate crimes. None, however, feel that the college's security force is supportive. Consequently, most of the students do not feel safe on the campus as gays, lesbians, and bisexuals.

Gay, lesbian, and bisexual students between the ages of 20–22 responded to the survey. Students are juniors, seniors, and graduate students with SAT scores 900 or higher and grade point averages of 2.5 or higher (graduate students have GPAs of 3.5 or higher). Students have majors in the liberal arts and speech communication.

All of the students are openly gay on the campus but most are not out to their parents and families. None are considered out-of-state students and all live off campus, some with their families. All of the students responding came out before attending college, and none said that being gay, lesbian, or bisexual affected their choosing Bridgewater State. However, if information on the climate for gay, lesbian, and bisexual students at Bridgewater State had been available, all of the respondents would have chosen to go elsewhere.

The respondents are involved in the gay, lesbian, and bisexual student group, which has an average membership of 10–15 students and sponsors speakers, safe-sex education, and Pride and National Coming Out Day activities. The group receives funding from the student government. In addition, students are active in other organizations such as the AIDS Task Force, the Campus Programming Committee, and the Board of Governors. The students date other Bridgewater State students and indicate that their dating activity takes place off campus, where they congregate in private homes and apartments.

All of the students view the lack of role models as the largest problem at Bridgewater State, with the lack of student organization and coming out following second.

Gay men's and lesbians' cultural contributions are not a part of

regular courses, nor does the college offer courses on gay, lesbian, and bisexual issues. The college does provide free, anonymous HIV testing, counseling for those who are HIV+ or have AIDS, and condoms free of charge. Both the Health Center and the student group provide safe-sex education.

None of the respondents recommend Bridgewater State to other gay, lesbian, and bisexual students.

Brooklyn College of the City University of New York •
Brooklyn, New York

Students define Brooklyn College's position on gay, lesbian, and bisexual issues as noncommittal. The college has a committee on gay, lesbian, and bisexual issues, and sexual orientation is included in the college's affirmative action policy. In addition, counseling services are available for gay, lesbian, and bisexual students. Housing for cohabitating couples is not available. According to the students, the municipality in which the college is located does not have a civil rights law that includes sexual orientation.

Unanimously, students believe that homophobia is a serious problem on the campus. One third of those responding report being victims of harassment and vandalism. Moreover, all of the students have knowledge of hate crimes committed on the campus. Students do not know who, if anyone, maintains hate-crime statistics.

In addition, students do not know how Brooklyn College reacts to hate crimes. Most feel that the college's security force is not supportive. However, all of the students feel safe on the campus as gays, lesbians, and bisexuals.

Gay, lesbian, and bisexual students between the ages of 18–20 responded to the survey. Students are freshmen and sophomores with SAT scores of 899 or higher and grade point averages of 3.5 or higher. Students have majors in biology, business administration, and TV and radio production.

The majority of the students are openly gay on the campus. Those who are not cite fear of reprisal as the primary reason. The majority of students, however, are not out to their parents and families. None are considered out-of-state students and all live off campus, some with their families. Most of the students responding came out before attending college, and none said that being gay, lesbian, or bisexual affected their choosing Brooklyn College. Furthermore, if information on the climate for gays, lesbians, and bisexuals at Brooklyn College had been available, few of the respondents' choices would have been different.

The respondents are involved in the gay, lesbian, and bisexual student group, which has an average membership of 30–40 students and sponsors dances, speakers, safe-sex education, and Pride and National Coming Out Day activities. The group receives funding from the student government. In addition, students are active in athletics. The students tend not to date other Brooklyn College students. Off campus, students congregate in bars and the community center.

All of the students view coming out as the largest problem at Brooklyn College, with the lack of role models following second.

Although gay men's and lesbians' cultural contributions are not a part of regular courses, the college does offer courses on gay, lesbian, and bisexual issues in English. The college does not provide free, anonymous HIV testing or counseling for those who are HIV+ or have AIDS. Condoms, however, are provided free of charge. Both the Health Center and the student group provide safe-sex education.

The majority of the respondents do not recommend Brooklyn College to other gay, lesbian, and bisexual students.

Brown University • *Providence, Rhode Island*

Students define Brown's position on gay, lesbian, and bisexual issues as proactive. The university has a committee on gay, lesbian, and bisexual issues, and sexual orientation is included in the university's affirmative action policy. In addition, counseling services are available for gay, lesbian, and bisexual students. Housing for cohabitating couples is not available. According to the students, the municipality in which the university is located does not have a civil rights law that includes sexual orientation.

Unanimously, students believe strongly that homophobia is a serious problem on the campus. Those responding report being victims

of harassment and verbal abuse. Moreover, all of the students have knowledge of hate crimes committed on the campus, including assault. Both the university and the student group maintain hate-crime statistics.

All of the students believe that Brown takes action in response to hate crimes, and all agree that the university's security force is supportive. Consequently, all of the students feel safe on the campus as gays, lesbians, and bisexuals.

Gay, lesbian, and bisexual students between the ages of 19–21 responded to the survey. Students are sophomores and juniors with SAT scores of 1100 or higher and grade point averages of 3.0 or higher. Students have majors in the liberal arts.

All of the students are openly gay on the campus as well as to their parents and families. None are considered out-of-state students and all live in residence halls or sorority housing. All of the students responding came out before attending college, and none said that being gay, lesbian, or bisexual affected their choosing Brown. Furthermore, if information on the climate for gays, lesbians, and bisexuals at Brown had been available, the respondents' choices would not have been different.

The respondents are involved in the gay, lesbian, and bisexual student group, which has an average membership of 200 students and sponsors dances, speakers, safe-sex education, and Pride and National Coming Out Day activities. The group receives funding from the student government. In addition, students are active in peer education and counseling, Greek letter organizations, and athletics. The students date other Brown students and state that their dating activity takes place on the campus. Off campus, students congregate in bars.

All of the students view coming out as the largest problem at Brown, with alcohol abuse following second.

Gay men's and lesbians' cultural contributions are a part of regular courses. In addition, the university offers courses on gay, lesbian, and bisexual issues in history, American civilization, English, women's studies, and the social sciences. The university provides free HIV testing, counseling for those who are HIV+ or have AIDS, and condoms free of charge. Both the Health Center and the student group provide safe-sex education.

All of the respondents recommend Brown to other gay, lesbian, and bisexual students.

Bryn Mawr College • *Bryn Mawr, Pennsylvania*

Students define Bryn Mawr's position on gay, lesbian, and bisexual issues as noncommittal. The college does not have a committee on gay, lesbian, and bisexual issues, and sexual orientation is not included in its affirmative action policy. In addition, counseling services are not available for gay, lesbian, and bisexual students nor is housing for cohabitating couples. According to the students, the municipality in which the college is located does not have a civil rights law that includes sexual orientation.

Unanimously, however, students do not believe that homophobia is a serious problem on the campus. None of those responding report being victims of hate crimes. However, all of the students have knowledge of hate crimes committed on the campus. The college maintains hate-crime statistics.

All of the students believe that Bryn Mawr takes action in response to hate crimes and agree that the college's security force is supportive. As a result, all of the students feel safe on the campus as gays, lesbians, and bisexuals.

Gay, lesbian, and bisexual students between the ages of 21–23 responded to the survey. Students are juniors and seniors with SAT scores of 1100 or higher and grade point averages of 3.5 or higher. Students have majors in the liberal arts.

All of the students are openly gay on the campus as well as to their parents and families. All are considered out-of-state students and live in residence halls. The students responding came out before attending college, and said that being gay, lesbian, or bisexual affected their choosing Bryn Mawr. Consequently, if information on the climate for gays, lesbians, and bisexuals at Bryn Mawr had been available, the respondents' choices would not have been different.

The respondents are involved in the gay, lesbian, and bisexual student group, which sponsors dances, Pride and National Coming Out Day activities, and safe-sex education. The group receives funding from the student government. The students tend not to date other Bryn Mawr students. Off campus, students congregate in bars.

All of the students view the lack of student organization as the largest problem at Bryn Mawr, with coming out and alcohol abuse following second.

Although gay men's and lesbians' cultural contributions are not a part of regular courses, the college does offer courses on gay, lesbian, and bisexual issues in English and the social sciences. The college provides free, anonymous HIV testing and condoms free of charge. Counseling is not available for those who are HIV+ or have AIDS. The student group provides safe-sex education.

All of the respondents recommend Bryn Mawr to other gay, lesbian, and bisexual students.

Bucknell University • *Lewisberg, Pennsylvania*

Fifty percent of the students responding define Bucknell's position on gay, lesbian, and bisexual issues as noncommittal. The university has a committee on gay, lesbian, and bisexual issues, and sexual orientation is included in the university's affirmative action statement. Bucknell, in addition, provides counseling services for gay, lesbian, and bisexual students; however, students do not know if housing for cohabitating couples is available, nor if the municipality in which the university is located has a civil rights law that includes sexual orientation.

Unanimously, students believe that homophobia is a serious problem on the campus. Fifty percent of those responding report being victims of verbal abuse, harassment, and assault. Moreover, all the students have knowledge of hate crimes committed on the campus. The university maintains hate-crime statistics.

Half of the students do not know how the administration reacts to incidents of hate crimes, while half believe the university is supportive of victims. In contrast, none of the students feel supported by the university's security force. Furthermore, none of the students feel safe on the campus as gays, lesbians, and bisexuals.

Gay, lesbian, and bisexual students between the ages of 19–21 responded to the survey. Students are freshmen and juniors with SAT scores of 1100 or higher and grade point averages of 3.5 and higher. Students have majors in the liberal arts and computer science.

Half of the students surveyed are openly gay on the campus; those who are not state fear of reprisal and knowledge of others' bad experiences as the reasons. Those who are not open are freshmen. All of the students are out to some family members, half are out to their parents. All of the respondents are considered out-of-state students and live in residence halls. None of the students responding came out before attending college, and none said that being gay, lesbian, or bisexual affected their choosing Bucknell. However, if information on the climate for gays, lesbians, and bisexuals at Bucknell had been available, all would have made a different choice.

The respondents are involved in the gay, lesbian, and bisexual student group, which has an average membership of 10–25 students and sponsors speakers, safe-sex education and Pride and National Coming Out Day activities. The group receives funding from the student government. All of the respondents date other Bucknell students; however, only half of those say that their dating activity takes place on the campus. Some of the respondents have life partners attending the university. Off campus, students tend to congregate in bars.

All of the students view coming out as the largest problem at Bucknell, with the lack of role models and student organization following second.

Although gay men's and lesbians' cultural contributions are not a part of some regular courses, the university does offer courses on gay, lesbian, and bisexual issues in the English department. The university does provide free, anonymous HIV testing and counseling for those who are HIV+ or have AIDS, but it does not provide condoms free of charge. Both the university and the student group provide safe-sex education.

None of the respondents recommend Bucknell to other gay, lesbian, and bisexual students.

California Polytechnic State University •
San Luis Obispo, California

Students define Cal Poly's position on gay, lesbian, and bisexual issues as negative. The university does not have a committee on gay, lesbian, and bisexual issues, nor is sexual orientation included in its affirmative action policy. However, counseling services are available for gay, lesbian, and bisexual students. Housing for cohabitating couples is not available. According to the students, the municipality in which the university is located does not have a civil rights law that includes sexual orientation.

Unanimously, students believe that homophobia is a serious problem on the campus. Those responding report being victims of blackmail and verbal abuse. Moreover, all of the students have knowledge of hate crimes committed on the campus, including assault. Students do not know who, if anyone, maintains hate-crime statistics.

Some of the students believe that Cal Poly takes action in response to hate crimes; others believe the school does nothing. Students are also divided concerning the security force's support. All of the students, however, feel safe on the campus as gays, lesbians, and bisexuals.

Gay, lesbian, and bisexual students between the ages of 19–30 responded to the survey. Students are freshmen, sophomores, juniors, seniors, and graduate students with SAT scores of 1100 or higher and grade point averages of 3.5 or higher. Students have majors in the liberal arts and sciences.

Most of the students are openly gay on the campus as well as to their parents and families. Those who are not open cite the fear of their parents finding out as the primary reason. None are considered out-of-state students and all live off campus, some with their families. All of the students responding came out before attending college, and none said that being gay, lesbian, or bisexual affected their choosing Cal Poly. Furthermore, if information on the climate for gays, lesbians, and bisexuals had been available, half of the respondents would have chosen to go elsewhere.

The respondents are involved in the gay, lesbian, and bisexual student group, which has an average membership of 30–35 students and sponsors dances, speakers, safe-sex education, and Pride and National Coming Out Day activities. The group receives funding from the student government. Most students date other Cal Poly students and state that their dating activity takes place on the campus. Off campus, students congregate in bars and cafes.

All of the students view alcohol abuse as the largest problem at Cal Poly, with the lack of role models and other substance abuse following second.

Gay men's and lesbians' cultural contributions are not a part of regular courses, nor does the university offer courses on gay, lesbian, and bisexual issues. The university provides free, anonymous HIV testing, counseling for those who are HIV+ or have AIDS, and condoms free of charge. Both the Health Center and the student group provide safe-sex education.

Half of the respondents recommend Cal Poly to other gay, lesbian, and bisexual students.

California State University, Fullerton • *Fullerton, California*

Students define the position of Cal State, Fullerton, on gay, lesbian, and bisexual issues as proactive. Although the university does not have a committee on gay, lesbian, and bisexual issues, sexual orientation is included in its affirmative action policy. In addition, counseling services are available for gay, lesbian, and bisexual students. Students do not know if housing for cohabitating couples is available. According to the students, the municipality in which the university is located does not have a civil rights law that includes sexual orientation.

Unanimously, students believe that homophobia is a serious problem on the campus. However, none of those responding report being victims of hate crimes. Yet all of the students have knowledge of hate crimes committed on the campus. The university maintains hate-crime statistics.

All of the students believe that Cal State takes action in response to hate crimes and agree that the university's security force is supportive. All of the students feel safe on the campus as gays, lesbians, and bisexuals.

Gay, lesbian, and bisexual students between the ages of 19–21 responded to the survey. Students are sophomores and juniors with SAT scores of 1100 or higher and grade point averages of 3.5 or higher. Students have majors in the liberal arts.

Most of the students are openly gay on the campus but are not out to their parents and families. None are considered out-of-state students and all live off campus, some with their families. None of the students responding came out before attending college, and none said that being gay, lesbian, or bisexual affected their choosing Cal State at Fullerton. Furthermore, if information on the climate for gays, lesbians, and bisexuals at Cal State had been available, the respondents' choices would not have been different.

The respondents are involved in the gay, lesbian, and bisexual student group, which has an average membership of 80–100 students and sponsors support groups and safe-sex education. The group receives no funding from the student government. In addition, students are active in the Student Environmental Action League. The students tend not to date other Cal State students. Off campus, students congregate in the community center.

All of the students view coming out as the largest problem at Cal State with the lack of role models and student organization following second.

Gay men's and lesbians' cultural contributions are not a part of regular courses, nor does the university offer courses on gay, lesbian, and bisexual issues. Students do not know if the university provides free, anonymous HIV testing or counseling for those who are HIV+ or have AIDS. Condoms, however, are available free of charge. Both the Health Center and the student group provide safe-sex education.

All of the respondents recommend Cal State at Fullerton to other gay, lesbian, and bisexual students.

California State University, Northridge •
Northridge, California

Students vary in defining the position of Cal State, Northridge, on gay, lesbian, and bisexual issues as proactive and noncommittal. Although the university has a committee on gay, lesbian, and bisexual issues, sexual orientation is not included in the university's affirmative action statement. Counseling services are available for gay, lesbian, and bisexual students, but housing for cohabitating couples is not. Students' answers vary widely on whether the municipality in which the university is located has a civil rights law that includes sexual orientation.

Unanimously, students believe that homophobia is a serious problem on the campus. However, none of those responding report being victims of hate crimes; yet, all of the students have knowledge of hate crimes committed on the campus, including assault. The university maintains hate-crime statistics.

All of the students believe that Cal State takes action in response to these incidents and feel supported by the university's security force. As a result, all of the students feel safe on the campus as gays, lesbians, and bisexuals.

Gay, lesbian, and bisexual students between the ages of 20–23 responded to the survey. Students are freshmen, sophomores, and seniors with SAT scores of 899 or higher and grade point averages of 2.5 and higher. Students declaring majors are studying in the liberal arts and journalism.

All of the students surveyed are openly gay on the campus as well as to their parents and families. None are considered out-of-state students and all live off campus. Half of the students responding came out before attending college, and none said that being gay, lesbian, or bisexual affected their choosing Cal State at Northridge. However, if information on the climate for gays, lesbians, and bisexuals at Cal State had been available, some of the respondents would have made a different choice.

The respondents are involved in the gay, lesbian, and bisexual student group, which has an average membership of 50–80 students and sponsors dances, speakers, safe-sex education and Pride and National Coming Out Day activities. The group receives funding from the student government. The students date other Cal State students and indicate that their dating activity takes place on the campus. Off campus, students congregate in bars, religious organizations, and the community center.

All of the students view coming out as the largest problem at Cal State, with lack of role models and student organization following second.

Although gay men's and lesbians' cultural contributions are not a part of regular courses, the university offers courses on gay, lesbian, and bisexual issues in English and women's studies. The university provides free, anonymous HIV testing and condoms free of charge. Students do not know if counseling is available for those who are HIV+ or have AIDS. Both the Health Center and the student group provide safe-sex education.

Fifty percent of the respondents recommend Cal State at Northridge to other gay, lesbian, and bisexual students.

California State University, Sacramento •
Sacramento, California

Fifty percent of the students responding define the position of Cal State, Sacramento, on gay, lesbian, and bisexual issues as proactive. The remaining students do not know the school's position. Although the university does not have a committee on gay, lesbian, and bisexual issues, sexual orientation is included in its affirmative action statement. Cal State does, however, provide counseling services for gay, lesbian, and bisexual students. Students do not know if housing for cohabitating couples is available. According to the students, the municipality in which the university is located has a civil rights law that includes sexual orientation.

Unanimously, students believe that homophobia is a serious problem on the campus. None of those responding report being victims of hate crimes, but many activity posters are torn down and "hate literature" can be found on the campus. No one maintains hate-crime statistics.

None of the students know how Cal State reacts to hate crimes, but half feel supported by the university's security force. In addition, all students feel moderately safe on the campus as gays, lesbians, and bisexuals.

Gay, lesbian, and bisexual students between the ages of 24–29 responded to the survey. Students are juniors and seniors with SAT scores of 1100 or higher and grade point averages of 3.0 and higher. Students have majors in the liberal arts, nursing, and psychology.

The majority of the students surveyed are openly gay on the campus, and all are out to parents and family members. None of the respondents are considered out-of-state students and all live off campus, some live with life partners. All of the students responding came out before attending college and said that being gay, lesbian, or bisexual affected their choosing Cal State at Sacramento. But if information on the climate for gays, lesbians, and bisexuals at Cal State had been available, 50 percent of the respondents would have made a different choice.

The respondents are involved in the gay, lesbian, and bisexual student group, which has an average membership of 10–12 students and sponsors speakers, safe-sex education, and Pride and National Coming Out Day activities. The group receives funding from the student government. In addition, students are active in other organizations such as the Council for Equality and area organizations for gays and lesbians. Half of the students responding indicate that they date other Cal State students and that their dating activity typically takes place on campus. Off campus, students congregate in bars, at the community center, and in various coffeehouses.

All of the students view the lack of student organization as the largest problem at Cal State, with the lack of role models and alcohol abuse following second.

Gay men's and lesbians' cultural contributions are not a part of some regular courses, but the university does offer courses on gay, lesbian, and bisexual issues in the psychology department. The university provides free, anonymous HIV testing but does not provide condoms. Students do not know if counseling is available for those who are HIV+ or have AIDS. Both the Health Center and the student group provide safe-sex education.

All of the respondents recommend Cal State at Sacramento to other gay, lesbian, and bisexual students, with one student remarking that "there are good, supportive teachers and a large gay community in the city itself."

Carleton College • *Northfield, Minnesota*

Students define Carleton's position on gay, lesbian, and bisexual issues somewhere between negative and noncommittal. The college has a committee on gay, lesbian, and bisexual issues, and sexual orientation is included in the college's affirmative action policy. Counseling services are not available for gay, lesbian, and bisexual students nor is housing for cohabitating couples. According to the students, the municipality in which the college is located does not have a civil rights law that includes sexual orientation.

Unanimously, students believe that homophobia is a serious problem on the campus. Those responding report being victims of hate mail, vandalism, and verbal abuse. Moreover, all of the students have knowledge of hate crimes committed on the campus, including assault. The student group maintains hate-crime statistics.

All of the students believe that Carleton does nothing in response to hate crimes, and all agree that the college's security force is not supportive. Consequently, most of the students do not feel safe on the campus as gays, lesbians, and bisexuals.

Gay, lesbian, and bisexual students between the ages of 18–20 responded to the survey. Students are freshmen, sophomores, and juniors with SAT scores of 900 or higher and grade point averages of 3.0 or higher. Students have majors in the liberal arts.

All of the students are openly gay on the campus as well as to their parents and families. All are considered out-of-state students and live in residence halls. Most of the students responding came out before attending college, and some said that being gay, lesbian, or bisexual affected their choosing Carleton. But if information on the climate for gays, lesbians, and bisexuals at Carleton had been available, all of the respondents would have chosen to go elsewhere.

The respondents are involved in the gay, lesbian, and bisexual student group, which has an average membership of 85 students and sponsors dances, speakers, safe-sex education, and Pride and National Coming Out Day activities. The group receives funding from the student government. In addition, students are active in other organizations such as the women's a cappella singing group, Resources Against Pornography, and the Activist Coalition for Multicultural Education. The students date other Carleton students and state that their dating activity takes place on the campus. Some of the respondents have life partners attending the school. Off campus, students congregate in bars and religious organizations.

All of the students view coming out as the largest problem at Carleton, with the lack of role models and alcohol abuse following second.

Gay men's and lesbians' cultural contributions are not a part of regular courses, nor does the college offer courses on gay, lesbian, and bisexual issues. The college does not provide free, anonymous

HIV testing or counseling for those who are HIV+ or have AIDS. Condoms, however, are provided free of charge. Both the Health Center and the student group provide safe-sex education.

All of the respondents recommend Carleton to other gay, lesbian, and bisexual students.

Carnegie-Mellon University • *Pittsburgh, Pennsylvania*

Students define Carnegie-Mellon's position on gay, lesbian, and bisexual issues between proactive and noncommittal. The university has a committee on gay, lesbian, and bisexual issues, and sexual orientation is included in the university's affirmative action policy. In addition, counseling services are available for gay, lesbian, and bisexual students. Housing for cohabitating couples is not available. According to the students, the municipality in which the university is located does not have a civil rights law that includes sexual orientation.

Unanimously, students believe that homophobia is a serious problem on the campus. Those responding report being victims of vandalism. Moreover, all of the students have knowledge of hate crimes committed on the campus. The university maintains hate-crime statistics.

All of the students believe that Carnegie-Mellon takes action in response to hate crimes and agree strongly that the university's security force is supportive. All of the students feel basically safe on the campus as gays, lesbians, and bisexuals.

Gay, lesbian, and bisexual students between the ages of 21–23 responded to the survey. Students are juniors and seniors with SAT scores of 1100 or higher and grade point averages of 3.0 or higher. Some students have majors in architecture.

All of the students are openly gay on the campus but not to their parents and families. None are considered out-of-state students and all live in off-campus apartments and houses. All of the students responding came out before attending college, and none said that being gay, lesbian, or bisexual affected their choosing Carnegie-Mellon. Furthermore, if information on the climate for gays, lesbians, and bisexuals at Carnegie-Mellon had been available, the respondents' choices would not have been different.

The respondents are involved in the gay, lesbian, and bisexual

student group, which has an average membership of 20+ students and sponsors dances, speakers, safe-sex education, and Pride and National Coming Out Day activities. The group receives funding from the student government. In addition, students are active in other organizations such as the student government and the alternative press. The students tend not to date other Carnegie-Mellon students. Off campus, students tend to congregate in bars.

All of the students view coming out as the largest problem at Carnegie-Mellon, with the lack of role models and student organization following second.

Although gay men's and lesbians' cultural contributions are not a part of regular courses, the university does offer courses on gay, lesbian, and bisexual issues in the English department. Students do not know if the University provides free, anonymous HIV testing, but counseling is available for those who are HIV+ or have AIDS. Condoms are not provided. Both the Health Center and the student group provide safe-sex education.

Students are not sure if they would recommend Carnegie-Mellon to other gay, lesbian, and bisexual students.

Catholic University of America • *Washington, D.C.*

Students define Catholic U's position on gay, lesbian, and bisexual issues as noncommittal. Although the university does not have a committee on gay, lesbian, and bisexual issues, sexual orientation is included in its affirmative action policy. Counseling services are not available for gay, lesbian, and bisexual students nor is housing for cohabitating couples. According to the students, the municipality in which the university is located has a civil rights law that includes sexual orientation.

Unanimously, students believe strongly that homophobia is a serious problem on the campus. Those responding report being victims of verbal abuse. Moreover, all of the students have knowledge of hate crimes committed on the campus. The student group maintains hate-crime statistics.

All of the students believe that Catholic U takes action in response to hate crimes, but they do not agree that the university's security force is supportive. None of the students feel safe on the campus as gays, lesbians, and bisexuals.

Gay, lesbian, and bisexual students between the ages of 23–31 responded to the survey. Students are seniors and graduate students with grade point averages of 3.5 or higher. Students have majors in the liberal arts and theology.

All of the students are openly gay on the campus as well as to their parents and families. None are considered out-of-state students and all live in off-campus houses and apartments. All of the students responding came out before attending college, and none said that being gay, lesbian, or bisexual affected their choosing Catholic U. However, if information on the climate for gays, lesbians, and bisexuals at Catholic U had been available, all of the respondents would have made a different choice.

The respondents are involved in the gay, lesbian, and bisexual student group, which has an average membership of 10 students and sponsors speakers and safe-sex education. The group receives funding from the student government. The students tend not to date other Catholic U students, but state that their dating activity takes place on the campus. Off campus, students congregate in bars and religious organizations.

All of the students view coming out as the largest problem at Catholic U, with the lack of student organization and role models following second.

Gay men's and lesbians' cultural contributions are not a part of regular courses, nor does the university offer courses on gay, lesbian, and bisexual issues. The university does not provide free, anonymous HIV testing, counseling for those who are HIV+ or have AIDS, or condoms. The student group provides safe-sex education.

None of the respondents recommend Catholic U to other gay, lesbian, and bisexual students.

City University of New York • *New York, New York*

Students define CUNY's position on gay, lesbian, and bisexual issues as proactive. Although the university does not have a committee on gay, lesbian, and bisexual issues, sexual orientation is included in its affirmative action policy. Counseling services are not available for gay, lesbian, and bisexual students nor is housing for cohabitating couples. According to the students, the municipality in which the university is located has a civil rights law that includes sexual orientation.

Unanimously, students believe strongly that homophobia is a serious problem on the campus. Those responding report being victims of hate mail, vandalism, and verbal abuse. Moreover, all of the students have knowledge of hate crimes committed on the campus. The university maintains hate-crime statistics.

All of the students believe that CUNY takes action in response to hate crimes but do not agree that the University's security force is supportive. Yet all of the students feel safe on the campus as gays, lesbians, and bisexuals.

Gay, lesbian, and bisexual students between the ages of 19–21 responded to the survey. Students are sophomores with grade point averages of 3.5 or higher. Students have majors in the liberal arts and lesbian and gay studies.

All of the students are openly gay on the campus as well as to their parents and families. None are considered out-of-state students and all live off campus, some with life partners. All of the students responding came out before attending college, and said that being gay, lesbian, or bisexual affected their choosing CUNY. Furthermore, if information on the climate for gays, lesbians, and bisexuals at CUNY had been available, the respondents' choices would not have been different.

The respondents are involved in the gay, lesbian, and bisexual student group, which has an average membership of 35 students and sponsors dances, speakers, safe-sex education, and Pride and National Coming Out Day activities. The group receives funding from the student government. The students date other CUNY students and state that their dating activity takes place on the campus.

All of the students view the lack of role models as the largest problem at CUNY, with the lack of student organization and coming out following second.

Gay men's and lesbians' cultural contributions are not a part of regular courses, nor does the university offer courses on gay, lesbian, and bisexual issues except in the lesbian and gay studies program. The university does not provide free, anonymous HIV testing, counseling for those who are HIV+ or have AIDS, or condoms free of charge. The student group provides safe-sex education.

All of the respondents recommend CUNY to other gay, lesbian, and bisexual students.

Colby College • *Waterville, Maine*

Students define Colby's position on gay, lesbian, and bisexual issues as proactive. The college has a committee on gay, lesbian, and bisexual issues, and sexual orientation is included in the college's affirmative action policy. In addition, counseling services are available for gay, lesbian, and bisexual students, as is housing for cohabitating couples (according to one third of the students). According to the students, the municipality in which the college is located has a civil rights law that includes sexual orientation.

Unanimously, students believe that homophobia is a serious problem on the campus. One third of those responding report being victims of harassment, vandalism, and verbal abuse. Moreover, all of the students have knowledge of hate crimes committed on the campus. The college maintains hate-crime statistics.

All of the students believe that Colby takes action in response to hate crimes and all agree that the college's security force is supportive. As a result, all of the students feel safe on the campus as gays, lesbians, and bisexuals.

Gay, lesbian, and bisexual students between the ages of 18–22 responded to the survey. Students are freshmen, sophomores, juniors, and seniors with SAT scores of 900 or higher and grade point averages of 3.0 or higher. Students have majors in art history, performing arts, and American studies.

Most of the students are openly gay on the campus as well as to their parents and families. All are considered out-of-state students and live in residence halls. None of the students responding came out before attending college, and none said that being gay, lesbian, or bisexual affected their choosing Colby. Furthermore, if information on the climate for gays, lesbians, and bisexuals at Colby had been available, the respondents' choices would not have been different.

The respondents are involved in the gay, lesbian, and bisexual student group, which has an average membership of 50–100 students

and sponsors dances, speakers, safe-sex education, and Pride and National Coming Out Day activities. The group receives funding from the student government. In addition, students are active in theater groups and women's groups. The students date other Colby students and state that their dating activity takes place on the campus. Off campus, students tend to congregate in the community center.

All of the students view coming out as the largest problem at Colby, with the lack of role models and student organization following second.

Although gay men's and lesbians' cultural contributions are not a part of regular courses, the college does offer courses on gay, lesbian, and bisexual issues in English, women's studies, and American studies. The college provides free HIV testing, counseling for those who are HIV+ or have AIDS, and condoms free of charge. Both the Health Center and the student group provide safe-sex education.

All of the respondents recommend Colby to other gay, lesbian, and bisexual students.

Colorado College • *Colorado Springs, Colorado*

Students define Colorado's position on gay, lesbian, and bisexual issues as noncommittal. Although the college does not have a committee on gay, lesbian, and bisexual issues, sexual orientation is included in its affirmative action policy. In addition, counseling services are available for gay, lesbian, and bisexual students. Housing for cohabiting couples is not available. According to the students, the municipality in which the college is located does not have a civil rights law that includes sexual orientation.

Unanimously, students believe that homophobia is a serious problem on the campus. Those responding report being victims of verbal abuse. Moreover, all of the students have knowledge of hate crimes committed on the campus, including assault. No one maintains hate-crime statistics.

All of the students believe that Colorado does nothing in response to hate crimes. Students are divided over the security force's support, but feel relatively safe on the campus as gays, lesbians, and bisexuals.

Gay, lesbian, and bisexual students between the ages of 21–22 responded to the survey. Students are seniors with SAT scores of 1100

or higher and grade point averages of 3.5 or higher. They have majors in the liberal arts and sciences.

All of the students are openly gay on the campus as well as to their parents and families. None are considered out-of-state students and all live in off-campus houses and apartments. None of the students responding came out before attending college, and none said that being gay, lesbian, or bisexual affected their choosing Colorado. If information on the climate for gays, lesbians, and bisexuals had been available, the respondents' choices would have been different.

The respondents are involved in the gay, lesbian, and bisexual student group, which has an average membership of 40 students and sponsors dances, speakers, safe-sex education, and Pride and National Coming Out Day activities. The group receives funding from the student government. Additionally, students are active in other organizations such as biology journal club, psychology society, and feminist groups. The students date other Colorado students and state that their dating activity takes place on the campus. Off campus, students congregate in bars, political groups, and community dances.

All of the students view coming out as the largest problem at Colorado, with the lack of role models following second.

Although gay men's and lesbians' cultural contributions are not a part of regular courses, the college does offer courses on gay, lesbian, and bisexual issues in English and women's studies. The college provides free, anonymous HIV testing and condoms. Students do not know if counseling is available for those who are HIV+ or have AIDS or if condoms are available. Both the Health Center and the student group provide safe-sex education.

All of the respondents recommend Colorado to other gay, lesbian, and bisexual students, although most find the city of Colorado Springs very hostile.

Columbia University, Columbia College •
New York, New York

Students define Columbia's position on gay, lesbian, and bisexual issues somewhere between proactive and noncommittal. The college has a committee on gay, lesbian, and bisexual issues, and sexual orientation is included in the college's affirmative action policy. In addition, counseling services are available for gay, lesbian, and bisexual students. Housing for cohabitating couples is not available. According to the students, the municipality in which the college is located has a civil rights law that includes sexual orientation.

Students are divided on whether homophobia is a serious problem on the campus. Half of those responding report being victims of harassment, vandalism, and verbal abuse. All of the students have knowledge of hate crimes committed on the campus, including physical and sexual assault. An off-campus group maintains hate-crime statistics on the campus.

All of the students believe that Columbia does nothing in response to hate crimes, and are divided concerning the security force's support. However, all of the students feel safe on the campus as gays, lesbians, and bisexuals.

Gay, lesbian, and bisexual students between the ages of 20–23 responded to the survey. Students are juniors and seniors with SAT scores of 1100 or higher and grade point averages of 3.0 or higher. Students have majors in the liberal arts.

All of the students are openly gay on the campus as well as to their parents and families. None are considered out-of-state students and all live in residence halls or off-campus apartments. None of the students responding came out before attending college, and none said that being gay, lesbian, or bisexual affected their choosing Columbia. Furthermore, if information on the climate for gays, lesbians, and bisexuals at Columbia had been available, the respondents' choices would not have been different.

The respondents are involved in the gay, lesbian, and bisexual student group, which has an average membership of 25–100 students and sponsors dances, speakers, safe-sex education, and Pride and National Coming Out Day activities. The group receives funding from the student government. In addition, students are active in peer education and counseling. The students date other Columbia students and state that some of their dating activity takes place on the campus. Off campus, students congregate in bars, the community center, and religious organizations.

All of the students view alcohol and substance abuse as the largest problem at Columbia, with the lack of role models and coming out following second.

Gay men's and lesbians' cultural contributions are a part of some regular courses. In addition, the college also offers courses on gay, lesbian, and bisexual issues in history, English, women's studies, and the social sciences. The college provides free, anonymous HIV testing, counseling for those who are HIV+ or have AIDS, and condoms free of charge. Both the Health Center and the student group provide safe-sex education.

All of the respondents recommend Columbia to other gay, lesbian, and bisexual students.

Columbia University, School of Law • *New York, New York*

Students define Columbia School of Law's position on gay, lesbian, and bisexual issues as noncommittal. The university does not have a committee on gay, lesbian, and bisexual issues, nor is sexual orientation included in its affirmative action policy. However, counseling services are available for gay, lesbian, and bisexual students, as is housing for cohabitating couples. According to the students, the municipality in which the university is located has a civil rights law that includes sexual orientation.

Unanimously, students believe that homophobia is a serious problem on the campus, though none of those responding report being victims of hate crimes. However, all of the students have knowledge of hate crimes committed on the campus, including assault. The university maintains hate-crime statistics.

All of the students believe that Columbia takes action in response to hate crimes and agree that the university's security force is supportive. All of the students feel safe on the campus as gays, lesbians, and bisexuals.

Gay, lesbian, and bisexual students between the ages of 24–28 responded to the survey. Students are Juris Doctor candidates with SAT scores of 1100 or higher and high grade point averages.

All of the students are openly gay on the campus as well as to their parents and families. None are considered out-of-state students and all live off campus, some with life partners. None of the students responding came out before attending college, and none said that being gay, lesbian, or bisexual affected their choosing Columbia Law School. Furthermore, if information on the climate for gays, lesbians, and bisexuals at Columbia had been available, the respondents' choices would not have been different, although some are unsure.

The respondents are involved in the gay, lesbian, and bisexual student group, which has an average membership of 15 students and sponsors speakers, Pride and National Coming Out Day activities, and safe-sex education. The group receives funding from the student government. In addition, students are active in the various law student associations, including the Law Review. The students tend not to date other Columbia students. Off campus, students congregate in the community center.

All of the students view coming out as the largest problem at Columbia, with the lack of role models following second.

Although gay men's and lesbians' cultural contributions are not a part of regular courses, the university does offer courses on gay, lesbian, and bisexual issues in English, history, and law. The university provides free, anonymous HIV testing, counseling for those who are HIV+ or have AIDS, and condoms free of charge. Both the Health Center and the student group provide safe-sex education.

All of the respondents recommend Columbia to other gay, lesbian, and bisexual students.

Columbia University, Teachers College •
New York, New York

Students define Columbia's position on gay, lesbian, and bisexual issues as proactive. Although the university does not have a committee on gay, lesbian, and bisexual issues, sexual orientation is included in its affirmative action policy. In addition, counseling services are available for gay, lesbian, and bisexual students, as is housing for cohabitating couples. According to the students, the municipality in which the university is located does not have a civil rights law that includes sexual orientation.

Unanimously, students believe that homophobia is a serious problem on the campus, although none of those responding report being victims of hate crimes. However, all of the students have knowledge of hate crimes committed on the campus, including assault. The student group maintains hate-crime statistics.

All of the students believe that Columbia takes action in response to hate crimes and agree that the university's security force is support-ive. All of the students feel safe on the campus as gays, lesbians, and bisexuals.

Gay, lesbian, and bisexual students between the ages of 20–34 responded to the survey. Students are juniors, seniors, and graduate students with SAT scores of 1100 or higher and grade point averages of 3.5 or higher. Students have majors in education.

All of the students are openly gay on the campus as well as to their parents and families. None are considered out-of-state students and all live off campus. All of the students responding came out before attending college, and none said that being gay, lesbian, or bisexual affected their choosing Columbia. Furthermore, if information on the climate for gays, lesbians, and bisexuals had been available, respon-dents' choices would not have been different.

The respondents are involved in the gay, lesbian, and bisexual student group, which has an average membership of 30+ students and sponsors dances, speakers, and safe-sex education. The group receives funding from the student government. The students date other Columbia students and state that their dating activity takes place off campus, where they tend to congregate in bars.

All of the students view the lack of role models as the largest problem at Columbia, with coming out and substance abuse follow-ing second.

Gay men's and lesbians' cultural contributions are a part of regular courses. In addition, the university also offers courses on gay, lesbian, and bisexual issues in English, women's studies, history, art, educa-tion, and the social sciences. The university provides free, anonymous HIV testing, counseling for those who are HIV+ or have AIDS, and condoms free of charge. Both the Health Center and the student group provide safe-sex education.

All of the respondents recommend Columbia to other gay, lesbian, and bisexual students.

Connecticut College • *New London, Connecticut*

Students define Connecticut College's position on gay, lesbian, and bisexual issues as proactive. The college has a committee on gay, lesbian, and bisexual issues, and sexual orientation is included in the college's affirmative action policy. In addition, counseling services are available for gay, lesbian, and bisexual students. Housing for cohabitating couples is not available. According to the students, the municipality in which the college is located has a civil rights law that includes sexual orientation.

Unanimously, students believe that homophobia is a serious problem on the campus. Twenty-five percent of those responding report being victims of harassment, vandalism, and verbal abuse. Moreover, all of the students have knowledge of hate crimes committed on the campus, including assault. The college maintains hate-crime statistics.

All of students believe that Connecticut College takes action in response to hate crimes and agree that the college's security force is supportive. Consequently, all of the students feel safe on the campus as gays, lesbians, and bisexuals.

Gay, lesbian, and bisexual students between the ages of 20–22 responded to the survey. Students are juniors and seniors with SAT scores of 1100 or higher and grade point averages of 2.5 or higher. Students have majors in psychology, art history, religious studies, and history.

All of the students are openly gay on the campus and the majority are out to their parents and families. Half are considered out-of-state students. Seventy-five percent of the students live in residence halls; the remaining students live off campus, some with life partners. None of the students responding came out before attending college, and none said that being gay, lesbian, or bisexual affected their choosing Connecticut College. Furthermore, if information on the climate for gays, lesbians, and bisexuals had been available, few of the respondents would have made a different choice.

The respondents are involved in the gay, lesbian, and bisexual student group, which has an average membership of 15–25 students and sponsors dances, speakers, safe-sex education, and Pride and National Coming Out Day activities. The group receives funding from the student government. In addition, students are active in other organizations such as SOAR (Society Organized Against Racism), Psi Chi, and the Asian Student Union. Twenty-five percent of the students date other Connecticut College students and state that their dating activity takes place on the campus. Off campus, students typically congregate in bars.

All of the students view coming out as the largest problem at Connecticut College, with the lack of role models and alcohol abuse following second.

Gay men's and lesbians' cultural contributions are not a part of regular courses, nor does the college offer courses on gay, lesbian, and bisexual issues. The college does not provide free, anonymous HIV testing. Students do not know if counseling is available for those who are HIV+ or have AIDS. Condoms are available for a nominal charge. Both the Health Center and the student group provide safe-sex education.

Half of the respondents recommend Connecticut College to other gay, lesbian, and bisexual students.

Curry College • *Milton, Massachusetts*

Students define Curry's position on gay, lesbian, and bisexual issues as proactive. The college does not have a committee on gay, lesbian, and bisexual issues, but sexual orientation is included in its affirmative action statement. Students do not know if counseling services are available for gay, lesbian, and bisexual students. Housing for cohabitating couples is not available. According to the students, the municipality in which the college is located has a civil rights law that includes sexual orientation.

Unanimously, students strongly believe that homophobia is a serious problem on the campus. Those responding report being victims of hate mail, verbal abuse, assault, vandalism, and harassment. Moreover, all of the students have knowledge of hate crimes committed on the campus. Both the college and the student group maintain hate-crime statistics.

All of the students believe that Curry takes action in response to hate crimes. All of the students, in addition, feel supported by the college's security force. Consequently, the majority of students feel safe on the campus as gays, lesbians, and bisexuals.

Gay, lesbian, and bisexual students between the ages of 20–22 responded to the survey. Students are freshmen and sophomores with SAT scores of 900 or higher and grade point averages of 3.5 and higher. Students have majors in the liberal arts and mass communication.

All of the students surveyed are openly gay on the campus as well as to their parents and families. None are considered out-of-state students and all live in residence halls. All of the students responding came out before attending college, and none said that being gay, lesbian, or bisexual affected their choosing Curry. Furthermore, if information on the climate for gays, lesbians, and bisexuals at Curry had been available, the respondents' choices would not have been different.

The respondents are involved in the gay, lesbian, and bisexual student group, which has an average membership of 20 students and sponsors speakers, safe-sex education, and Pride and National Coming Out Day activities. The group receives no funding from the student government. The students tend not to date other Curry students. Off campus, students congregate in bars and the community center.

All of the students view coming out as the largest problem at Curry, with substance abuse following second.

Although gay men's and lesbians' cultural contributions are not a part of regular courses, the college offers courses on gay, lesbian, and bisexual issues in women's studies. Students do not know if the college provides free, anonymous HIV testing, nor whether counseling is available for those who are HIV+ or have AIDS. Condoms are provided free of charge. Both the college and the student group provide safe-sex education.

All of the respondents recommend Curry to other gay, lesbian, and bisexual students.

C. W. Post Center, Long Island University •
Brookville, New York

Students at C. W. Post do not know the school's position on gay, lesbian, and bisexual issues, nor whether sexual orientation is included in the university's affirmative action statement. In addition, the university does not have a committee on gay, lesbian, and bisexual issues, nor does it provide counseling services for gay, lesbian, and bisexual students; housing for cohabiting couples is not available. According to the students, the municipality in which the university is located has a civil rights law that includes sexual orientation.

Unanimously, students believe that homophobia is a serious problem on the campus, though none of those responding report being victims of hate crimes. However, all the students have knowledge of hate crimes committed on the campus, including verbal abuse and vandalism. The university maintains hate-crime statistics.

None of the respondents know how C. W. Post reacts to hate crimes. Most, in addition, do not feel supported by the university's security force. Most of the students, however, do feel safe on the campus as gays, lesbians, and bisexuals.

Gay, lesbian, and bisexual students between the ages of 19–21 responded to the survey. Students are sophomores, juniors, and seniors with SAT scores of 900 or higher and grade point averages of 3.5 and higher. All have majors in the liberal arts.

None of the students surveyed are openly gay on the campus primarily due to fear of reprisal; however, most are out to parents and family members. None are considered out-of-state students and most live at home with their families. Few of the students responding came out before attending college, and none said that being gay, lesbian, or bisexual affected their choosing C. W. Post. However, if information on the climate for gays, lesbians, and bisexuals at C. W. Post had been available, the respondents' choices would have been different.

The respondents are involved in the gay, lesbian, and bisexual student group at Hofstra University since there is no active group at C. W. Post. All of the students responding state that they tend not to date other C. W. Post students. Off campus, students congregate in bars and the community center.

All of the students view coming out as the largest problem at C. W. Post, with alcohol and other substance abuse following second.

Gay men's and lesbians' cultural contributions are not a part of regular courses, nor are courses offered on gay, lesbian, and bisexual issues. The university does not provide free, anonymous HIV testing, condoms, or counseling for those who are HIV+ or have AIDS. The student group provides safe-sex education.

None of respondents recommend C. W. Post to other gay, lesbian, and bisexual students.

Dartmouth College • *Hanover, New Hampshire*

Students define Dartmouth's position on gay, lesbian, and bisexual issues as noncommittal. Students do not know if Dartmouth has a committee on gay, lesbian, and bisexual issues. However, sexual orientation is included in the college's nondiscrimination policy and counseling services are available to gay, lesbian, and bisexual students. Housing for cohabitating couples is not available. According to the students, the municipality in which the university is located does not have a civil rights law that includes sexual orientation.

Unanimously, students strongly believe that homophobia is a serious problem on the Dartmouth campus. Those responding report being victims of hate mail, verbal abuse, harassment, and vandalism. Moreover, all of the students have knowledge of hate crimes committed on the campus, including assault. No one maintains hate-crime statistics.

All of the students believe that Dartmouth does nothing in response to these incidents. In fact, one student states that the college "changed the policy to protect perpetrators after one incident." Additionally, none of the students feel supported by the college's security force. Consequently, most students do not feel safe on the campus.

Gay, lesbian, and bisexual students between the ages of 21–23 responded to the survey. Students are juniors and seniors with SAT scores of 1100 or higher and grade point averages of 3.5 and higher. All have majors in the liberal arts.

All of the students are openly gay on the campus, but only a minority of the respondents are out to their parents and families. All are considered out-of-state students and live off campus. Few of the students responding came out before attending college, and none said that being gay, lesbian, or bisexual affected their choosing Dartmouth. Furthermore, if information on the climate for gays, lesbians, and bisexuals at Dartmouth had been available, most of the respondents would not have made a different choice.

All of the students are involved in the gay, lesbian, and bisexual student groups (DAGLO and In Your Face), which have an average membership of 40 students and sponsors dances, speakers, safe-sex education, and Pride and National Coming Out Day activities. The group receives funding from the student government. The students date other Dartmouth students and their dating activity takes place on the campus. Off campus, students congregate in restaurants and in other students' apartments.

All of the students view coming out as the largest problem at Dartmouth, with lack of role models and alcohol abuse following second.

Although gay men's and lesbians' cultural contributions are not a part of regular courses, the college does offer courses on gay, lesbian, and bisexual issues in the English and drama departments. The college offers free, anonymous HIV testing and condoms. Students do not know whether counseling is available for those who are HIV+ or have AIDS. Both the Health Center and the student group provide safe-sex education.

Only one of the respondents recommends Dartmouth to other gay, lesbian, and bisexual students "only because this college needs more people who are willing to come out. But gay students should know that among other schools with a similar background, Dartmouth is not an easy place for gays, lesbians, and bisexuals. In fact, I'm convinced that it is as homophobic as the rest of the American culture."

De Anza Junior College • *De Anza, California*

Students define De Anza's position on gay, lesbian, and bisexual issues as noncommittal. Students do not know if the college has a committee on gay, lesbian, and bisexual issues, or if counseling services are available for gay, lesbian, and bisexual students. Sexual orientation, however, is included in the college's affirmative action statement. Students do not know if the municipality in which the college is located has a civil rights law that includes sexual orientation.

Unanimously, students believe that homophobia is a somewhat serious problem on the campus. None of those responding report being victims of hate crimes, or have knowledge of hate crimes committed on the campus. Students do not know who, if anyone, maintains hate-crime statistics.

Students do not know how De Anza reacts to hate crimes and are ambivalent concerning the college's security force. However, all of the students feel safe on the campus as gays, lesbians, and bisexuals.

Gay, lesbian, and bisexual students between the ages of 19–20 responded to the survey. Students are freshmen and sophomores with SAT scores of 900 or higher and grade point averages of 3.0 and higher. Students have majors in the liberal arts.

All of the students surveyed are openly gay on the campus as well as to some family members. None are considered out-of-state students and all live off campus, some with their families. None of the students responding came out before attending college, and none said that being gay, lesbian, or bisexual affected their choosing De Anza. Furthermore, if information on the climate for gays, lesbians, and bisexuals at De Anza had been available, the respondents' choices would not have been different.

The respondents are involved in the gay, lesbian, and bisexual student group, which has an average membership of 10–20 students and sponsors speakers and safe-sex education. The group receives funding from the student government. In addition, students are active in political groups. Students date other De Anza students, but their dating activity takes place off campus, where they congregate in bars, dance clubs, and the community center.

All of the students view the lack of role models as the largest problem at De Anza, with coming out and the lack of student organization following second.

Gay men's and lesbians' cultural contributions are a part of some regular courses within certain departments; however, the college does not offer courses on gay, lesbian, and bisexual issues. Students do not know if the college provides HIV testing or counseling for those who are HIV+ or have AIDS. Condoms, however, are provided free of charge. Both the Health Center and the student group provide safe-sex education.

All of the respondents recommend De Anza to other gay, lesbian, and bisexual students.

Denison University • *Granville, Ohio*

Students define Denison's position on gay, lesbian, and bisexual issues as proactive. The university does not have a committee on gay, lesbian, and bisexual issues, but sexual orientation is included in its affirmative action statement, and counseling services are available for gay, lesbian, and bisexual students. Students do not know if housing for cohabitating couples is available. According to the students, the municipality in which the university is located does not have a civil rights law that includes sexual orientation.

Unanimously, students strongly believe that homophobia is a serious problem on the campus. Those responding report being victims of hate mail, verbal abuse, vandalism, and harassment. Moreover, all of the students have knowledge of hate crimes committed on the campus. The university maintains hate-crime statistics.

All of the students believe that Denison takes action in response to hate crimes but they do not feel supported by the university's security force. However, the majority of students feel safe on the campus as gays, lesbians, and bisexuals.

Gay, lesbian, and bisexual students between the ages of 20–22 responded to the survey. Students are sophomores and juniors with SAT scores of 900 or higher and grade point averages of 3.0 and higher. Students have majors in the liberal arts.

All of the students surveyed are openly gay on the campus as well as to their parents and families. None are considered out-of-state students and all live in residence halls. None of the students responding came out before attending college, and none said that being gay, lesbian, or bisexual affected their choosing Denison. Furthermore, if information on the climate for gays, lesbians, and bisexuals at Denison had been available, the respondents' choices would not have been different.

The respondents are involved in the gay, lesbian, and bisexual student group, which has an average membership of 60 (5 core) students and sponsors speakers, safe-sex education, and Pride and National Coming Out Day activities. The group receives no funding from the student government. The students tend not to date other Denison students. Off campus, students typically congregate in bars.

All of the students view coming out as the largest problem at Denison, with lack of role models and student organization following second.

Gay men's and lesbians' cultural contributions are not a part of regular courses, nor does the university offer courses on gay, lesbian, and bisexual issues. The university does not provide free, anonymous HIV testing or counseling for those who are HIV+ or have AIDS.

Condoms are provided free of charge. Both the university and the student group provide safe-sex education.

All of the respondents recommend Denison to other gay, lesbian, and bisexual students, but "only if they want to fight."

Earlham College • *Richmond, Indiana*

Students define Earlham's position on gay, lesbian, and bisexual issues as noncommittal. The college does not have a committee on gay, lesbian, and bisexual issues, nor is sexual orientation included in its affirmative action statement. Earlham does, however, provide counseling services for gay, lesbian, and bisexual students. Students do not know if housing for cohabitating couples is available. According to the students, the municipality in which the college is located does not have a civil rights law that includes sexual orientation.

Unanimously, students believe that homophobia is not a serious problem on the campus. None of those responding report being victims of hate crimes, but all of the students have knowledge of hate crimes committed on the campus, including assault. No one maintains hate-crime statistics.

All of the students believe that Earlham takes action in response to hate crimes and all feel supported by the college's security force. Consequently, all students feel safe on the campus as gays, lesbians, and bisexuals.

Gay, lesbian, and bisexual students between the ages of 19–21 responded to the survey. Students are juniors and seniors with SAT scores of 1100 or higher and grade point averages of 3.0 and higher. Students have majors in the liberal arts.

All of the students surveyed are openly gay on the campus as well as to their parents and families. All of the respondents are considered out-of-state students and live off campus. None of the students responding came out before attending college and none said that being gay, lesbian, or bisexual affected their choosing Earlham. Furthermore, if information on the climate for gays, lesbians, and bisexuals at Earlham had been available, the respondents' choices would not have been different.

The respondents are involved in the gay, lesbian, and bisexual student group, which has an average membership of 30 students and

sponsors dances, speakers, safe-sex education, and Pride and National Coming Out Day activities. The group does not receive funding from the student government. Students state that they tend not to date other Earlham students. Off campus, students congregate in bars.

All of the students view the lack of role models as the largest problem at Earlham, with coming out and lack of student organization following second.

Gay men's and lesbians' cultural contributions are not a part of regular courses, nor does the college offer courses on gay, lesbian, and bisexual issues. However, the college provides free, anonymous HIV testing and counseling for those who are HIV+ or have AIDS. The college does not provide condoms free of charge. Both the Health Center and student groups provide safe-sex education.

All of the respondents recommend Earlham to other gay, lesbian, and bisexual students.

Emerson College • *Boston, Massachusetts*

Students responding divide evenly in defining Emerson's position on gay, lesbian, and bisexual issues as proactive and noncommittal. Although the college does not have a committee on gay, lesbian, and bisexual issues, sexual orientation is included in its affirmative action statement. Emerson does, however, provide counseling services for gay, lesbian, and bisexual students. Students do not know if housing for cohabitating couples is available. According to the students, the municipality in which the college is located has a civil rights law that includes sexual orientation.

Unanimously, students believe that homophobia is a serious problem on the campus. Those responding report being victims of verbal abuse, harassment, hate mail and vandalism. Moreover, all the students have knowledge of hate crimes committed on the campus, but no one maintains hate-crime statistics.

Twenty-five percent of the students believe that Emerson supports victims in response to hate crimes; the remaining students do not know how the administration reacts. Students split evenly about feeling supported by the college's security force. However, all students feel safe on the campus as gays, lesbians, and bisexuals.

Gay, lesbian, and bisexual students between the ages of 23–29

responded to the survey. Students are juniors, seniors, and graduate students with SAT scores of 1100 or higher and grade point averages of 3.5 and higher. Students have majors in mass communication, creative writing, and the liberal arts.

Fifty percent of the students surveyed are openly gay on the campus; those who are not open cite fear of reprisal and labeling as the primary reasons. All are out to their parents and some family members. None of the respondents are considered out-of-state students and all live off campus, some in fraternity/sorority housing. Those living in Greek housing are not openly gay. All of the students responding came out before attending college, and 50 percent said that being gay, lesbian, or bisexual affected their choosing Emerson. If information on the climate for gays, lesbians, and bisexuals at Emerson had been available, half of the respondents would have chosen to go elsewhere.

The respondents are involved in the gay, lesbian, and bisexual student group, which has an average membership of 10–20 students and sponsors speakers, safe-sex education, and Pride and National Coming Out Day activities. The group receives funding from the student government. In addition, students are active in other organizations such as the school broadcasting groups, the literary magazine, and Greek-letter organizations. Half of the students responding state that they date other Emerson students and that their dating activity typically takes place on campus. Off campus, students congregate in bars.

All of the students view coming out as the largest problem at Emerson, with the lack of student organization following second.

Gay men's and lesbians' cultural contributions are not a part of some regular courses, nor does the college offer courses on gay, lesbian, and bisexual issues. The college does not provide free, anonymous HIV testing but does provide condoms. Students do not know if counseling is available for those who are HIV+ or have AIDS. Both the Health Center and the student group provide safe-sex education.

Ninety percent of the respondents recommend Emerson to other gay, lesbian, and bisexual students.

Emory University • *Atlanta, Georgia*

Students define Emory's position on gay, lesbian, and bisexual issues as noncommittal. The university has a committee on gay, lesbian, and bisexual issues, but sexual orientation is not included in the university's affirmative action policy. However, counseling services are available for gay, lesbian, and bisexual students. Housing for cohabitating couples is not available. According to the students, the municipality in which the university is located does not have a civil rights law that includes sexual orientation.

Most students believe strongly that homophobia is a serious problem on the campus. One third of those responding report being victims of verbal abuse. Moreover, all of the students have knowledge of hate crimes committed on the campus, including assault. Both the university and the student group maintain hate-crime statistics.

Students believe that Emory takes action in response to hate crimes when pushed by the student group; however, action is slow and minimal. But all agree that the university's security force is supportive and all feel safe on the campus as gays, lesbians, and bisexuals.

Gay, lesbian, and bisexual students between the ages of 21–32 responded to the survey. Students are seniors and graduate students with SAT scores of 900 or higher and grade point averages of 3.0 or higher. Students have majors in the liberal arts.

All of the students are openly gay on the campus as well as to their parents and families. Most are considered out-of-state students and all live off campus, some with life partners. Few of the students responding came out before attending college, and none said that being gay, lesbian, or bisexual affected their choosing Emory. Furthermore, if information on the climate for gays, lesbians, and bisexuals at Emory had been available, the respondents' choices would not have been different.

The respondents are involved in the gay, lesbian, and bisexual student group, which has an average membership of 50–75 students and sponsors dances, speakers, safe-sex education, and Pride and National Coming Out Day activities. The group receives funding from the student government. Additionally, students are active on the Student Programming Council. The students date other Emory students and state that their dating activity takes place on the campus. Off campus, students congregate in bars.

All of the students view the lack of role models as the largest problem at Emory, with coming out following second.

Gay men's and lesbians' cultural contributions are a part of some regular courses. In addition, the university also offers courses on gay, lesbian, and bisexual issues in English, women's studies, history, and the social sciences. The university does not provide free, anonymous HIV testing or counseling for those who are HIV+ or have AIDS, but condoms are provided free of charge. Both the Health Center and the student group provide safe-sex education.

All of the respondents recommend Emory to other gay, lesbian, and bisexual students. "Emory has just opened up a Gay, Lesbian, and Bisexual Office in Student Life. The campus is in a new stage of political and social awareness. For a campus in the Deep South, Emory is a strong supportive community for bisexual, lesbian, and gay students, faculty, and staff."

Florida State University • *Tallahassee, Florida*

Two thirds of the students responding define Florida State's position on gay, lesbian, and bisexual issues as proactive, while one third view the university as noncommittal. The university has a committee on gay, lesbian, and bisexual issues, and sexual orientation is included in its affirmative action statement. In addition, counseling services are provided for gay, lesbian, and bisexual students. Students do not know if housing for cohabitating couples is available. According to the students, the municipality in which the university is located does not have a civil rights law that includes sexual orientation.

Unanimously, students believe that homophobia is a serious problem on the campus. Two thirds of those responding report being victims of verbal abuse, and all of the students have knowledge of hate crimes committed on the campus, including assault. The student group maintains hate-crime statistics.

The majority of the students believe that Florida State takes action in response to hate crimes. However, two thirds of the respondents state that they do not feel supported by the university's security force.

Yet all of the students feel safe on the campus as gays, lesbians, and bisexuals.

Gay, lesbian, and bisexual students between the ages of 20–24 responded to the survey. Students are juniors and seniors with SAT scores of 900 or higher and grade point averages of 3.0 and higher. Most students have majors in music and music therapy.

Two thirds of the students surveyed are openly gay on the campus; those who are not cite fear of reprisal as the primary reason. None of the students are out to their parents and families. None are considered out-of-state students and all live off campus. All of the students responding came out before attending college, and none said that being gay, lesbian, or bisexual affected their choosing Florida State. If information on the climate for gays, lesbians, and bisexuals at Florida State had been available, the respondents' choices would not have been different.

The respondents are involved in the gay, lesbian, and bisexual student group, which has an average membership of 100 students and sponsors dances, speakers, safe-sex education and Pride and National Coming Out Day activities. The group receives funding from the student government. Two thirds of the students responding indicate that they date other Florida State students and that their dating activity takes places on the campus. Off campus, students congregate in bars, the community center, and religious organizations.

All of the students view coming out as the largest problem at Florida State, with alcohol abuse and the lack of role models following second.

Gay men's and lesbians' cultural contributions are a part of some regular courses; the university also offers courses on gay, lesbian, and bisexual issues in the social sciences and humanities. The university provides free, anonymous HIV testing, counseling services for those who are HIV+ or have AIDS, and condoms free of charge. Both the Health Center and the student group provide safe-sex education.

The majority of the respondents recommend Florida State to other gay, lesbian, and bisexual students.

George Washington University • *Washington, D.C.*

Students define George Washington University's position on gay, lesbian, and bisexual issues as noncommittal. Although the university does not have a committee on gay, lesbian, and bisexual issues, sexual orientation is included in its affirmative action statement. The university provides some counseling services for gay, lesbian, and bisexual students. Students do not know if housing for cohabitating couples is available. According to the students, the municipality in which the university is located has a civil rights law that includes sexual orientation.

Unanimously, students believe that homophobia is a serious problem on the campus. Those responding report being victims of verbal abuse, harassment, hate mail, and threats. Moreover, all the students have knowledge of hate crimes committed on the campus, including assault. No one maintains hate-crime statistics.

Most of the students believe that George Washington University does nothing in response to hate crimes, and the majority do not feel supported by its security force. However, most students feel safe on the campus as gays, lesbians, and bisexuals.

Gay, lesbian, and bisexual students between the ages of 18–28 responded to the survey. Students are freshman, sophomores, juniors, seniors, and graduate students with SAT scores of 900 or higher and grade point averages of 2.0 and higher. Students have majors in journalism, psychology, computer science, and international affairs.

Eighty percent of the students surveyed are openly gay on the campus; those who are not open cite fear of being labeled as the primary reason. All are out to some family members, with 60 percent out to their parents. The majority of respondents are considered out-of-state students. Half of the students live in residence halls while the remainder live off campus, a few with their families. Eighty percent of the students responding came out before attending college, and 30 percent said that being gay, lesbian, or bisexual affected their choosing George Washington. Furthermore, if information on the climate for gays, lesbians, and bisexuals at George Washington had been available, 60 percent of the respondents would have made a different choice.

The respondents are involved in the gay, lesbian, and bisexual

student group, which has an average membership of 40–60 students and sponsors dances, speakers, safe-sex education, and Pride and National Coming Out Day activities. The group receives funding from the student government. In addition, students are active in other organizations such as the school newspaper, College Democrats, the campus radio station, and Greek-letter organizations. Twenty percent of the students responding state that they date other George Washington students, but their dating activity typically takes place off campus, where students congregate in bars, the community center, and religious organizations.

All of the students view coming out as the largest problem at George Washington, with the lack of student organization and role models following second.

Gay men's and lesbians' cultural contributions are not a part of some regular courses, nor does the university offer courses on gay, lesbian, and bisexual issues. The university does not provide free, anonymous HIV testing or condoms. Students do not know if counseling is available for those who are HIV+ or have AIDS. Both the Health Center and the student group provide safe-sex education.

All of the respondents recommend George Washington University to other gay, lesbian, and bisexual students.

Georgia Institute of Technology • *Atlanta, Georgia*

Students define Georgia Tech's position on gay, lesbian, and bisexual issues as noncommittal. The Institute does not have a committee on gay, lesbian, and bisexual issues, and sexual orientation is not included in the Institute's affirmative action statement. Housing for cohabitating couples is not available. Counseling services, however, are available for gay, lesbian, and bisexual students. According to the students, the municipality in which the Institute is located does not have a civil rights law that includes sexual orientation.

Unanimously, students strongly believe that homophobia is a serious problem on the campus. Those responding report being victims of hate mail, verbal abuse, assault, harassment, and vandalism. Moreover, all of the students have knowledge of hate crimes committed on the campus. Both the Institute and the student group maintain hate-crime statistics.

None of the students know how Georgia Tech reacts to hate crimes. None of the students feel supported by the Institute's security force, so the majority do not feel safe on the campus as gays, lesbians, and bisexuals.

Gay, lesbian, and bisexual students between the ages of 20–23 responded to the survey. Students are juniors and seniors with SAT scores of 1100 or higher and grade point averages of 2.5 and higher. Students have majors in engineering.

None of the students surveyed are openly gay on the campus, citing fear of reprisal as the primary reason. Students, however, are out to their parents and families. None are considered out-of-state students and all live off campus, some with their families. All of the students responding came out before attending college, and none said that being gay, lesbian, or bisexual affected their choosing Georgia Tech. Furthermore, if information on the climate for gays, lesbians, and bisexuals at Georgia Tech had been available, the respondents' choices would not have been different.

The respondents are involved in the gay, lesbian, and bisexual student group, which has an average membership of 30 students and sponsors Pride and National Coming Out Day activities and safe-sex education. The group receives no funding from the student government. The students tend not to date other Georgia Tech students. Off campus, students congregate in bars.

All of the students view coming out as the largest problem at Georgia Tech.

Gay men's and lesbians' cultural contributions are not a part of regular courses, nor does the Institute offer courses on gay, lesbian, and bisexual issues. Students do not know if the Institute provides free, anonymous HIV testing, but counseling is available for those who are HIV+ or have AIDS, and condoms are provided free of charge. The student group provides safe-sex education.

All of the respondents recommend Georgia Tech to other gay, lesbian, and bisexual students.

Gettysburg College • *Gettysburg, Pennsylvania*

Students define Gettysburg's position on gay, lesbian, and bisexual issues as noncommittal. The college does not have a committee on gay, lesbian, and bisexual issues, sexual orientation is not included in its affirmative action statement, and housing for cohabitating couples is not available. Counseling services, however, are available for gay, lesbian, and bisexual students. According to the students, the municipality in which the college is located does not have a civil rights law that includes sexual orientation.

Unanimously, students strongly believe that homophobia is a serious problem on the campus. None of those responding report being victims of hate crimes, but all of the students have knowledge of hate crimes committed on the campus. No one maintains hate-crime statistics.

None of the students know how Gettysburg reacts to hate crimes, but none of the students feel supported by the college's security force. Consequently, the majority of students do not feel safe on the campus as gays, lesbians, and bisexuals.

Gay, lesbian, and bisexual students between the ages of 20–23 responded to the survey. Students are juniors and seniors with SAT scores of 1100 or higher and grade point averages of 3.5 and higher. Students have majors in the liberal arts.

All of the students surveyed are openly gay on the campus as well as to their parents and families. None are considered out-of-state students and all live in off-campus apartments and houses. All of the students responding came out before attending college, and none said that being gay, lesbian, or bisexual affected their choosing Gettysburg. However, if information on the climate for gays, lesbians, and bisexuals at Gettysburg had been available, the majority of the respondents would have chosen to go elsewhere.

The respondents are involved in the gay, lesbian, and bisexual student group, which has an average membership of 4 students and sponsors speakers. The group receives no funding from the student government. In addition, students are active in other organizations such as the Debate Society. The students tend not to date other Gettysburg students. Off campus, students typically congregate in bars.

All of the students view coming out as the largest problem at Gettysburg, with lack of role models and alcohol abuse following second.

Gay men's and lesbians' cultural contributions are not a part of

regular courses, nor does the college offer courses on gay, lesbian, and bisexual issues. The college does not provide free, anonymous HIV testing or counseling for those who are HIV+ or have AIDS. Condoms, however, are provided free of charge. The Health Center provides safe-sex education.

None of the respondents recommend Gettysburg to other gay, lesbian, and bisexual students.

Goldey Beacom College • *Wilmington, Delaware*

Students define Goldey Beacom's position on gay, lesbian, and bisexual issues as noncommittal. The college does not have a committee on gay, lesbian, and bisexual issues, sexual orientation is not included in its affirmative action policy, and counseling services are not available for gay, lesbian, and bisexual students. Students do not know if housing for cohabitating couples is available. According to the students, the municipality in which the college is located does not have a civil rights law that includes sexual orientation.

Unanimously, students believe strongly that homophobia is a serious problem on the campus, but none of those responding report being victims of hate crimes. However, all of the students have knowledge of hate crimes committed on the campus. Students do not know who, if anyone, maintains hate-crime statistics.

All of the students believe that Goldey Beacom does nothing in response to hate crimes. All agree that the college's security force is not supportive. Still, all of the students feel safe on the campus as gays, lesbians, and bisexuals.

Gay, lesbian, and bisexual students between the ages of 20–24 responded to the survey. Students are juniors and seniors with grade point averages of 3.0 or higher. Students have majors in the liberal arts and business administration.

All of the students are openly gay on the campus as well as to their parents and families. None are considered out-of-state students and all live off campus, some with their families. None of the students responding came out before attending college, and none said that being gay, lesbian, or bisexual affected their choosing Goldey Beacom. However, if information on the climate for gays, lesbians, and bisexuals at Goldey Beacom had been available, all of the respondents would have chosen to go elsewhere.

Goldey Beacom does not have a gay, lesbian, and bisexual student group. Students are, however, active in the University of Delaware Lesbian, Gay, and Bisexual Student Union. The students tend not to date other Goldey Beacom students. Off campus, students congregate in bars and at other area colleges.

All of the students view the lack of role models as the largest problem at Goldey Beacom, with the lack of student organization and coming out following second.

Gay men's and lesbians' cultural contributions are not a part of regular courses, nor does the college offer courses on gay, lesbian, and bisexual issues. The college does not provide free, anonymous HIV testing, counseling for those who are HIV+ or have AIDS, or condoms. No one provides safe-sex education for the students.

None of the respondents recommend Goldey Beacom to other gay, lesbian, and bisexual students.

Gustavus Adolphus College • *St. Peter, Minnesota*

Students define Gustavus Adolphus College's position on gay, lesbian, and bisexual issues as noncommittal. The college does not have a committee on gay, lesbian, and bisexual issues, nor is sexual orientation included in its affirmative action policy. Counseling services, however, are available for gay, lesbian, and bisexual students. Housing for cohabitating couples is not available. According to the students, the municipality in which the college is located does not have a civil rights law that includes sexual orientation.

Unanimously, students believe strongly that homophobia is a serious problem on the campus. Those responding report being victims of hate mail and harassment. Moreover, all of the students have knowledge of hate crimes committed on the campus. Students do not know who, if anyone, maintains hate-crime statistics.

All of the students believe that Gustavus Adolphus does nothing in response to hate crimes, and all agree that the college's security force is not supportive. Students are ambivalent concerning their safety on the campus as gays, lesbians, and bisexuals.

Gay, lesbian, and bisexual students between the ages of 20–21

responded to the survey. Students are sophomores with SAT scores of 1100 or higher and grade point averages of 3.0 or higher. Students have majors in the liberal arts and psychology.

None of the students are openly gay on the campus, nor are they out to their parents and families. All are considered out-of-state students and live in residence halls. None of the students responding came out before attending college, and none said that being gay, lesbian, or bisexual affected their choosing Gustavus Adolphus. Furthermore, if information on the climate for gays, lesbians, and bisexuals at Gustavus Adolphus had been available, the respondents' choices would not have been different.

The respondents are involved in the gay, lesbian, and bisexual student group, which has an average membership of 5 students. The group receives no funding from the student government. In addition, students are active in the Women's Awareness Center. The students date other Gustavus Adolphus students and state that their dating activity takes place on the campus. Students typically congregate in each other's rooms.

All of the students view the lack of student organization as the largest problem at Gustavus Adolphus, with coming out and the lack of role models following second.

Gay men's and lesbians' cultural contributions are not a part of regular courses, nor does the college offer courses on gay, lesbian, and bisexual issues. Students do not know if the College provides free, anonymous HIV testing, or condoms. However, counseling is available for those who are HIV+ or have AIDS. Students do not know who provides safe-sex education.

None of the respondents recommend Gustavus Adolphus to other gay, lesbian, and bisexual students.

Hamilton College • *Clinton, New York*

Students vary defining Hamilton's position on gay, lesbian, and bisexual issues: half say it is noncommittal, one quarter says proactive and one quarter says negative. The college has a committee on gay, lesbian, and bisexual issues, and sexual orientation is included in its affirmative action policy. In addition, counseling services are available for gay, lesbian, and bisexual students. Housing for cohabitating couples is not available. Students do not know if the municipality in which the college is located has a civil rights law that includes sexual orientation.

Unanimously, students believe that homophobia is a serious problem on the campus. Those responding report being victims of verbal abuse and harassment. Moreover, all of the students have knowledge of hate crimes committed on the campus, including assault. Students do not know who, if anyone, maintains hate-crime statistics.

The majority of students believe that Hamilton takes some kind of action in response to hate crimes, but all agree that the college's security force is not supportive. Consequently, most of the students do not feel safe on the campus as gays, lesbians, and bisexuals.

Gay, lesbian, and bisexual students between the ages of 20–21 responded to the survey. Students are sophomores and seniors with SAT scores of 1100 or higher and grade point averages of 3.0 or higher. Students have majors in comparative literature, creative writing, computer science, art history, and French.

Half of the students are openly gay on the campus as well as to their parents and families. Those who are not cite fear of reprisal as the primary reason. Few are considered out-of-state students. The majority of students live in residence halls. Very few students responding came out before attending college, and none said that being gay, lesbian, or bisexual affected their choosing Hamilton. But if information on the climate for gays, lesbians, and bisexuals at Hamilton had been available, half of the respondents would have made a different choice.

The respondents are involved in the gay, lesbian, and bisexual student group, which has an average membership of 15–20 students and sponsors dances, speakers, safe-sex education, and Pride and National Coming Out Day activities. The group receives no funding from the student government. Additionally, students are active in other organizations such as the Women's Center, the Hamilton Organization for Peace on Earth, and the Emerson Literary Society. Most students date other Hamilton students and state that their dating activity takes place off campus, where they tend to congregate in bars.

All of the students view coming out as the largest problem at Hamilton, with the lack of role models following second.

Although gay men's and lesbians' cultural contributions are not a

part of regular courses, the college does offer courses on gay, lesbian, and bisexual issues in English, women's studies, and the social sciences. The college provides free, anonymous HIV testing, counseling for those who are HIV+ or have AIDS, and condoms. Both the Health Center and the student group provide safe-sex education.

The majority of the respondents emphatically do not recommend Hamilton to other gay, lesbian, and bisexual students. One student, however, does for the reason that "we are stronger in larger numbers."

Hampshire College • *Amherst, Massachusetts*

Students define Hampshire's position on gay, lesbian, and bisexual issues as proactive. The college has a committee on gay, lesbian, and bisexual issues, and sexual orientation is included in the college's affirmative action policy. In addition, counseling services are available for gay, lesbian, and bisexual students. One third of the students state that housing for cohabitating couples is available. According to the students, the municipality in which the college is located has a civil rights law that includes sexual orientation.

The majority of students believe that homophobia is not a serious problem on the campus. None of those responding report being victims of hate crimes. However, all of the students have knowledge of hate crimes committed on the campus, including assault. Both the college and the student group maintain hate-crime statistics.

All of the students believe that Hampshire takes action in response to hate crimes, and most agree that the college's security force is supportive. All of the students feel safe on the campus as gays, lesbians, and bisexuals.

Gay, lesbian, and bisexual students between the ages of 20–22 responded to the survey. Students are juniors and seniors with SAT scores of 1100 or higher. Hampshire does not have grades. Students have majors in sexuality and gender roles, community-supported agriculture, environmental design, and urban studies.

All of the students are openly gay on the campus and the majority are out to their parents and families. Some are considered out-of-state students and all live in residence halls or in on-campus apartments. One third of the students responding came out before attending college, and some said that being gay, lesbian, or bisexual affected their choosing Hampshire. If information on the climate for gay, lesbian, and bisexuals at Hampshire had been available, the respondents' choices would not have been different.

The respondents are involved in the gay, lesbian, and bisexual student group, which has an average membership of 45–120 students and sponsors dances, speakers, safe-sex education, and Pride and National Coming Out Day activities. The group receives funding from the student government. In addition, students are active in AIDS organizations and the farm policy committee. Two thirds of the students date other Hampshire students and state that their dating activity takes place on the campus. Off campus, students congregate in bars.

All of the students view coming out as the largest problem at Hampshire, with the lack of student organization and alcohol abuse following second.

Gay men's and lesbians' cultural contributions are a part of regular courses. In addition, the college offers courses on gay, lesbian, and bisexual issues in English, women's studies, history, film, education, and the social sciences. The college provides free, anonymous HIV testing and condoms free of charge. Students do not know if counseling is available for those who are HIV+ or have AIDS. Both the Health Center and the student group provide safe-sex education.

All of the respondents highly recommend Hampshire to other gay, lesbian, and bisexual students, with one student commenting: "I would rate Hampshire's queer atmosphere very high. There's a large degree of visibility for bisexuals, lesbians, and gay men. Our student group is active and the faculty is supportive of gay studies. The five colleges in the area provide lots of room for interaction with other gay students. Hampshire isn't perfect. It's small. There's a low enrollment of minorities, homophobic things do happen, the LGBA is only mildly organized at times. But I'd still encourage other queer students to look at Hampshire."

Harvard Divinity School • *Cambridge, Massachusetts*

Students define Harvard Divinity School's position on gay, lesbian, and bisexual issues as proactive. The school has a committee on gay, lesbian, and bisexual issues, and sexual orientation is included in the school's affirmative action policy. Students do not know if counseling services are available for gay, lesbian, and bisexual students. Housing for cohabitating couples is available. According to the students, the municipality in which the Divinity School is located does not have a civil rights law that includes sexual orientation.

Unanimously, students do not believe that homophobia is a serious problem on the campus. None of those responding report being victims of hate crimes. However, all of the students have knowledge of hate crimes committed on the Harvard campus, but not at the Divinity School specifically. Students do not know who, if anyone, maintains hate-crime statistics.

All of students believe that Harvard takes action in response to hate crimes, and all agree that the school's security force is supportive. All of the students feel safe on the campus as gays, lesbians, and bisexuals.

Gay, lesbian, and bisexual students between the ages of 22–24 responded to the survey. Students are graduates with SAT scores of 900 or higher and grade point averages of 3.5 or higher.

All of the students are openly gay on the campus as well as to their parents and families. All are considered out-of-state students and all live in residence halls. Most of the students responding came out before attending college, and some said that being gay, lesbian, or bisexual affected their choosing Harvard. Furthermore, if information on the climate for gays, lesbians, and bisexuals at Harvard Divinity had been available, the respondents' choices would not have been different.

The respondents are involved in the gay, lesbian, and bisexual student group, which has an average membership of 15–30 students and sponsors dances, speakers, safe-sex education, and Pride and National Coming Out Day activities. The group receives funding from the student government. Students are also active in student government. The students tend not to date other Harvard students. Off campus, students congregate in bars and religious organizations.

All of the students view the lack of student organization as the largest problem at Harvard Divinity School, with coming out following second.

Although gay men's and lesbians' cultural contributions are not a

part of regular courses, the school does offer courses on gay, lesbian, and bisexual issues in English, history, and divinity classes. The school provides free, but not anonymous, HIV testing, and counseling for those who are HIV+ or have AIDS. But students point out that Fenway Medical and Cambridge Cares are the best places to go in the area. Students do not know if condoms are provided free of charge. Both the Health Center and the student group provide safe-sex education.

All of the respondents recommend Harvard Divinity School to other gay, lesbian, and bisexual students.

Harvard University • *Cambridge, Massachusetts*

Students define Harvard's position on gay, lesbian, and bisexual issues as proactive. The university does not have a committee on gay, lesbian, and bisexual issues, but sexual orientation is included in its affirmative action statement, and counseling services are available for gay, lesbian, and bisexual students. Students do not know if housing for cohabitating couples is available. According to the students, the municipality in which the university is located has a civil rights law that includes sexual orientation.

Unanimously, students believe that homophobia is a serious problem on the campus. Those responding report being victims of verbal abuse, assault, and harassment. Moreover, all of the students have knowledge of hate crimes committed on the campus. The student group maintains hate-crime statistics.

None of the students know how Harvard reacts to hate crimes. All of the students, though, feel strongly that they are supported by the university's security force. Consequently, the majority of students feel safe on the Harvard campus as gays, lesbians, and bisexuals.

Gay, lesbian, and bisexual students between the ages of 20–22 responded to the survey. Students are freshmen and juniors with SAT scores of 1100 or higher and grade point averages of 3.5 and higher. Students have majors in the liberal arts.

All of the students surveyed are openly gay on the campus as well as to their parents and families. None are considered out-of-state students and all live off campus. All of the students responding came out before attending college, and said that being gay, lesbian, or bisexual affected their choosing Harvard. If information on the climate for gays, lesbians, and bisexuals at Harvard had been available, the respondents' choices would not have been different.

The respondents are involved in the gay, lesbian, and bisexual student group, which has an average membership of 30 students and sponsors dances, speakers, safe-sex education, and Pride and National Coming Out Day activities. The group receives no funding from the student government. The students tend not to date other Harvard students. Off campus, students congregate in bars, the community center, and religious organizations.

All of the students view alcohol abuse as the largest problem at Harvard, with other substance abuse and the lack of role models following second.

Gay men's and lesbians' cultural contributions are not a part of regular courses, nor does the university offer courses on gay, lesbian, and bisexual issues. Students do not know if the university provides free, anonymous HIV testing, nor whether counseling is available for those who are HIV+ or have AIDS or if condoms are provided free of charge. The student group provides safe-sex education.

All of the respondents recommend Harvard to other gay, lesbian, and bisexual students.

Hobart and William Smith College • *Geneva, New York*

Ninety percent of the students responding define Hobart and Smith's position on gay, lesbian, and bisexual issues as proactive. The college has a committee on gay, lesbian, and bisexual issues, and sexual orientation is included in the college's affirmative action policy. In addition, counseling services are available for gay, lesbian, and bisexual students. Housing for cohabiting couples is not available. Students do not know if the municipality in which the college is located has a civil rights law that includes sexual orientation.

Unanimously, students believe that homophobia is a serious problem on the campus. Sixty percent of those responding report being victims of harassment and verbal abuse. Moreover, all of the students have knowledge of hate crimes committed on the campus, including assault. The college maintains hate-crime statistics.

All of students believe that Hobart and Smith takes action in response to hate crimes and agree that the college's security force is supportive. However, only 40 percent of the students feel safe on the campus as gays, lesbians, and bisexuals.

Gay, lesbian, and bisexual students between the ages of 18–21 responded to the survey. Students are freshmen, sophomores, juniors, and seniors with SAT scores of 900 or higher and grade point averages of 2.0 or higher. Students have majors in sociology, anthropology, wellness, English, women's studies, French, and political science.

Sixty percent of the students are not openly gay on the campus, citing fear of reprisal as the primary reason. Half are out to their parents and families. Fifty-five percent are considered out-of-state students and all live in residence halls. One fifth of the students responding came out before attending college, and none said that being gay, lesbian, or bisexual affected their choosing Hobart and Smith. If information on the climate for gays, lesbians, and bisexuals at Hobart and Smith had been available, half of the respondents would have made a different choice.

The respondents are involved in the gay, lesbian, and bisexual student group, which has an average membership of 20–25 students and sponsors speakers, safe-sex education, and Pride and National Coming Out Day activities. The group receives funding from the student government. In addition, students are active in other organizations such as the Latin American Organization, the Women's Resource Center, residential life, the student newspaper, and athletics. Most students tend not to date other Hobart and Smith students. Off campus, students congregate in bars.

All of the students view coming out as the largest problem at Hobart and Smith, with the lack of role models and alcohol abuse following second.

Although gay men's and lesbians' cultural contributions are not a part of regular courses, the college does offer courses on gay, lesbian, and bisexual issues in English, history, film, American studies, women's studies, and political science. The college provides free, anonymous HIV testing and counseling for those who are HIV+ or have AIDS. Students do not know if condoms are provided. The Health Center, Residence Life, and the student group provide safe-sex education for the campus.

All of the respondents recommend Hobart and Smith to other gay, lesbian, and bisexual students. Students agree that the student group is very strong and visible, providing a "healthy environment in which to come out." The students view the president and deans of the college as very supportive. The group also has a resource center funded in part by the administration. The only drawbacks, according to students, are that homophobia is a problem and that any major city is an hour's drive away.

Hofstra University • *Hempstead, New York*

Three quarters of the students responding define Hofstra's position on gay, lesbian, and bisexual issues as negative. Although the university does not have a committee on gay, lesbian, and bisexual issues, sexual orientation is included in its affirmative action policy. In addition, counseling services are available for gay, lesbian, and bisexual students. Housing for cohabitating couples is not available. According to the students, the municipality in which the university is located does not have a civil rights law that includes sexual orientation.

Unanimously, students believe that homophobia is a serious problem on the campus. Three quarters of those responding report being victims of harassment and verbal abuse. Moreover, all of the students have knowledge of hate crimes committed on the campus, including assault. Students do not know who, if anyone, maintains hate-crime statistics.

All of the students believe that Hofstra does nothing in response to hate crimes, and all agree that the university's security force is not supportive. Consequently only one quarter of the students feel safe on the campus as gays, lesbians, and bisexuals.

Gay, lesbian, and bisexual students between the ages of 18–24 responded to the survey. Students are freshmen, sophomores, juniors, and seniors with SAT scores of 900 or higher and grade point averages of 2.0 or higher. Students have majors in psychology, business administration, and mass communications.

The majority of the students are openly gay on the campus and most are out to their parents and families. Those who are not out cite the fear that fraternity brothers may find out. None are considered out-of-state students. Students live both in residence halls and off campus. Half of the students responding came out before attending college, and none said that being gay, lesbian, or bisexual affected their choosing Hofstra. If information on the climate for gays, lesbians, and bisexuals at Hofstra had been available, half of the respondents would have made a different choice.

The respondents are involved in the gay, lesbian, and bisexual student group, which has an average membership of 15–20 students and sponsors dances, speakers, safe-sex education, and Pride and National Coming Out Day activities. The group receives funding from the student government. In addition, students are active in other organizations such as the psychology group, Hillel, and the Program Board. The students date other Hofstra students and state that their dating activity takes place on the campus. Off campus, students congregate in bars and the community center.

All of the students view coming out as the largest problem at Hofstra, with the lack of role models and following second.

Gay men's and lesbians' cultural contributions are not a part of regular courses, nor does the university offer courses on gay, lesbian, and bisexual issues. The university does not provide free, anonymous HIV testing or counseling for those who are HIV+ or have AIDS. Condoms are provided free of charge. The student group provides safe-sex education.

Half of the respondents recommend Hofstra to other gay, lesbian, and bisexual students. One student comments: "I would recommend the school because I have had no major problems, but there are many students who have. It is not really good here on campus. If I had it to do over, I would have gone to a school where the gay people on campus are out and one that has a large gay group as well as support for the group. We really don't get that."

Holyoke Community College • *Holyoke, Massachusetts*

Students define Holyoke's position on gay, lesbian, and bisexual issues as noncommittal. The college does not have a committee on gay, lesbian, and bisexual issues, sexual orientation is not included in its affirmative action policy, nor are counseling services available for gay, lesbian, and bisexual students. Housing for cohabitating couples is also not available. According to the students, the municipality in which the college is located has a civil rights law that includes sexual orientation.

Unanimously, students believe strongly that homophobia is a serious problem on the campus. Those responding report being victims of verbal abuse, hate mail, assault, and harassment. Moreover, all of the students have knowledge of hate crimes committed on the campus. The student group maintains hate-crime statistics.

All of the students believe that Holyoke takes action in response to hate crimes. None, however, agree that the college's security force is supportive. None of the students feel safe on the campus as gays, lesbians, and bisexuals.

Gay, lesbian, and bisexual students between the ages of 19–21 responded to the survey. Students are sophomores and juniors with SAT scores of 900 or higher and grade point averages of 2.5 or higher. Students have majors in the liberal arts.

All of the students are openly gay on the campus as well as to their parents and families. None are considered out-of-state students and all live off campus. All of the students responding came out before attending college, and none said that being gay, lesbian, or bisexual affected their choosing Holyoke. Furthermore, if information on the climate for gays, lesbians, and bisexuals at Holyoke had been available, the respondents' choices would not have been different.

The respondents are involved in the gay, lesbian, and bisexual student group, which has an average membership of 25 students and sponsors speakers, safe-sex education, and Pride and National Coming Out Day activities. The group receives funding from the student government. The students date other Holyoke students and state that their dating activity takes place on the campus. Off campus, students congregate in bars.

All of the students view the lack of student organization as the largest problem at Holyoke, with coming out and the lack of role models following second.

Gay men's and lesbians' cultural contributions are a part of regular courses. The college also offers courses on gay, lesbian, and bisexual issues in English. The college does not provide free, anonymous HIV testing or counseling for those who are HIV+ or have AIDS. Condoms, however, are provided free of charge. Both the Health Center and the student group provide safe-sex education for the campus.

All of the respondents recommend Holyoke to other gay, lesbian, and bisexual students.

Hunter College of the City University of New York •
New York, New York

Students define Hunter's position on gay, lesbian, and bisexual issues as proactive. The college has a committee on gay, lesbian, and bisexual issues and sexual orientation is included in the college's affirmative action statement. Respondents do not know whether the college provides counseling services for gay, lesbian, and bisexual students, or if housing for cohabitating couples is available. According to the students, the municipality in which the college is located has a civil rights law that includes sexual orientation.

Unanimously, students believe that homophobia is a serious problem on the campus. Most of those responding report being victims of verbal abuse and harassment. Moreover, all the students have knowledge of hate crimes committed on the campus. The college maintains hate-crime statistics.

Some of the students believe that Hunter takes action in response to these incidents but most do not know how the administration reacts. The majority of the students, however, do feel supported by the college's security force. The majority, as well, feel safe on the Hunter campus as gays, lesbians, and bisexuals.

Gay, lesbian, and bisexual students between the ages of 18–24 responded to the survey. Students are freshmen and sophomores with SAT scores of 900 or higher and grade point averages of 2.5 and higher. All have majors in the liberal arts.

Two thirds of the students surveyed are openly gay on the campus; those who are not state fear of reprisal as the reason. Those students who are out on campus are also open with their parents and families. None are considered out-of-state students, and all live off campus. All of the students responding came out before attending college, and none said that being gay, lesbian, or bisexual affected their choosing Hunter. However, if information on the climate for gays, lesbians, and bisexuals at Hunter had been available, one third of the respondents would have made a different choice.

The respondents are involved in the gay, lesbian, and bisexual

student group, which has an average membership of 100 students and sponsors dances, speakers, safe-sex education and Pride and National Coming Out Day activities. The group also receives funding from the student government. Two thirds of the respondents state that they do not date other Hunter students; those that do indicate that their dating activity takes place on the Hunter campus. In addition, those students who are life partners met at the college. Off campus, students congregate in bars and the community center.

All of the students view the lack of role models as the largest problem at Hunter, with coming out and the lack of student organization following second.

Gay men's and lesbians' cultural contributions are a part of some regular courses, but no courses are offered on gay, lesbian, and bisexual issues. None of the respondents know if the college provides free, anonymous HIV testing, condoms, or counseling for those who are HIV+ or have AIDS. However, both the college and the student group provide safe-sex education.

All of the respondents recommend Hunter to other gay, lesbian, and bisexual students.

Indiana University • *Bloomington, Indiana*

Students define Indiana's position on gay, lesbian, and bisexual issues as relatively proactive. The university has a committee on gay, lesbian, and bisexual issues, sexual orientation is included in the university's affirmative action policy, and counseling services are available for gay, lesbian, and bisexual students. Students do not know if housing for cohabitating couples is available. According to the students, the municipality in which the university is located has a civil rights law that includes sexual orientation.

Unanimously, students believe that homophobia is a serious problem on the campus. Those responding report being victims of verbal abuse and harassment. Moreover, all of the students have knowledge of hate crimes committed on the campus, including assault. The university maintains hate-crime statistics.

All of the students believe that Indiana takes action in response to hate crimes, but all agree that the university's security force is not supportive. Most of the time, students feel safe on the campus as gays, lesbians, and bisexuals.

Gay, lesbian, and bisexual students between the ages of 21–23 responded to the survey. Students are seniors with SAT scores of 1100 or higher and grade point averages of 3.5 or higher. Students have majors in the liberal arts.

All of the students are openly gay on the campus as well as to their parents and families. None are considered out-of-state students and all live off campus. None of the students responding came out before attending college, and none said that being gay, lesbian, or bisexual affected their choosing Indiana. However, if information on the climate for gays, lesbians, and bisexuals at Indiana had been available, all of the respondents would have made a different choice.

The respondents are involved in the gay, lesbian, and bisexual student group, which has an average membership of 75 students and sponsors dances, speakers, safe-sex education, and Pride and National Coming Out Day activities. The group receives funding from the student government. The students date other Indiana students and state that their dating activity takes place on the campus. Off campus, students congregate in bars.

All of the students view alcohol abuse as the largest problem at Indiana, with other substance abuse and the lack of role models following second.

Although their sexual orientation is never discussed, gay men's and lesbians' cultural contributions are a part of regular courses. The university also offers, although rarely, courses on gay, lesbian, and bisexual issues in English, women's studies, history, and the social sciences. The university does not provide free, anonymous HIV testing or counseling for those who are HIV+ or have AIDS. Bloomington's Mental Health Center provides these services. Students do not know if condoms are available free of charge. Both the Health Center and the student group provide safe-sex education.

All of the respondents recommend Indiana to other gay, lesbian, and bisexual students.

Iowa State University • *Ames, Iowa*

Students define Iowa State's position on gay, lesbian, and bisexual issues as noncommittal. Student do not know if the university has a committee on gay, lesbian, and bisexual issues or if sexual orientation is included in the university's affirmative action policy. Iowa State, however, provides counseling services for gay, lesbian, and bisexual students. Housing for cohabitating couples is not available. According to the students, the municipality in which the university is located has a civil rights law that includes sexual orientation.

Unanimously, students believe that homophobia is a serious problem on the campus. Two thirds of those responding report being victims of verbal abuse and hate mail. Moreover, all the students have knowledge of hate crimes committed on the campus, including assault. Both the university and the student group maintain hate-crime statistics.

One third of the students believe that Iowa State takes action in response to these incidents, and most feel supported by the university security force. The remaining students do not know the administration's position. Most of the students do feel safe on the campus as gays, lesbians, and bisexuals; one third of the students feel safe on the campus sometimes.

Gay, lesbian, and bisexual students between the ages of 21–23 responded to the survey. Students are sophomores and juniors with SAT scores of 900 or lower and grade point averages from 3.0 and higher. Students have majors in art, communications, and business.

All of the students are openly gay on the campus as well as to some family members. Half are out to their parents. None are considered out-of-state students and all live off campus, half with their families. All of the students responding came out before attending college, and none said that being gay, lesbian, or bisexual affected their choosing Iowa State. Furthermore, if information on the climate for gays, lesbians, and bisexuals at Iowa State had been available, the respondents' choices would not have been different.

The respondents are involved in the gay, lesbian, and bisexual student group which has an average membership of 60 students and sponsors dances, speakers, safe-sex education, and Pride and National Coming Out Day activities. The group receives funding from the student government. Seventy-five percent of the students responding indicate that they date other Iowa State students but their dating activity takes place off campus, where students congregate in bars.

All of the students view coming out as the largest problem at Iowa State, with the lack of role models and alcohol abuse following second.

Gay men's and lesbians' cultural contributions are not a part of regular courses, nor are courses offered on gay, lesbian, and bisexual issues. The university does, however, provide free, anonymous HIV testing, condoms, and counseling for those who are HIV+ or have AIDS. Both the Health Center and the student group provide safe-sex education.

All of the respondents recommend Iowa State to other gay, lesbian, and bisexual students who are very out and active.

Jacksonville University • *Jacksonville, Florida*

Students define Jacksonville's position on gay, lesbian, and bisexual issues as negative. The university does not have a committee on gay, lesbian, and bisexual issues, nor is sexual orientation included in its affirmative action statement. Jacksonville, in addition, does not provide counseling services for gay, lesbian, and bisexual students or housing for cohabitating couples. According to the students, the municipality in which the university is located does have a civil rights law that includes sexual orientation.

Unanimously, students believe that homophobia is a serious problem on the campus. None of those responding report being victims of hate crimes; however, all the students have knowledge of hate crimes committed on the campus. None of the students know if the university maintains hate-crime statistics.

Most of the students believe that Jacksonville supports victims of hate crimes, but they are noncommittal about their perception of the university's security force. The students are also ambivalent about their safety on the campus as gays, lesbians, and bisexuals.

Gay, lesbian, and bisexual students between the ages of 21–34 responded to the survey. Students are juniors and seniors with SAT scores of 900 or higher and grade point averages of 3.5 and higher. Students have majors in the liberal arts and computer science.

All of the students surveyed are openly gay on the campus as well as to their parents and families. None of the respondents are considered out-of-state students and all live off campus. None of the students responding came out before attending college, and none said that being gay, lesbian, or bisexual affected their choosing Jacksonville. Furthermore, if information on the climate for gays, lesbians, and bisexuals at Jacksonville had been available, the respondents' choices would not have been different.

The respondents are not involved in a gay, lesbian, and bisexual student group at Jacksonville and tend not to date other Jacksonville students. Off campus, students congregate in bars and religious organizations.

All of the students view the lack of student organization as the largest problem at Jacksonville, with the lack of role models and alcohol abuse following second.

Gay men's and lesbians' cultural contributions are not a part of some regular courses, nor does the university offer courses on gay, lesbian, and bisexual issues. The students do not know if the university provides free, anonymous HIV testing, condoms, or counseling for those who are HIV+ or have AIDS. It does not provide condoms free of charge.

All of the respondents recommend Jacksonville to other gay, lesbian, and bisexual students.

James Madison University • *Harrisonburg, Virginia*

Students define James Madison University's position on gay, lesbian, and bisexual issues as proactive. Although the university has a committee on gay, lesbian, and bisexual issues, sexual orientation is not included in the university's affirmative action policy. Counseling services, however, are available for gay, lesbian, and bisexual students. Housing for cohabitating couples is not available. According to the students, the municipality in which the university is located does not have a civil rights law that includes sexual orientation.

Unanimously, students believe that homophobia is not a serious problem on the campus. None of those responding report being victims of hate crimes. However, all of the students have knowledge of hate crimes committed on the campus, including assault. The university maintains hate-crime statistics.

All of the students believe that the university takes action in response to hate crimes and agree that its security force is supportive. All of the students feel safe on the campus as gays, lesbians, and bisexuals.

Gay, lesbian, and bisexual students between the ages of 21–28 responded to the survey. Students are seniors and graduate students with SAT scores of 1100 or higher and grade point averages of 3.0 or higher. Students have majors in the liberal arts and theater arts.

All of the students are openly gay on the campus as well as to their parents and families. None are considered out-of-state students and all live off campus. None of the students responding came out before attending college, and none said that being gay, lesbian, or bisexual affected their choosing James Madison University. Furthermore, if information on the climate for gays, lesbians, and bisexuals at James Madison had been available, the respondents' choices would not have been different.

The respondents are involved in the gay, lesbian, and bisexual student group, which has an average membership of 20–30 students and sponsors speakers, safe-sex education, and Pride and National Coming Out Day activities. The group receives funding from the student government. In addition, students are active in student government. The students date other James Madison students and state that their dating activity takes place on the campus. Some have life partners attending the school. Off campus, students congregate in restaurants and private homes and apartments.

All of the students view coming out as the largest problem at James Madison, with the lack of role models and student organization following second.

Although gay men's and lesbians' cultural contributions are a part of regular courses, the university does not offer courses on gay, lesbian, and bisexual issues. The university provides free HIV testing but no counseling for those who are HIV+ or have AIDS; condoms are not provided free of charge. Both the Health Center and the student group provide safe-sex education.

All of the respondents recommend James Madison to other gay, lesbian, and bisexual students.

John Jay College of Criminal Justice of the City University of New York • *New York, New York*

Seventy-five percent of the students responding define John Jay's position on gay, lesbian, and bisexual issues as noncommittal. Although the college does not have a committee on gay, lesbian, and bisexual issues, sexual orientation is included in its affirmative action statement, and counseling services are available for gay, lesbian, and bisexual students. Students do not know if housing for cohabitating couples is available. According to the students, the municipality in which the college is located has a civil rights law that includes sexual orientation.

Unanimously, students believe that homophobia is a serious problem on the campus. Seventy-five percent of those responding report being victims of hate mail, verbal abuse, and harassment. Moreover, all of the students have knowledge of hate crimes committed on the campus, with the exception of assault. The student group maintains hate-crime statistics.

Half of the students believe that John Jay College takes action in response to hate crimes, but 75 percent do not feel supported by the college's security force. Most students feel relatively safe on the John Jay campus as gays, lesbians, and bisexuals.

Gay, lesbian, and bisexual students between the ages of 25–40 responded to the survey. Students are sophomores, juniors, and seniors with grade point averages of 2.5 and higher. Students have majors in sociology, substance abuse counseling, criminology, CRJ planning, and legal studies.

All of the students surveyed are openly gay on the campus and are out to some family members. Half are out to their parents. None are considered out-of-state students and all live off campus, some with their families. All of the students responding came out before attending college, and none said that being gay, lesbian, or bisexual affected their choosing John Jay. However, if information on the climate for gays, lesbians, and bisexuals at John Jay had been available, the choice of 25 percent of the respondents would have been different.

The respondents are involved in the gay, lesbian, and bisexual student group, which has an average membership of 35–40 students

and sponsors dances, speakers, safe-sex education, and Pride and National Coming Out Day activities. The group receives funding from the student government. Students tend not to date other John Jay students. Off campus, students congregate in bars, at the community center, and in religious organizations.

All of the students view the lack of role models and coming out as the largest problem at John Jay.

Gay men's and lesbians' cultural contributions are not a part of regular courses, nor does the college offer courses on gay, lesbian, and bisexual issues. The college does not provide free, anonymous HIV testing or counseling for those who are HIV+ or have AIDS. Condoms, however, are provided free of charge. The student group provides safe-sex education.

Seventy-five percent of the respondents recommend John Jay to other gay, lesbian, and bisexual students.

Kalamazoo College • *Kalamazoo, Michigan*

Students define Kalamazoo's position on gay, lesbian, and bisexual issues as proactive, even though the college does not have a committee on gay, lesbian, and bisexual issues, and sexual orientation is not included in its affirmative action policy. However, counseling services are available for gay, lesbian, and bisexual students. Housing for cohabitating couples is not available. According to the students, the municipality in which the college is located does not have a civil rights law that includes sexual orientation.

Unanimously, students believe that homophobia is a serious problem on the campus. Those responding report being victims of hate mail. Moreover, all of the students have knowledge of hate crimes committed on the campus. Students do not know who, if anyone, maintains hate-crime statistics.

All of the students believe that Kalamazoo takes action in response to hate crimes but are ambivalent about the college's security force. All of the students feel relatively safe on the campus as gays, lesbians, and bisexuals.

Gay, lesbian, and bisexual students between the ages of 19–29 responded to the survey. Students are freshmen and sophomores with

SAT scores of 1100 or higher and grade point averages of 3.5 or higher. Students have majors in the liberal arts and environmental studies.

All of the students are openly gay on the campus but not to their parents and families. None are considered out-of-state students and all live in residence halls. All of the students responding came out before attending college, and none said that being gay, lesbian, or bisexual affected their choosing Kalamazoo. However, if information on the climate for gays, lesbians, and bisexuals at Kalamazoo had been available, choices of all the respondents would have been different.

The respondents are involved in the gay, lesbian, and bisexual student group, which has an average membership of 5–25 students and sponsors dances, speakers, and safe-sex education. The group receives funding from the student government. In addition, students are active in other organizations such as the student newspaper and the Women's Equity Coalition. The students date other Kalamazoo students and state that their dating activity takes place off campus, where they congregate in bars and religious organizations.

All of the students view alcohol abuse and the lack of student organization as the largest problems at Kalamazoo.

Gay men's and lesbians' cultural contributions are not a part of regular courses, nor does the college offer courses on gay, lesbian, and bisexual issues. The college does provide free, anonymous HIV testing, counseling for those who are HIV+ or have AIDS, and condoms. Both the Health Center and the student group provide safe-sex education for the campus.

All of the respondents recommend Kalamazoo to other gay, lesbian, and bisexual students "only if you don't mind having virtually no 'gay' social life. The school itself is rather cooperative."

Keene State College • *Keene, New Hampshire*

Students define Keene's position on gay, lesbian, and bisexual issues as noncommittal. The college does not have a committee on gay, lesbian, and bisexual issues, nor is sexual orientation included in its affirmative action policy. Counseling services, however, are available for gay, lesbian, and bisexual students; housing for cohabitating couples is not. According to the students, the municipality in which the college is located does not have a civil rights law that includes sexual orientation.

Unanimously, students believe strongly that homophobia is a serious problem on the campus. Those responding report being victims of harassment, vandalism, and verbal abuse. Moreover, all of the students have knowledge of hate crimes committed on the campus. No one maintains hate-crime statistics.

All of the students believe that Keene takes action in response to hate crimes and agree that the college's security force is supportive. However, none of the students feel safe on the campus as gays, lesbians, and bisexuals.

Gay, lesbian, and bisexual students between the ages of 19–21 responded to the survey. Students are sophomores and juniors with SAT scores of 1100 or higher and grade point averages of 2.0 or higher. Students have majors in the liberal arts and sciences.

All of the students are openly gay on the campus as well as to their parents and families. None are considered out-of-state students and all live off campus. None of the students responding came out before attending college, and none said that being gay, lesbian, or bisexual affected their choosing Keene. But if information on the climate for gays, lesbians, and bisexuals at Keene had been available, most of the respondents would have made a different choice.

The respondents are involved in the gay, lesbian, and bisexual student group, which has an average membership of 5 students and sponsors dances, speakers, and safe-sex education. The group receives funding from the student government. In addition, students are active in student government. The students date other Keene students and state that their dating activity takes place off campus.

All of the students view coming out as the largest problem at Keene, with the lack of role models following second.

Gay men's and lesbians' cultural contributions are not a part of regular courses, nor does the college offer courses on gay, lesbian, and bisexual issues. Students do not know if the college provides free, anonymous HIV testing; however, counseling is available for those who are HIV+ or have AIDS. Condoms are not provided. Both the Health Center and the student group provide safe-sex education.

None of the respondents recommend Keene to other gay, lesbian, and bisexual students.

Lehigh University • *Bethlehem, Pennsylvania*

Students define Lehigh's position on gay, lesbian, and bisexual issues as proactive. Students do not know if the university has a committee on gay, lesbian, and bisexual issues, but sexual orientation is not included in the university's affirmative action policy. However, counseling services are available for gay, lesbian, and bisexual students. Students do not know if housing for cohabitating couples is available or if the municipality in which the university is located has a civil rights law that includes sexual orientation.

Unanimously, students believe strongly that homophobia is a serious problem on the campus. Those responding report being victims of harassment and verbal abuse. Moreover, all of the students have knowledge of hate crimes committed on the campus, including assault. Students do not know who, if anyone, maintains hate-crime statistics.

All of the students believe that Lehigh takes action in response to hate crimes and agree that the university's security force is supportive. All of the students feel safe on the campus as gays, lesbians, and bisexuals.

Gay, lesbian, and bisexual students between the ages of 19–21 responded to the survey. Students are sophomores and juniors with SAT scores of 1100 or higher and grade point averages of 2.5 or higher. Students have majors in the liberal arts.

All of the students are openly gay on the campus as well as to their parents and families. None are considered out-of-state students and all live off campus. None of the students responding came out before attending college, and none said that being gay, lesbian, or bisexual affected their choosing Lehigh. Furthermore, if information on the climate for gays, lesbians, and bisexuals at Lehigh had been available, the respondents' choices would not have been different.

The respondents are involved in the gay, lesbian, and bisexual student group, which has an average membership of 5 students and sponsors dances and speakers. The group receives funding from the student government. The students tend not to date other Lehigh students. Off campus, students typically congregate in bars.

All of the students view the lack of role models as the largest problem at Lehigh, with coming out and alcohol abuse following second.

Gay men's and lesbians' cultural contributions are not a part of regular courses, nor does the university offer courses on gay, lesbian, and bisexual issues. The university provides free, anonymous HIV testing, but not counseling for those who are HIV+ or have AIDS; it provides condoms free of charge. Students do not know who provides safe-sex education.

None of the respondents recommend Lehigh to other gay, lesbian, and bisexual students.

Lewis and Clark College • Portland, Oregon

Students define Lewis and Clark College's position on gay, lesbian, and bisexual issues as noncommittal. The college has a committee on gay, lesbian, and bisexual issues, sexual orientation is included in its affirmative action policy, and counseling services are available for gay, lesbian, and bisexual students. Housing for cohabitating couples is not available. According to the students, the municipality in which the college is located has a civil rights law that includes sexual orientation.

Two thirds of the students do not believe that homophobia is a serious problem on the campus. However, those responding report being victims of verbal abuse, vandalism, and harassment. Moreover, all of the students have knowledge of hate crimes committed on the campus including assault. The college maintains hate-crime statistics.

Student opinion varies widely as to how Lewis and Clark reacts to hate crimes, although most agree that the college does do something. All agree that the college's security force is supportive, and all of the students feel safe on the campus as gays, lesbians, and bisexuals.

Gay, lesbian, and bisexual students between the ages of 18–21 responded to the survey. Students are freshmen, sophomores, and seniors with SAT scores of 900 or higher and grade point averages of 3.0 or higher. Students have majors in sociology, psychology, health, and gender and sexuality.

All of the students are openly gay on the campus as well as to their parents and families. Two thirds of the students are considered out-of-state students. The majority of the respondents live off campus, some with life partners, and the remaining students live in residence halls. Most of the students responding came out before attending college, and none said that being gay, lesbian, or bisexual affected their choosing Lewis and Clark. However, if information on the climate for gays, lesbians, and bisexuals at Lewis and Clark had been available, two thirds of the respondents said their choices would have been different.

The respondents are involved in the gay, lesbian, and bisexual student group, which has an average membership of 15–40 students and sponsors dances, speakers, safe-sex education, and Pride and National Coming Out Day activities. The group receives funding from the student government. In addition, students are active in athletics and political organizations. Most of the students date other Lewis and Clark students and state that their dating activity takes place on the campus. Off campus, students congregate in bars and private homes and apartments.

All of the students view alcohol abuse as the largest problem at Lewis and Clark, with coming out and the lack of role models following second.

Although gay men's and lesbians' cultural contributions are not a part of regular courses, the college does offer courses on gay, lesbian, and bisexual issues in women's studies, history, and health. The college provides free, anonymous HIV testing and condoms free of charge. Students do not know if counseling is available for those who are HIV+ or have AIDS. Both the Health Center and the student group provide safe-sex education.

All of the respondents recommend Lewis and Clark College to other gay, lesbian, and bisexual students.

Lock Haven University • *Lock Haven, Pennsylvania*

Students define Lock Haven's position on gay, lesbian, and bisexual issues as proactive. The university has a committee on gay, lesbian, and bisexual issues and sexual orientation is included in the university's affirmative action statement. In addition, the university provides counseling services for gay, lesbian, and bisexual students. Respondents do not know whether housing for cohabiting couples is available or if the municipality in which the university is located has a civil rights law that includes sexual orientation.

Unanimously, students believe that homophobia is a serious problem on the campus. None of those responding report being victims of hate crimes, but all have knowledge of hate crimes committed on the campus, primarily harassment. Students do not know who, if anyone, maintains hate-crime statistics.

None of the respondents know how Lock Haven reacts to hate crimes. Most, however, do feel supported by the university's security force. Consistently, all of the students do feel safe on the Lock Haven campus as gays, lesbians, and bisexuals.

Gay, lesbian, and bisexual students between the ages of 20–22 responded to the survey. Students are juniors and seniors with SAT scores of 900 or higher and grade point averages of 2.0 and higher. All have majors in the liberal arts and sciences.

None of the students surveyed are openly gay on the campus, primarily due to fear of reprisal; however, most are out to some family members. None are considered out-of-state students, and all live off campus or in fraternity/sorority housing. Few of the students responding came out before attending college, and none said that being gay, lesbian, or bisexual affected their choosing Lock Haven. Furthermore, if information on the climate for gays, lesbians, and bisexuals at Lock Haven had been available, the respondents' choices would not have been different.

The respondents are involved in the gay, lesbian, and bisexual student group, which has an average membership of 30 students and sponsors safe-sex education and Pride and National Coming Out Day activities. The group does not receive funding from the student government. None of the students date other Lock Haven students, and their dating activity does not take place on the campus. All of the students view coming out as the largest problem at Lock Haven, with lack of role models and student organization following second.

Gay men's and lesbians' cultural contributions are not a part of regular courses, nor are courses offered on gay, lesbian, and bisexual issues. The university does provide free, anonymous HIV testing and condoms, but respondents do not know if the university provides counseling for those who are HIV+ or have AIDS. Both the university and the student group provide safe-sex education for the campus.

Most of respondents recommend Lock Haven to other gay, lesbian, and bisexual students but recommend the school primarily to women.

Manhattan School of Music • *New York, New York*

Students vary widely defining Manhattan's position on gay, lesbian, and bisexual issues as proactive and noncommittal. Although the school does not have a committee on gay, lesbian, and bisexual issues, sexual orientation is included in its affirmative action statement, and counseling services are available for gay, lesbian, and bisexual students. Students do not know if housing for cohabitating couples is available. According to the students, the municipality in which the school is located does have a civil rights law that includes sexual orientation.

Two thirds of the students do not believe that homophobia is a serious problem on the campus. None of those responding report being victims of hate crimes. Moreover, only two thirds all of the students have knowledge of hate crimes committed on the campus, specifically vandalism and verbal abuse. No one knows who maintains hate-crime statistics.

One third of the students believe that Manhattan takes action in response to these incidents, and two thirds state that they feel supported by the school's security force. All of the students feel safe on the Manhattan campus as gays, lesbians, and bisexuals.

Gay, lesbian, and bisexual students between the ages of 20–25 responded to the survey. Students are sophomores, juniors, and graduate students with SAT scores of 899 or higher and grade point averages of 3.0 and higher. Students have majors in voice and classical music performance.

All of the students surveyed are openly gay on the campus as well as to some family members. Few are out to their parents. None are considered out-of-state students, and all of the students live off campus. Fifty percent of the students responding came out before attending college, but none said that being gay, lesbian, or bisexual affected their choosing Manhattan. Furthermore, if information on the climate for gays, lesbians, and bisexuals at Manhattan had been available, the respondents' choices would not have been different.

There is no active gay, lesbian, and bisexual student group, but one is being formed and will sponsor speakers, safe-sex education, and Pride and National Coming Out Day activities. Two thirds of the students are active in the Pan-African Students Union. The majority of students date other Manhattan students and state that their dating activity takes place off campus. A minority of the students have life partners attending the school. Off campus, students congregate in bars.

All of the students view the lack of student organization and coming out as the largest problems at Manhattan.

Gay men's and lesbians' cultural contributions are not a part of regular courses, nor does the school offer courses on gay, lesbian, and bisexual issues. Students do not know if the school provides free, anonymous HIV testing or condoms free of charge. Most agree, though, that counseling is not available for those who are HIV+ or have AIDS. The school's Health Center provides safe-sex education.

All of the respondents recommend the Manhattan School of Music to other gay, lesbian, and bisexual students.

Mankato State University • *Mankato, Minnesota*

Students define Mankato State's position on gay, lesbian, and bisexual issues as both negative and noncommittal. Although the university does not have a committee on gay, lesbian, and bisexual issues, sexual orientation is included in its affirmative action policy. In addition, counseling services are available for gay, lesbian, and bisexual students. Housing for cohabitating couples is not available. According to the students, the municipality in which the university is located does not have a civil rights law that includes sexual orientation.

Unanimously, students believe that homophobia is a serious problem on the campus. Those responding report being victims of verbal abuse and harassment. Moreover, all of the students have knowledge of hate crimes committed on the campus, including assault. The university maintains hate-crime statistics.

Most of students believe that Mankato State takes action in response to hate crimes, although some say the school does nothing.

Most agree that the university's security force is not supportive, and the majority do not feel safe on the campus as gays, lesbians, and bisexuals.

Gay, lesbian, and bisexual students between the ages of 21–47 responded to the survey. Students are sophomores and graduate students with SAT scores of 1100 or higher and grade point averages of 2.5 or higher (undergraduate) and 3.5 or higher (graduate). Students have majors in women's studies, open studies, and the liberal arts.

The majority of the students are openly gay on the campus as well as to their parents and families. Those who are not cite fear of reprisal as the primary reason. Half are considered out-of-state students and all live off campus. All of the students responding came out before attending college, and half said that being gay, lesbian, or bisexual affected their choosing Mankato State. If information on the climate for gay, lesbian, and bisexuals at Mankato State had been available, the choice of some of the respondents would have been different.

The respondents are involved in the gay, lesbian, and bisexual student group, which has an average membership of 20+ students and sponsors dances, speakers, safe-sex education, and Pride and National Coming Out Day activities. The group receives funding from the student government. In addition, some students are active in Greek-letter organizations. Most of the students date other Mankato State students and indicate that some of their dating activity takes place on the campus. Off campus, students congregate in bars and coffeehouses.

All of the students view coming out as the largest problem at Mankato State, with the lack of student organization and alcohol abuse following second.

Although gay men's and lesbians' cultural contributions are not a part of regular courses, the university does offer courses on gay, lesbian, and bisexual issues in women's studies. Students do not know if the university provides free, anonymous HIV testing or counseling for those who are HIV+ or have AIDS. Condoms are not provided. Both the Health Center and the student group provide safe-sex education.

Half of the respondents recommend Mankato State to other gay, lesbian, and bisexual students.

Marquette University • *Milwaukee, Wisconsin*

Students define Marquette's position on gay, lesbian, and bisexual issues somewhere between noncommittal and negative. The university does not have a committee on gay, lesbian, and bisexual issues, nor is sexual orientation included in its affirmative action policy. However, counseling services are available for gay, lesbian, and bisexual students. Housing for cohabitating couples is not available. According to the students, the municipality in which the university is located has a civil rights law that includes sexual orientation.

Unanimously, students believe strongly that homophobia is a serious problem on the campus. Those responding report being victims of harassment and verbal abuse. Moreover, all of the students have knowledge of hate crimes committed on the campus, including assault. Students do not know who, if anyone, maintains hate-crime statistics.

The majority of students believe that Marquette does nothing in response to hate crimes, but all agree that the university's security force is supportive. Sixty percent of the students feel safe on the campus as gays, lesbians, and bisexuals.

Gay, lesbian, and bisexual students between the ages of 19–25 responded to the survey. Students are sophomores, seniors, and graduate students with SAT scores of 1100 or higher and grade point averages of 3.0 or higher. Students have majors in theater, biomedical engineering, and theology.

All of the students are openly gay on the campus and most are out to their parents and families. Two thirds are considered out-of-state students and all live off campus. Sixty percent of the students responding came out before attending college, and none said that being gay, lesbian, or bisexual affected their choosing Marquette. However, if information on the climate for gay, lesbian, and bisexuals at Marquette been available, 70 percent of the respondents' choices would have been different.

The respondents are involved in the gay, lesbian, and bisexual student group, which has an average membership of 40–50 students and sponsors speakers and safe-sex education. The group receives funding from the student government. The students date other Marquette students and state that most of their dating activity takes place on the campus. Off campus, students congregate in bars.

All of the students view coming out as the largest problem at Marquette, with the lack of role models and student organization following second.

Gay men's and lesbians' cultural contributions are not a part of regular courses, nor does the university offer courses on gay, lesbian, and bisexual issues. The university provides free, anonymous HIV testing, but students do not know if counseling is available for those who are HIV+ or have AIDS. Condoms are not provided. Both the Health Center and the student group provide safe-sex education.

The majority of the respondents do not recommend Marquette to other gay, lesbian, and bisexual students.

Mary Washington College • *Fredericksburg, Virginia*

Students define Mary Washington College's position on gay, lesbian, and bisexual issues somewhere between negative and noncommittal, although the college has a committee on gay, lesbian, and bisexual issues, and sexual orientation is included in the college's affirmative action policy. In addition, counseling services are available for gay, lesbian, and bisexual students. Housing for cohabitating couples is not available. According to the students, the municipality in which the college is located does not have a civil rights law that includes sexual orientation.

Unanimously, students believe that homophobia is a serious problem on the campus. Those responding report being victims of harassment and verbal abuse. Moreover, all of the students have knowledge of hate crimes committed on the campus, including assault. Both the college and the student group maintain hate-crime statistics.

All of the students believe that Mary Washington College does nothing in response to hate crimes. Fifty percent agree that its security force is supportive, and all of the students feel relatively safe on the campus as gays, lesbians, and bisexuals.

Gay, lesbian, and bisexual students between the ages of 20–22 responded to the survey. Students have SAT scores of 1100 or higher and grade point averages of 2.5 or higher. Students have majors in English, chemistry, and international affairs.

All of the students are openly gay on the campus as well as to their parents and families. Some are considered out-of-state students and all live either in residence halls or off campus. Three quarters of the students responding came out before attending college, and none said that being gay, lesbian, or bisexual affected their choosing Mary Washington College. Furthermore, if information on the climate for gay, lesbian, and bisexuals at Mary Washington had been available, one quarter of the respondents would have made a different choice.

The respondents are involved in the gay, lesbian, and bisexual student group, which has an average membership of 20–45 students and sponsors dances, speakers, safe-sex education, and Pride and National Coming Out Day activities. The group receives funding from the student government. In addition, students are active in other organizations such as the school newspaper, honor societies, the American Chemical Society, and the literary magazine. Few (about one quarter) of the students date other Mary Washington students and state that their dating activity takes place off campus, where students congregate in bars.

All of the students view coming out as the largest problem at Mary Washington, with the lack of role models and alcohol abuse following second.

Gay men's and lesbians' cultural contributions are not a part of regular courses, nor does the college offer courses on gay, lesbian, and bisexual issues. The college provides free, anonymous HIV testing, counseling for those who are HIV+ or have AIDS, and condoms free of charge. Both the Health Center and the student group provide safe-sex education.

Seventy-five percent of the respondents recommend Mary Washington College to other gay, lesbian, and bisexual students.

Massachusetts College of Art • *Boston, Massachusetts*

Students define Mass College of Art's position on gay, lesbian, and bisexual issues as proactive. Although the college does not have a committee on gay, lesbian, and bisexual issues, sexual orientation is included in its affirmative action policy. In addition, counseling services are available for gay, lesbian, and bisexual students. Students do not know if housing for cohabiting couples is available. According to the students, the municipality in which the college is located does not have a civil rights law that includes sexual orientation.

Unanimously, students believe that homophobia is a serious problem on the campus. Those responding report being victims of verbal abuse and harassment. Moreover, all of the students have knowledge of hate crimes committed on the campus. Students do not know who, if anyone, maintains hate-crime statistics.

None of students know how the college reacts to hate crimes, but all agree that the college's security force is supportive. All of the students feel safe on the campus as gays, lesbians, and bisexuals.

Gay, lesbian, and bisexual students between the ages of 20–22 responded to the survey. Students are juniors and seniors with SAT scores of 1100 or higher and grade point averages of 3.0 or higher. Students have majors in studio art.

All of the students are openly gay on the campus as well as to their parents and families. None are considered out-of-state students and all live off campus. All of the students responding came out before attending college, and none said that being gay, lesbian, or bisexual affected their choosing Mass College of Art. Furthermore, if information on the climate for gay, lesbian, and bisexuals at the college had been available, the respondents' choices would not have been different.

The respondents are involved in the gay, lesbian, and bisexual student group, which has an average membership of 25–30 students and sponsors speakers, safe-sex education, and Pride and National Coming Out Day activities. The group receives funding from the student government, in which some of them are active. Students tend not to date other students from the school. Off campus, students congregate in bars.

All of the students view coming out as the largest problem at the college, with the lack of role models and student organization following second.

Gay men's and lesbians' cultural contributions are not a part of regular courses, nor does the college offer courses on gay, lesbian, and bisexual issues. Students do not know if the college provides free, anonymous HIV testing or condoms. Counseling, however, is available for those who are HIV+ or have AIDS. Both the Health Center and the student group provide safe-sex education.

All of the respondents recommend Mass College of Art to other gay, lesbian, and bisexual students.

Massachusetts Institute of Technology •
Cambridge, Massachusetts

Students define MIT's position on gay, lesbian, and bisexual issues somewhere between proactive and noncommittal. MIT has a committee on gay, lesbian, and bisexual issues, and sexual orientation is included in the Institute's affirmative action policy. In addition, counseling services are available for gay, lesbian, and bisexual students. Housing for cohabitating couples is not available. According to the students, the municipality in which MIT is located has a civil rights law that includes sexual orientation.

The majority students believe that homophobia is a serious problem on the campus. Eighty percent of those responding report being victims of harassment, vandalism, and verbal abuse. Moreover, all of the students have knowledge of hate crimes committed on the campus, including assault. The Institute maintains hate-crime statistics.

All of the students believe that MIT takes action in response to hate crimes, and the majority agree that its security force is supportive. Most of the students feel relatively safe on the campus as gays, lesbians, and bisexuals.

Gay, lesbian, and bisexual students between the ages of 18–25 responded to the survey. Students are freshmen, sophomores, juniors, seniors, and graduate students with SAT scores of 1100 or higher and grade point averages of 3.0 or higher. Students have majors in brain and cognitive science, chemistry, women's studies, political science, electrical engineering, and computer engineering.

Ninety percent of the students are openly gay on the campus. Those who are not cite fear of reprisal as the primary reason. Seventy-five percent are out to their parents and families. Ninety percent are considered out-of-state students. Eighty percent of the students live in residence halls, the remaining students live off campus. The majority of the students responding came out before attending college, and few said that being gay, lesbian, or bisexual affected their choosing MIT. Furthermore, if information on the climate for gay, lesbian, and bisexuals at MIT had been available, only 10 percent of the respondents would have made a different choice.

The respondents are involved in the gay, lesbian, and bisexual student group, which has an average membership of 100 + students and sponsors dances, speakers, safe-sex education, and Pride and National Coming Out Day activities. The group receives funding from the student government. In addition, students are active in AIDS education, the Black Student Union, MIT radio, the National Society for Black Engineers, the Association for Women Students, athletics, and Greek life. Less than 10 percent identify themselves as cross dressers. The students date other MIT students and state that most of their dating activity takes place on the campus. Off campus, students congregate in bars and dance clubs.

All of the students view coming out as the largest problem at MIT, with the lack of role models and alcohol abuse following second.

Gay men's and lesbians' cultural contributions are a part of some regular courses. MIT also offers courses on gay, lesbian, and bisexual issues in history, English, women's studies, and in the social sciences. It provides free, anonymous HIV testing and condoms free of charge. Students do not know if counseling is available for those who are HIV + or have AIDS. Both the Health Center and the student group provide safe-sex education.

All of the respondents recommend MIT to other gay, lesbian, and bisexual students.

Metropolitan State College of Denver • *Denver, Colorado*

Students define Metro State's position on gay, lesbian, and bisexual issues as proactive. Although the college does not have a committee on gay, lesbian, and bisexual issues, sexual orientation is included in its affirmative action policy. In addition, counseling services are available for gay, lesbian, and bisexual students. Students do not know if housing for cohabitating couples is available. According to the students, the municipality in which the college is located has a civil rights law that includes sexual orientation.

Unanimously, students do not believe that homophobia is a serious problem on the campus. None of those responding report being victims of hate crimes. However, all of the students have knowledge of hate crimes committed on the campus. The college maintains hate-crime statistics.

All of the students believe that Metro State takes action in response to hate crimes, and all agree that the college's security force is supportive. Consequently all feel relatively safe on the campus as gays, lesbians, and bisexuals.

Gay, lesbian, and bisexual students between the ages of 19–22 responded to the survey. Students are sophomores, juniors, and seniors with grade point averages of 3.0 or higher. Students have majors in the liberal arts.

All of the students are openly gay on the campus as well as to their parents and families. None are considered out-of-state students and all live off campus. All of the students responding came out before attending college, and none said that being gay, lesbian, or bisexual affected their choosing Metro State. Furthermore, if information on the climate for gay, lesbian, and bisexuals at Metro State had been available, the respondents' choices would not have been different.

The respondents are involved in the gay, lesbian, and bisexual student group, which has an average membership of 40 students and sponsors speakers, safe-sex education, and Pride and National Coming Out Day activities. The group receives funding from the student government. The students tend not to date other Metro State students. Off campus, students congregate in bars and at socials.

All of the students view coming out as the largest problem at Metro State, with the lack of role models and student organization following second.

Gay men's and lesbians' cultural contributions are not a part of regular courses, nor does the college offer courses on gay, lesbian, and bisexual issues. The college provides free, anonymous HIV testing, counseling for those who are HIV+ or have AIDS, and condoms free of charge. Both the Health Center and the student group provide safe-sex education.

All of the respondents recommend Metro State to other gay, lesbian, and bisexual students.

Miami University • *Oxford, Ohio*

Students define Miami's position on gay, lesbian, and bisexual issues somewhere between proactive and noncommittal. Although the university does not have a committee on gay, lesbian, and bisexual issues, sexual orientation is included in its affirmative action policy. In addition, counseling services are available for gay, lesbian, and bisexual students. Housing for cohabitating couples is not available. Students do not know if the municipality in which the university is located has a civil rights law that includes sexual orientation.

Unanimously, students believe that homophobia is a serious problem on the campus. Those responding report being victims of hate mail. Moreover, all of the students have knowledge of hate crimes committed on the campus, including assault. The university maintains hate-crime statistics.

All of the students believe that Miami takes action in response to hate crimes and agree that the university's security force is supportive. All feel safe on the campus as gays, lesbians, and bisexuals.

Gay, lesbian, and bisexual students between the ages of 21–22 responded to the survey. Students are juniors with SAT scores of 900 or higher and grade point averages of 3.0 or higher. Students have majors in the liberal arts.

All of the students are openly gay on the campus as well as to their parents and families. None are considered out-of-state students and all live in residence halls. None of the students responding came out before attending college, and none said that being gay, lesbian, or bisexual affected their choosing Miami. Furthermore, if information on the climate for gay, lesbian, and bisexuals at Miami had been available, the respondents' choices would not have been different.

The respondents are involved in the gay, lesbian, and bisexual student group, which has an average membership of 40–60 students and sponsors dances, speakers, safe-sex education, and Pride and National Coming Out Day activities. The group receives funding from the student government. The students tend not to date other Miami students. Off campus, students congregate in private homes and apartments.

All of the students view coming out as the largest problem at

Miami, with the lack of role models and alcohol abuse following second.

Although gay men's and lesbians' cultural contributions are not a part of regular courses, the university does offer courses on gay, lesbian, and bisexual issues in English and religious studies. The university does not provide free, anonymous HIV testing, counseling for those who are HIV+ or have AIDS, or condoms free of charge. Both the Health Center and the student group provide safe-sex education.

All of the respondents recommend Miami to other gay, lesbian, and bisexual students, with one student summing up his thoughts: "I'm sure there are better universities for gays, lesbians, and bisexuals, but I'm sure there are also a lot worse."

Middlebury College • *Middlebury, Vermont*

Students define Middlebury's position on gay, lesbian, and bisexual issues as noncommittal. The college does not have a committee on gay, lesbian, and bisexual issues, and sexual orientation is not included in its affirmative action policy. But counseling services are available for gay, lesbian, and bisexual students. Housing for cohabiting couples is not available. Students do not know if the municipality in which the college is located has a civil rights law that includes sexual orientation.

Unanimously, students believe that homophobia is a serious problem on the campus. None of those responding report being victims of hate crimes, but all of the students have knowledge of hate crimes committed on the campus. No one maintains hate-crime statistics.

All of the students believe that Middlebury does nothing in response to hate crimes, and all agree that the college's security force is not supportive. Yet most of the time, students do feel safe on the campus as gays, lesbians, and bisexuals.

Gay, lesbian, and bisexual students between the ages of 18–20 responded to the survey. Students are freshmen and sophomores with ACT scores of 31 or higher and grade point averages of 3.0 or higher. Students have majors in the liberal arts.

All of the students are openly gay on the campus as well as to their parents and families. None are considered out-of-state students and all live in residence halls. All of the students responding came out before attending college, and none said that being gay, lesbian, or bisexual affected their choosing Middlebury. But if information on the climate for gays, lesbians, and bisexuals at Middlebury had been available, all of the respondents would have made a different choice.

The respondents are involved in the gay, lesbian, and bisexual student group, which has an average membership of 15 students and sponsors dances, speakers, and safe-sex education. The group receives no funding from the student government. The students date other Middlebury students and state that their dating activity takes place on the campus. Off campus, students congregate in private homes and apartments.

All of the students view coming out as the largest problem at Middlebury, with the lack of role models and alcohol abuse following second.

Gay men's and lesbians' cultural contributions are not a part of regular courses, nor does the college offer courses on gay, lesbian, and bisexual issues. The college provides free but not anonymous HIV testing, and condoms free of charge. Students do not know if counseling is available for those who are HIV+ or have AIDS. Both the Health Center and the student group provide safe-sex education.

All of the respondents recommend Middlebury to other gay, lesbian, and bisexual students, "since we are trying to change the scene, and we need more students to help."

Mills College • *Oakland, California*

Students define Mills's position on gay, lesbian, and bisexual issues somewhere between proactive and noncommittal. The college has a committee on gay, lesbian, and bisexual issues, and sexual orientation is included in the college's affirmative action policy. In addition, counseling services are available for lesbian and bisexual students, as is housing for cohabitating couples. According to the students, the municipality in which the college is located does not have a civil rights law that includes sexual orientation.

Most students do not believe that homophobia is a serious problem on the campus. None of those responding report being victims of hate crimes. However, all of the students have knowledge of hate crimes committed on the campus. The student group maintains hate-crime statistics.

All of the students believe that Mills takes action in response to hate crimes, and all agree that the college's security force is supportive. All feel safe on the campus as lesbians and bisexuals.

Lesbian and bisexual students between the ages of 28–37 responded to the survey. Students are freshmen and sophomores with SAT scores of 1100 or higher and grade point averages of 3.5 or higher. Students have majors in English, creative writing, and political, legal, and economic analysis.

All of the students are openly gay on the campus and half are out to their parents and families. None are considered out-of-state students and all live off campus, some with life partners. All of the students responding came out before attending college, and half said that being lesbian, or bisexual affected their choosing Mills. If information on the climate for gay, lesbian, and bisexuals at Mills had been available, the respondents' choices would not have been different.

The respondents are involved in the lesbian and bisexual student group, which has an average membership of 30–50 students and sponsors dances, speakers, safe-sex education, and Pride and National Coming Out Day activities. The group receives funding from the student government. Students are active in athletics. The students date other Mills students and state that their dating activity takes place on the campus. Off campus, students congregate in dance clubs, coffeehouses, and book stores.

All of the students view the lack of role models as the largest problem at Mills, with the lack of student organization and coming out following second.

Gay men's and lesbians' cultural contributions are not a part of regular courses, nor does the college offer courses on gay, lesbian, and bisexual issues. The college does not provide free, anonymous HIV testing or counseling for those who are HIV+ or have AIDS. The student store provides condoms free of charge. Both the Health Center and the student group provide safe-sex education.

All of the respondents recommend Mills to other lesbian and bisexual students.

Montana State University • *Bozeman, Montana*

Students define Montana's position on gay, lesbian, and bisexual issues as noncommittal. Although the university does not have a committee on gay, lesbian, and bisexual issues, sexual orientation is included in its affirmative action statement, and counseling services are available for gay, lesbian, and bisexual students. Students do not know if housing for cohabitating couples is available or if the municipality in which the university is located has a civil rights law that includes sexual orientation.

Unanimously, students believe that homophobia is a serious problem on the campus. Fifty percent of those responding report being victims of verbal abuse. Moreover, all of the students have knowledge of hate crimes committed on the campus, including assault. Students do not know who, if anyone, maintains hate-crime statistics.

The students do not know how Montana State reacts to hate crimes, and all of the respondents state that they do not feel supported by the university's security force. Consequently, most students feel marginally safe on the Montana State campus as gays, lesbians, and bisexuals.

Gay, lesbian, and bisexual students between the ages of 18–26 responded to the survey. Students are freshmen and sophomores with SAT scores of 900 or higher and grade point averages of 2.5 and higher. Students have majors in liberal arts, occupational therapy, and education.

Half of the students surveyed are openly gay on the campus; those who are not cite fear of reprisal as the primary reason. All of the students are out to their parents and families. None are considered out-of-state students. Students divide evenly between living in residence halls and living off campus. All of the students responding came out before attending college, and none said that being gay, lesbian, or bisexual affected their choosing Montana State. Furthermore, if information on the climate for gays, lesbians, and bisexuals at Montana had been available, the respondents' choices would not have been different.

The respondents are involved in the gay, lesbian, and bisexual student group, which has an average membership of 20–30 students

and sponsors dances, speakers, and safe-sex education. The group does not receive funding from the student government. Students date other Montana State students and indicate that their dating activity takes place off campus.

All of the students view coming out as the largest problem at Montana State, with the lack of student organization following second.

Gay men's and lesbians' cultural contributions are not a part of regular courses, and courses are not offered on gay, lesbian, and bisexual issues. The university provides HIV testing for ten dollars and does not provide condoms free of charge. Students do not know if counseling is available for those who are HIV+ or have AIDS. Both the Health Center and the student group provide safe-sex education.

Half of the respondents recommend Montana to other gay, lesbian, and bisexual students.

Mount Holyoke College • *South Hadley, Massachusetts*

Most students define Mount Holyoke's position on gay, lesbian, and bisexual issues as noncommittal, but some view its position as negative. The college does not have a committee on gay, lesbian, and bisexual issues, and sexual orientation is not included in its affirmative action policy. However, counseling services are available for lesbian and bisexual students. Housing for cohabitating couples is not available. According to the students, the municipality in which the college is located has a civil rights law that includes sexual orientation.

Unanimously, students believe that homophobia is a serious problem on the campus. One third of those responding report being victims of verbal abuse. Moreover, all of the students have knowledge of hate crimes committed on the campus, including assault. The student group maintains hate-crime statistics.

Most of the students believe that Mount Holyoke does nothing in response to hate crimes, and most agree that the college's security force is not supportive. The majority of the students feel relatively safe on the campus as lesbians and bisexuals, but many say they feel safe only in the company of other lesbians and bisexuals.

Lesbian and bisexual students between the ages of 19–21 responded to the survey. Students are sophomores and juniors with SAT scores of 1100 or higher and grade point averages of 2.5 or higher. Students have majors in sociology, psychology, math, philosophy, and anthropology.

All of the students are openly gay on the campus and most are out to their parents and families. All are considered out-of-state students and live in residence halls. None of the students responding came out before attending college, and none said that being lesbian or bisexual affected their choosing Mount Holyoke. Furthermore, if information on the climate for lesbians and bisexuals at Mount Holyoke had been available, the respondents' choices would not have been different.

The respondents are involved in the lesbian and bisexual student group, which has an average membership of 80 students and sponsors dances, speakers, safe-sex education, and Pride and National Coming Out Day activities. The group receives funding from the student government. In addition, students are active in other student organizations such as the Karate Club, Pottery Club, and Rape Crisis Counseling. One third of the students date other Mount Holyoke students and state that their dating activity takes place on the campus. Off campus, students congregate in bars.

All of the students view the lack of effective student organization as the largest problem at Mount Holyoke, with the lack of role models and coming out following second.

Lesbians' cultural contributions are a part of regular courses, and the college offers courses on gay, lesbian, and bisexual issues in women's studies. The college does not provide free, anonymous HIV testing, counseling for those who are HIV+ or have AIDS, or condoms. Both the Health Center and the student group provide safe-sex education.

All of the respondents recommend Mount Holyoke to other lesbian and bisexual students. "Although the administration gives little support, they believe that the lesbians on campus are quite friendly and supportive of each other. Most of the student body remains quiet about any disapproval."

New England Conservatory of Music • *Boston, Massachusetts*

Students define the Conservatory's position on gay, lesbian, and bisexual issues as noncommittal. The Conservatory does not have a committee on gay, lesbian, and bisexual issues, nor is sexual orientation included in its affirmative action policy. Counseling services are available for gay, lesbian, and bisexual students, but housing for cohabitating couples is not. According to the students, the municipality in which the Conservatory is located has a civil rights law that includes sexual orientation.

Unanimously, students believe strongly that homophobia is a serious problem on the campus. Those responding report being victims of verbal abuse and harassment. Moreover, all of the students have knowledge of hate crimes committed on the campus, including assault. Students do not know who, if anyone, maintains hate-crime statistics.

Students do not know how the Conservatory reacts to hate crimes. All agree that the Conservatory's security force is not supportive, yet all of the students feel safe on the campus as gays, lesbians, and bisexuals.

Gay, lesbian, and bisexual students between the ages of 20–23 responded to the survey. Students are juniors, seniors and graduate students with SAT scores of 1100 or higher and grade point averages of 3.5 or higher. Students have majors in performance, voice, and composition.

Most of the students are openly gay on the campus as well as to their parents and families. All are considered out-of-state students and live in residence halls. All of the students responding came out before attending college, and none said that being gay, lesbian, or bisexual affected their choosing the Conservatory. Furthermore, if information on the climate for gay, lesbian, and bisexuals at the Conservatory had been available, the respondents' choices would not have been different.

The Conservatory does not have a gay, lesbian, and bisexual student group. The students date other Conservatory students and state that their dating activity takes place off campus, where they congregate in bars and the community center.

All of the students view coming out as the largest problem at the

Conservatory, with the lack of student organization and alcohol abuse following second.

Gay men's and lesbians' cultural contributions are not a part of the Conservatory's regular courses, nor does it offer courses on gay, lesbian, and bisexual issues. The Conservatory does not provide free, anonymous HIV testing, counseling for those who are HIV + or have AIDS, or condoms. No one provides safe-sex education for students.

All of the respondents recommend the New England Conservatory of Music to other gay, lesbian, and bisexual students.

New Mexico Institute of Mining and Technology •
Socorro, New Mexico

Students define New Mexico Institute's position on gay, lesbian, and bisexual issues as proactive. The Institute does not have a committee on gay, lesbian, and bisexual issues, nor is sexual orientation included in its affirmative action statement. New Mexico Institute does, however, provide counseling services for gay, lesbian, and bisexual students. Housing for cohabitating couples is not available. According to the students, the municipality in which the Institute is located does not have a civil rights law that includes sexual orientation.

Unanimously, students believe that homophobia is a serious problem on the campus. Those responding report being victims of verbal abuse. Moreover, all the students have knowledge of hate crimes committed on the campus, including hate mail harassment and vandalism. No one maintains hate-crime statistics. Most of the students believe that New Mexico Institute does nothing in response to hate crimes, but they do feel supported by the Institute's security force. Yet most students do not really feel safe on the New Mexico Institute campus as gays, lesbians, and bisexuals.

Gay, lesbian, and bisexual students between the ages of 21–24 responded to the survey. Students are juniors and seniors with SAT scores of 1100 or higher and grade point averages of 2.0 and higher. Students have declared majors in technical communication.

All of the students surveyed are openly gay on the campus, but most are not out to their parents and families. None of the respondents are considered out-of-state students and all live in campus housing. None of the students responding came out before attending college, and none said that being gay, lesbian, or bisexual affected their choosing New Mexico Institute. If information on the climate for gays, lesbians, and bisexuals at New Mexico Institute had been available, the respondents' choices would not have been different.

The respondents are involved in a gay, lesbian, and bisexual student group, which has an average membership of 10 students. The students date other Institute students, and their dating activity typically takes place off campus.

All of the students view alcohol abuse as the largest problem at New Mexico Institute, with the lack of student organization and role models following second.

Gay men's and lesbians' cultural contributions are not a part of some regular courses, nor does the Institute offer courses on gay, lesbian, and bisexual issues. The Institute does not have a Health Center. The student group provides safe-sex education.

All of the respondents recommend New Mexico Institute to other gay, lesbian, and bisexual students.

New York University • *New York, New York*

Students define NYU's position on gay, lesbian, and bisexual issues as proactive. The university has a committee on gay, lesbian, and bisexual issues, and sexual orientation is included in the university's affirmative action policy. In addition, counseling services are available for gay, lesbian, and bisexual students. Students do not know if housing for cohabitating couples is available. According to the students, the municipality in which the university is located has a civil rights law that includes sexual orientation.

Students are divided as to whether homophobia is a serious problem on the campus. Those responding do report being victims of hate mail, harassment, vandalism, and verbal abuse. Moreover, all of the students have knowledge of hate crimes committed on the campus including assault. Students do not know who, if anyone, maintains hate-crime statistics.

All of the students believe that NYU takes action in response to hate crimes and agree that the university's security force is supportive. All of the students feel safe on the campus as gays, lesbians, and bisexuals.

Gay, lesbian, and bisexual students between the ages of 20–23 responded to the survey. Students are juniors and seniors with SAT scores of 900 or higher and grade point averages of 2.5 or higher. Students have majors in the liberal arts.

Most of the students are openly gay on the campus. Those who are not cite fear of isolation as the primary reason. None are out to their parents and families. None are considered out-of-state students and all live both in residence halls and off campus. All of the students responding came out before attending college, and most said that being gay, lesbian, or bisexual affected their choosing NYU. If information on the climate for gays, lesbians, and bisexuals at NYU had been available, few of the respondents would have made different choices.

The respondents are involved in the gay, lesbian, and bisexual student group, which has an average membership of 50–75 students and sponsors dances, speakers, safe-sex education, and Pride and National Coming Out Day activities. The group receives funding from the student government. Most students date other NYU students and state that their dating activity takes place off campus, where they congregate in bars and the community center.

All of the students view coming out as the largest problem at NYU, with the lack of role models and alcohol abuse following second.

Gay men's and lesbians' cultural contributions are a part of some regular courses. The university also offers courses on gay, lesbian, and bisexual issues in English and women's studies. The university does not provide free, anonymous HIV testing. Students do not know if counseling is available for those who are HIV+ or have AIDS. Condoms are provided free of charge. Both the Health Center and the student group provide safe-sex education.

All of the respondents recommend NYU to other gay, lesbian, and bisexual students.

Northeastern University • *Boston, Massachusetts*

Students define Northeastern's position on gay, lesbian, and bisexual issues as noncommittal. Although the university does not have a committee on gay, lesbian, and bisexual issues, sexual orientation is included in its affirmative action statement, and counseling services are available for gay, lesbian, and bisexual students. Students do not know if housing for cohabitating couples is available. According to the students, the municipality in which the university is located has a civil rights law that includes sexual orientation.

Unanimously, all of the students believe that homophobia is a serious problem on the campus. Eighty percent of those responding report being victims of hate mail, verbal abuse, harassment, and vandalism. Moreover, all of the students have knowledge of hate crimes committed on the campus, including assault. Forty percent state that both the university and the student group maintain hate-crime statistics.

Eighty percent of the students believe that Northeastern takes action in response to these incidents, but the majority of the respondents do not feel supported by the university's security force. Still, 80 percent feel safe on the campus as gays, lesbians, and bisexuals.

Gay, lesbian, and bisexual students between the ages of 19–22 responded to the survey. Students are freshmen and juniors with SAT scores of 900 or higher and grade point averages of 2.0 and higher. Students have majors in journalism, business administration, engineering, and psychology.

All of the students surveyed are openly gay on the campus as well as to their parents and families. A few are considered out-of-state students. Forty percent live in residence halls but most live off campus, some with their families. Sixty percent of the students responding came out before attending college, and 80 percent said that being gay, lesbian, or bisexual affected their choosing Northeastern. If information on the climate for gays, lesbians, and bisexuals at Northeastern had been available, 20 percent of the respondents would have made a different choice.

The respondents are involved in the gay, lesbian, and bisexual student group, which has an average membership of 10–20 students and sponsors dances, speakers, safe-sex education, and Pride and National Coming Out Day activities. The group receives funding from the student government. Students are also active in other organizations such as Coalition for Exposing and Ending Discrimination, the NU Times Student magazine, AIDS Peer Education, and student government. The majority of students date other Northeastern students and state that their dating activity takes place on campus. Off campus, students congregate in bars, the community center, religious organizations, and in houses or apartments of other students off campus.

All of the students view coming out as the largest problem at Northeastern, with lack of role models and alcohol abuse following second.

Although gay men's and lesbians' cultural contributions are not a part of regular courses, the university offers courses on gay, lesbian, and bisexual issues in English. The university does not provides free, anonymous HIV testing nor is counseling available for those who are HIV+ or have AIDS. Condoms are not provided. Both the Health Center and the student group provide safe-sex education for the campus.

All of the respondents recommend Northeastern to other gay, lesbian, and bisexual students.

Northeastern University, School of Law •
Boston, Massachusetts

Students define Northeastern Law's position on gay, lesbian, and bisexual issues as proactive. Although the School of Law does not have a committee on gay, lesbian, and bisexual issues, sexual orientation is included in its affirmative action policy. In addition, counseling services are available for gay, lesbian, and bisexual students. Housing for cohabitating couples is not available. According to the students, the municipality in which the university is located has a civil rights law that includes sexual orientation.

Sixty percent of the students do not believe that homophobia is a serious problem on the campus, but 40 percent of those responding report being victims of verbal abuse. Moreover, 60 percent of the students have knowledge of hate crimes committed on the campus, including assault. The student group maintains hate-crime statistics.

All of the students believe that Northeastern Law takes action in response to hate crimes. Most are noncommittal regarding its security force. All of the students feel safe in the law school as gays, lesbians, and bisexuals, but not necessarily on the Northeastern campus.

Gay, lesbian, and bisexual students between the ages of 25–27 responded to the survey. Students are graduates with SAT scores of

1100 or higher. Grades are not given; the program is pass/fail. Students are Juris Doctor candidates.

All of the students are openly gay on the campus as well as to their parents and families. Some are considered out-of-state students and all live off campus, some with life partners. All of the students responding came out before attending college, and most said that being gay, lesbian, or bisexual affected their choosing Northeastern Law. If information on the climate for gays, lesbians, and bisexuals at Northeastern Law had been available, very few of the respondents would have made a different choice.

The respondents are involved in the gay, lesbian, and bisexual student group, which has an average membership of 30–40 students and sponsors speakers and Pride and National Coming Out Day activities. The group receives funding from the law school. In addition, students are active in various law associations within the school. Half of the students date other Northeastern Law students and state that some of their dating activity takes place on the campus. Off campus, students congregate in bars, the community center, religious organizations, and in various political groups.

All of the students view the lack of role models as the largest problem at Northeastern Law.

Although gay men's and lesbians' cultural contributions are not a part of regular courses, the law school does offer courses on gay, lesbian, and bisexual issues in law. Students do not know if there is free, anonymous HIV testing, counseling for those who are HIV+ or have AIDS, or condoms free of charge. In addition, students do not know who provides safe-sex education.

All of the respondents unequivocally recommend Northeastern Law to other gay, lesbian, and bisexual students. All of the students, in various comments, said that the law school is a comfortable place for them. "Faculty and staff are very supportive."

Oberlin College • *Oberlin, Ohio*

Students define Oberlin's position on gay, lesbian, and bisexual issues as proactive. The college has a committee on gay, lesbian, and bisexual issues and sexual orientation is included in the college's affirmative action policy. Oberlin provides counseling services for gay, lesbian, and bisexual students as well as housing for cohabitating couples. The majority of students do not know if the municipality in which the college is located has a civil rights law that includes sexual orientation.

Unanimously, students strongly believe that homophobia is not a serious problem on the campus. Those responding report being victims of verbal abuse and harassment. Both the college and the student group maintain hate-crime statistics.

Fifty percent of the students believe that Oberlin takes action in response to these incidents, and the other 50 percent do not know; however, all feel supported by the college's security force. All of the students feel very safe on the campus as gays, lesbians, and bisexuals.

Gay, lesbian, and bisexual students between the ages of 19–21 responded to the survey. Students are first-year, sophomores, and juniors with SAT scores of 1100 or higher with grade point averages of 3.0 and higher. All have majors in the liberal arts and one is undecided.

All of the students are openly gay on the campus as well as to their parents and families. All are considered out-of-state students and live in residence halls. All of the students responding came out before attending college, and said that being gay, lesbian, or bisexual affected their choosing Oberlin. Furthermore, if information on the climate for gays, lesbians, and bisexuals at Oberlin had been available, the respondents' choices would not have been different.

The respondents are involved in the gay, lesbian, and bisexual student group, which has an average membership of 45 students and sponsors dances, speakers, safe-sex education, and Pride Day activities. The group receives funding from the student government. In addition, students are active in other organizations such as the Student Senate. The students date other Oberlin students and state that their dating activity takes place on the Oberlin campus. Off campus, students congregate in private homes. One quarter of the students are members of intercollegiate athletic teams.

The largest problem at Oberlin is the "lack of energy and time" for student activity. Otherwise, all of the students report no significant problems for gay, lesbian, and bisexual students at Oberlin.

Gay men's and lesbians' cultural contributions are a part of regular courses; the college also offers courses on gay, lesbian, and bisexual issues in English, history, art, women's studies, and the social sciences. The college does not provide free, anonymous HIV testing, but it does provide condoms and offers counseling for those who are HIV+ or have AIDS. Both the Health Center and the student group provide safe-sex education.

All of the respondents recommend Oberlin to other gay, lesbian, and bisexual students.

Occidental College • *Los Angeles, California*

Students define Occidental's position on gay, lesbian, and bisexual issues as proactive. The college has a committee on gay, lesbian, and bisexual issues. Sexual orientation is included in the college's affirmative action statement, and counseling services are available for gay, lesbian, and bisexual students. Housing for cohabitating couples is not available. According to the students, the municipality in which the college is located has a civil rights law that includes sexual orientation.

Unanimously, students believe that homophobia is a serious problem on the campus. Those responding report being victims of verbal abuse and harassment. Moreover, all of the students have knowledge of hate crimes committed on the campus, including assault. Both the college and the student group maintain hate-crime statistics.

All of the students believe that Occidental takes action in response to hate crimes, and all strongly agree that the college's security force is supportive. Consequently, all of the students feel safe on the campus as gays, lesbians, and bisexuals.

Gay, lesbian, and bisexual students between the ages of 19–20 responded to the survey. Students are juniors with SAT scores of 1100 or higher and grade point averages of 3.0 and higher. Students have majors in the liberal arts.

All of the students surveyed are openly gay on the campus as well as to their parents and families. Most are considered out-of-state students and all live in residence halls. Most of the students responding came out before attending college, and said that being gay, lesbian, or bisexual affected their choosing Occidental. If information on the climate for gays, lesbians, and bisexuals at Occidental had been available, the respondents' choices would not have been different.

The respondents are involved in the gay, lesbian, and bisexual student group, which has an average membership of 100+ students and sponsors dances, speakers, safe-sex education, and Pride and National Coming Out Day activities. The group receives funding from the student government. Students are also active in the student government. Students date other Occidental students and state that their dating activity takes place on the campus. Off campus, they congregate in clubs, the community center, awareness groups, and religious organizations.

All of the students view coming out as the largest problem at Occidental.

Gay men's and lesbians' cultural contributions are a part of regular courses, and the college offers courses on gay, lesbian, and bisexual issues in English, history, art, women's studies, education, the social sciences, and psychology. The college provides free, anonymous HIV testing, counseling for those who are HIV+ or have AIDS, and condoms free of charge. Both the college and the student group provide safe-sex education.

All of the respondents recommend Occidental to other gay, lesbian, and bisexual students. (*Note:* Students at Occidental have created a "the Lambda Emergency Scholarship Fund" to provide financial assistance to students cut off from family funds as a result of their coming out. For more information on this scholarship contact the college or reference the July 6, 1992, issue of the *National On-Campus Report*, vol. 20, no. 13.)

Ohio State University • *Columbus, Ohio*

Students define Ohio State's position on gay, lesbian, and bisexual issues as proactive. The university has a committee on gay, lesbian, and bisexual issues, and sexual orientation is included in the university's affirmative action policy. In addition, counseling services are available for gay, lesbian, and bisexual students. Housing for cohabitating couples is not available. According to the students, the municipality in which the university is located has a civil rights law that includes sexual orientation.

Unanimously, students believe strongly that homophobia is a serious problem on the campus. Those responding report being victims of verbal abuse, harassment, and vandalism. Moreover, all of the students have knowledge of hate crimes committed on the campus, including assault. Both the university and the student group maintain hate-crime statistics.

All of the students believe that Ohio State takes action in response to hate crimes, and all of the students agree that the university's security force is supportive. Half of the students feel safe on the campus as gays, lesbians, and bisexuals.

Gay, lesbian, and bisexual students between the ages of 22–29 responded to the survey. Students are seniors and graduate students with SAT scores of 1100 or higher and grade point averages of 3.0 or higher. Students have majors in the liberal arts.

All of the students are openly gay on the campus and most are out to their parents and families. None are considered out-of-state students and all live off campus, some with life partners. Most of the students responding came out before attending college, and none said that being gay, lesbian, or bisexual affected their choosing Ohio State. If information on the climate for gays, lesbians, and bisexuals at Ohio State had been available, most of the undergraduate respondents would have made a different choice.

The respondents are involved in the gay, lesbian, and bisexual student group, which has an average membership of 50 students and sponsors speakers, safe-sex education, and Pride and National Coming Out Day activities. The group receives no funding from the student government. In addition, students are active in other organizations such as the student government, the Hispanic Professional and Graduate Student Organization, and the engineering magazine. The students date other Ohio State students and indicate that most of their dating activity takes place on the campus. Off campus, students congregate in bars.

All of the students view the lack of role models as the largest problem at Ohio State, with coming out and alcohol abuse following second.

Gay men's and lesbians' cultural contributions are a part of some regular courses. The university also offers courses on gay, lesbian, and bisexual issues in English, women's studies, history, and the social sciences. The university does not provide free, anonymous HIV testing, but counseling is available for those who are HIV+ or have AIDS. Students do not know if condoms are provided. Both the Health Center and the student group provide safe-sex education.

All of the respondents recommend Ohio State to other gay, lesbian, and bisexual students.

Old Dominion University • *Norfolk, Virginia*

Students define Old Dominion's position on gay, lesbian, and bisexual issues as noncommittal. The university has a committee on gay, lesbian, and bisexual issues, and sexual orientation is included in its affirmative action policy. In addition, counseling services are available for gay, lesbian, and bisexual students. Housing for cohabitating couples is not available. According to the students, the municipality in which the university is located does not have a civil rights law that includes sexual orientation.

Unanimously, students believe strongly that homophobia is a serious problem on the campus. Those responding report being victims of hate mail, harassment, vandalism, and verbal abuse. Moreover, all of the students have knowledge of hate crimes committed on the campus, including assault. Students do not know who, if anyone, maintains hate-crime statistics.

All of the students believe that Old Dominion takes action in response to hate crimes, and all agree that the university's security force is supportive. All of the students feel relatively safe on the campus as gays, lesbians, and bisexuals.

Gay, lesbian, and bisexual students between the ages of 20–22 responded to the survey. Students are juniors with SAT scores of 900 or higher and grade point averages of 2.5 or higher. Students have majors in the liberal arts.

All of the students are openly gay on the campus as well as to their parents and families. None are considered out-of-state students and all live off campus. All of the students responding came out before attending college, and said that being gay, lesbian, or bisexual affected their choosing Old Dominion. Furthermore, if information on the climate for gays, lesbians, and bisexuals at Old Dominion had been available, the respondents' choices would not have been different.

The respondents are involved in the gay, lesbian, and bisexual student group, which has an average membership of 6 students and sponsors dances, speakers, safe-sex education, and Pride and National Coming Out Day activities. The group receives funding from the student government. In addition, students are active in the Science Fiction Club. The students tend not to date other Old Dominion students. Off campus, students congregate in bars.

All of the students view coming out as the largest problem at Old Dominion, with the lack of role models and alcohol abuse following second.

Gay men's and lesbians' cultural contributions are not a part of regular courses, nor does the university offer courses on gay, lesbian, and bisexual issues. The university does not provide free, anonymous HIV testing, but counseling for those who are HIV+ or have AIDS is available. Free condoms are also available. Both the Health Center and the student group provide safe-sex education.

All of the respondents recommend Old Dominion to other gay, lesbian, and bisexual students.

Oregon State University • *Corvallis, Oregon*

Students are divided in defining Oregon State's position on gay, lesbian, and bisexual issues as both proactive and noncommittal. Although the university does not have a committee on gay, lesbian, and bisexual issues, sexual orientation is included in its affirmative action policy. In addition, counseling services are available for gay, lesbian, and bisexual students. Housing for cohabitating couples is not available. According to the students, the municipality in which the university is located has a civil rights law that includes sexual orientation.

Unanimously, students believe that homophobia is a serious problem on the campus. Those responding report being victims of verbal abuse. Moreover, all of the students have knowledge of hate crimes committed on the campus, including assault. Both the university and the student group maintain hate-crime statistics.

All of students believe that Oregon State takes action in response to hate crimes. None, however, agree that the university's security force is supportive. Still, most of the students feel safe on the campus as gays, lesbians, and bisexuals.

Gay, lesbian, and bisexual students between the ages of 19–28 responded to the survey. Students are freshmen, sophomores, juniors, seniors, and graduate students with SAT scores of 900 or higher and grade point averages of 2.5 or higher. Students have majors in psychology, human development, family sciences, business administration, and forest recreation.

All of the students are openly gay on the campus and half are out to their parents and families. None are considered out-of-state students and all live off campus. All of the students responding came out before attending college, and none said that being gay, lesbian, or bisexual affected their choosing Oregon State. Furthermore, if information on the climate for gays, lesbians, and bisexuals at Oregon State had been available, one quarter of the respondents would have made a different choice.

The respondents are involved in the gay, lesbian, and bisexual student group, which has an average membership of 20–30 students and sponsors dances, speakers, safe-sex education, and Pride and National Coming Out Day activities. The group receives funding from the student government. Students are also active in other organizations such as the Women's Affairs Task Force, the Hispanic Student Union, and the MBA Association. Seventy-five percent of the students date other Oregon students, and 25 percent state that their dating activity takes place on the campus. Off campus, students congregate in bars and religious organizations.

All of the students view the lack of student organization as the largest problem at Oregon State, with coming out and the lack of role models following second.

Although gay men's and lesbians' cultural contributions are not a part of regular courses, the university does offer courses on gay, lesbian, and bisexual issues in women's studies. The university provides anonymous HIV testing (fee is applied) and counseling for those who are HIV+ or have AIDS. Condoms are not provided. Both the Health Center and the student group provide safe-sex education.

Seventy-five percent of the respondents recommend Oregon State to other gay, lesbian, and bisexual students.

Pace University • *New York, New York*

Those students responding do not know Pace's position on gay, lesbian, and bisexual issues. Nor do they know if the university has a committee on gay, lesbian, and bisexual issues, or if sexual orientation is included in its affirmative action policy. However, counseling services are available for gay, lesbian, and bisexual students. Students do not know if housing for cohabiting couples is available, or if the municipality in which the university is located has a civil rights law that includes sexual orientation.

Unanimously, students believe that homophobia is a serious problem on the campus. None of those responding report being victims of hate crimes. However, all of the students have knowledge of hate crimes committed on the campus, including assault. Students do not know who, if anyone, maintains hate-crime statistics.

Students do not know how Pace reacts to hate crimes and are ambivalent concerning the security force's support. Consequently, students question their safety on the campus as gays, lesbians, and bisexuals.

Gay, lesbian, and bisexual students between the ages of 19–21 responded to the survey. Students are sophomores and juniors with SAT scores of 900 or higher and grade point averages of 3.5 or higher. Students have majors in the liberal arts.

All of the students are openly gay on the campus as well as to their parents and families. None are considered out-of-state students and all live off campus, some with their families. All of the students responding came out before attending college, and none said that being gay, lesbian, or bisexual affected their choosing Pace. If information on the climate for gays, lesbians, and bisexuals at Pace had been available, some of the respondents might have made a different choice.

The respondents are involved in the gay, lesbian, and bisexual student group, which sponsors speakers and provides safe-sex education. The group receives funding from the student government. The students tend not to date other Pace students. Off campus, students congregate in bars and the community center.

All of the students view coming out as the largest problem at Pace, with the lack of role models and student organization following second.

Although gay men's and lesbians' cultural contributions are not a part of regular courses, the university does offer courses on gay, lesbian, and bisexual issues in English and women's studies. Students do not know if the university provides free, anonymous HIV testing or counseling for those who are HIV+ or have AIDS. Condoms, however, are provided free of charge. Both the Health Center and the student group provide safe-sex education.

All of the respondents recommend Pace to other gay, lesbian, and bisexual students.

Palomar Community College • *San Marcos, California*

Students define Palomar's position on gay, lesbian, and bisexual issues as noncommittal. The college does not have a committee on gay, lesbian, and bisexual issues, nor are counseling services available for gay, lesbian, and bisexual students. Students do not know if sexual orientation is included in the college's affirmative action policy. Housing for cohabitating couples is not available. Students also do not know if the municipality in which the college is located has a civil rights law that includes sexual orientation.

Unanimously, students believe that homophobia is a serious problem on the campus. Those responding report being victims of minor harassment. Moreover, all of the students have knowledge of hate crimes committed on the campus (minor harassment). Both the college and the student group maintain hate-crime statistics.

All of students believe that Palomar takes action in response to hate crimes, but none agree that the college's security force is supportive. Students do not always feel safe on the campus as gays, lesbians, and bisexuals.

Gay, lesbian, and bisexual students between the ages of 18–23 responded to the survey. Students are freshmen and sophomores with SAT scores of 1100 or higher and grade point averages of 2.5 or higher. Students have majors in the liberal arts.

All of the students are openly gay on the campus as well as to their parents and families. None are considered out-of-state students and all live off campus, some with their families. All of the students responding came out before attending college, and none said that being gay, lesbian, or bisexual affected their choosing Palomar. Furthermore, if information on the climate for gays, lesbians, and bisexuals at Palomar had been available, the respondents' choices would not have been different.

The respondents are involved in the gay, lesbian, and bisexual student group, which has an average membership of 25 students and sponsors speakers and provides safe-sex education. The group receives no funding from the student government. In addition, students are active in the National Organization for Women. The students tend not to date other Palomar students. Off campus, students congregate in private homes and apartments.

All of the students view the lack of student organization as the largest problem at Palomar, with the lack of role models and coming out following second.

Although gay men's and lesbians' cultural contributions are not a part of regular courses, the college does offer courses on gay, lesbian, and bisexual issues in women's studies, human sexuality, and the social sciences. The college provides free, anonymous HIV testing and condoms free of charge. Counseling is not available for those who are HIV+ or have AIDS. Both the Health Center and the student group provide safe-sex education.

All of the respondents recommend Palomar with some reservation to other gay, lesbian, and bisexual students, but they do say that it is a good community college.

Parkland College • *Champaign, Illinois*

Students responding do not know Parkland's position on gay, lesbian, and bisexual issues. The college does not have a committee on gay, lesbian, and bisexual issues. Students do not know if sexual orientation is included in its affirmative action policy or if counseling services are available for gay, lesbian, and bisexual students. Housing for cohabitating couples is not available. According to the students, the municipality in which the college is located does not have a civil rights law that includes sexual orientation.

Unanimously, students believe strongly that homophobia is a serious problem on the campus. Although none of those responding report being victims of hate crimes, all of the students have knowledge of hate crimes committed on the campus. The student group maintains hate-crime statistics.

Students do not know how Parkland reacts to hate crimes. However, all agree that the college's security force is not supportive. All of the students, though, feel relatively safe on the campus as gays, lesbians, and bisexuals.

Gay, lesbian, and bisexual students between the ages of 18–21 responded to the survey. Students are freshmen with grade point averages of 2.5 or higher. Students have majors in the liberal arts and sciences.

All of the students are openly gay on the campus as well as to their parents and families. None are considered out-of-state students and all live off campus. All of the students responding came out before attending college, and none said that being gay, lesbian, or bisexual affected their choosing Parkland. However, if information on the climate for gays, lesbians, and bisexuals at Parkland had been available, all of the respondents would have made different choices.

Parkland does not have an active gay, lesbian, and bisexual student group. Students tend not to date other Parkland students. Off campus, students congregate in bars.

All of the students view the lack of role models as the largest problem at Parkland, with coming out and the lack of students organization following second.

Gay men's and lesbians' cultural contributions are not a part of regular courses, nor does the college offer courses on gay, lesbian, and bisexual issues. The college does not provides free, anonymous HIV testing, counseling for those who are HIV+ or have AIDS, or condoms. The Health Center provides safe-sex education.

Still, all of the respondents recommend Parkland to other gay, lesbian, and bisexual students.

Pasadena City College • *Pasadena, California*

Students define Pasadena City College's position on gay, lesbian, and bisexual issues as negative. The college does not have a committee on gay, lesbian, and bisexual issues, and only half say that sexual orientation is included in its affirmative action policy. But counseling services are available for gay, lesbian, and bisexual students. Housing for cohabitating couples is not available. According to the students, the municipality in which the college is located has a civil rights law that includes sexual orientation.

Unanimously, students believe that homophobia is a serious problem on the campus. Those responding report being victims of verbal abuse and harassment. Moreover, all of the students have knowledge of hate crimes committed on the campus with the exception of assault. No one maintains hate-crime statistics.

Students are divided about whether Pasadena City takes action in response to hate crimes. All, however, agree that the college's security force is not supportive. Half of the students feel safe on the campus as gays, lesbians, and bisexuals.

Gay, lesbian, and bisexual students between the ages of 17–20 responded to the survey. Students are sophomores with grade point averages of 1.99 or higher. Students have majors in the liberal arts, theater, and music.

Most of the students are openly gay on the campus. Those who are not cite the knowledge of others' bad experiences as the primary reason. Half of the students are out to their parents and families. None are considered out-of-state students and all live off campus, some with their families. All of the students responding came out before attending college, and none said that being gay, lesbian, or bisexual affected their choosing Pasadena City. However, if information on the climate for gays, lesbians, and bisexuals at Pasadena City had been available, half of the respondents would have made a different choice.

The respondents are involved in the gay, lesbian, and bisexual student group, which has an average membership of 45–60 students and sponsors dances, speakers, safe-sex education, and Pride and National Coming Out Day activities. The group receives funding from the student government. Students are also active in Earthwise.

Some of the students date other Pasadena City students and state that their dating activity takes place on the campus. Off campus, students congregate in dance clubs.

All of the students view coming out and the lack of role models as the largest problems at Pasadena City.

Gay men's and lesbians' cultural contributions are not a part of regular courses, nor does the college offer courses on gay, lesbian, and bisexual issues. The college does not provide free, anonymous HIV testing or counseling for those who are HIV+ or have AIDS. It does provide condoms free of charge. The student group provides safe-sex education.

All of the respondents recommend Pasadena City to other gay, lesbian, and bisexual students.

Pennsylvania State University • *State College, Pennsylvania*

Students define Penn State's position on gay, lesbian, and bisexual issues as noncommittal. Although the university does not have a committee on gay, lesbian, and bisexual issues, sexual orientation is included in its affirmative action policy. Counseling services are not available for gay, lesbian, and bisexual students, nor is housing for cohabitating couples. According to the students, the municipality in which the university is located does not have a civil rights law that includes sexual orientation.

Unanimously, students believe strongly that homophobia is a serious problem on the campus. Those responding report being victims of hate mail, vandalism, and verbal abuse. Moreover, all of the students have knowledge of hate crimes committed on the campus, including assault. Both the university and the student group maintain hate-crime statistics.

All of the students believe that Penn State takes action in response to hate crimes and agree that the university's security force is supportive. All of the students usually feel safe on the campus as gays, lesbians, and bisexuals.

Gay, lesbian, and bisexual students between the ages of 19–21 responded to the survey. Students are sophomores and juniors with SAT scores of 1100 or higher and grade point averages of 3.5 or higher. Students have majors in the liberal arts.

All of the students are openly gay on the campus as well as to their parents and families. None are considered out-of-state students and all live off campus. All of the students responding came out before attending college, and none said that being gay, lesbian, or bisexual affected their choosing Penn State. Furthermore, if information on the climate for gays, lesbians, and bisexuals at Penn State had been available, none of the respondents would have made a different choice.

The respondents are involved in the gay, lesbian, and bisexual student group, which has an average membership of 50–100 students and sponsors dances, speakers, safe-sex education, and Pride and National Coming Out Day activities. The group receives funding from the student government. In addition, students are active in other organizations such as the women's center, the concert choir, and campus life. The students date other Penn State students and indicate that their dating activity takes place on the campus. Off campus, students congregate in religious organizations and coffeehouses.

All of the students view the lack of role models as the largest problem at Penn State, with alcohol abuse and coming out following second.

Gay men's and lesbians' cultural contributions are a part of some regular courses. The university also offer courses on gay, lesbian, and bisexual issues in history, women's studies, and human development. The university provides free, confidential HIV testing, counseling for those who are HIV+ or have AIDS, and condoms for a nominal charge. Both the Health Center and the student group provide safe-sex education for the campus.

All of the respondents recommend Penn State to other gay, lesbian, and bisexual students.

Plymouth State College of the University System of New Hampshire • *Plymouth, New Hampshire*

Students define Plymouth State's position on gay, lesbian, and bisexual issues as proactive. The college has a committee on gay, lesbian, and bisexual issues, and sexual orientation is included in the college's affirmative action policy. In addition, counseling services are available for gay, lesbian, and bisexual students. Students do not know if housing for cohabitating couples is available. According to the students, the municipality in which the college is located does not have a civil rights law that includes sexual orientation.

Unanimously, students believe that homophobia is a serious problem on the campus. Those responding report being victims of vandalism and verbal abuse. Moreover, all of the students have knowledge of hate crimes committed on the campus, including assault. Students do not know who, if anyone, maintains hate-crime statistics.

All of the students believe that Plymouth State takes action in response to hate crimes and agree that the college's security force is supportive. All of the students feel safe, more often than not, on the campus as gays, lesbians, and bisexuals.

Gay, lesbian, and bisexual students between the ages of 23–30 responded to the survey. Students are seniors with SAT scores of 900 or higher and grade point averages of 3.5 or higher. Students have majors in the fine arts.

All of the students are openly gay on the campus as well as to their parents and families. None are considered out-of-state students and all live off campus. None of the students responding came out before attending college, and none said that being gay, lesbian, or bisexual affected their choosing Plymouth State. Furthermore, if information on the climate for gays, lesbians, and bisexuals at Plymouth State had been available, some of the respondents would have made a different choice.

The respondents are involved in the gay, lesbian, and bisexual student group, which has an average membership of 12–15 students and sponsors speakers, safe-sex education, and Pride and National Coming Out Day activities. The group receives funding from the student government. Students are also active in the student art society. The students date other Plymouth State students and indicate that their dating activity takes place off campus, where they congregate in private homes and apartments.

All of the students view coming out as the largest problem at Plymouth State, with the lack of role models and alcohol abuse following second.

Gay men's and lesbians' cultural contributions are not a part of regular courses, nor does the college offer courses on gay, lesbian, and bisexual issues. The college does not provide free, anonymous

HIV testing, counseling for those who are HIV+ or have AIDS, or condoms free of charge. Both the Health Center and the student group provide safe-sex education.

None of the respondents recommend Plymouth State to other gay, lesbian, and bisexual students, primarily because the "majority of gay students are still closeted. The administration is more supportive of gay students and issues than the student body, which has an incredible emphasis on assimilation. However, the gay community at PSC is tolerated and to a great degree respected for their openness and educational contributions on campus. So, in this respect students are physically safe at PSC, yet emotional support is questionable."

Princeton University • *Princeton, New Jersey*

Students define Princeton's position on gay, lesbian, and bisexual issues as noncommittal. The university has a committee on gay, lesbian, and bisexual issues, sexual orientation is included in the university's affirmative action policy, counseling services are available for gay, lesbian, and bisexual students, and housing is available for co-habitating couples. According to the students, the municipality in which the university is located does have a civil rights law that includes sexual orientation.

Unanimously, students believe that homophobia is a serious problem on the campus. Those responding report being victims of verbal abuse. Moreover, all of the students have knowledge of hate crimes committed on the campus. Both the university and the student group maintain hate-crime statistics.

All of the students believe that Princeton does nothing in response to hate crimes, and students are ambivalent concerning the support of the university's security force. Consequently, students do not always feel safe on the campus as gays, lesbians, and bisexuals.

Gay, lesbian, and bisexual students between the ages of 22–31 responded to the survey. Students are seniors and graduate students with SAT scores 1100 or higher and grade point averages of 3.5 or higher. Students have majors in the liberal arts.

All of the students are openly gay on the campus as well as to some family members. Few are out to their parents. All are considered out-of-state students and live off campus. All of the students responding came out before attending college, and none said that being gay, lesbian, or bisexual affected their choosing Princeton. However, if information on the climate for gays, lesbians, and bisexuals at Princeton had been available, all of the respondents would have made a different choice.

The respondents are involved in the gay, lesbian, and bisexual student group, which has an average membership of 25 students and sponsors dances, speakers, safe-sex education, and Pride and National Coming Out Day activities. The group receives funding from the student government. The students date other Princeton students and state that their dating activity takes place on the campus. Off campus, students congregate in bars and religious organizations.

All of the students view coming out as the largest problem at Princeton, with the lack of role models and alcohol abuse following second.

Gay men's and lesbians' cultural contributions are a part of regular courses, and the university offers courses on gay, lesbian, and bisexual issues in history and women's studies. The university provides free, anonymous HIV testing, counseling for those who are HIV+ or have AIDS, and condoms free of charge. Both the Health Center and the student group provide safe-sex education.

All of the respondents recommend Princeton to other gay, lesbian, and bisexual students. "We need help here," one of the respondents said.

Purdue University • *West Lafayette, Indiana*

Students define Purdue's position on gay, lesbian, and bisexual issues as noncommittal. The university does not have a committee on gay, lesbian, and bisexual issues, nor is sexual orientation included in its affirmative action policy. In addition, counseling services are not available for gay, lesbian, and bisexual students, nor is housing available for cohabitating couples. Students do not know if the municipality in which the university is located has a civil rights law that includes sexual orientation.

Unanimously, students believe strongly that homophobia is a serious problem on the campus. Those responding report being victims

of harassment, vandalism, and verbal abuse. Moreover, all of the students have knowledge of hate crimes committed on the campus, including assault. No one maintains hate-crime statistics.

All of the students believe that Purdue does nothing in response to hate crimes, and none agree that the university's security force is supportive. Students do not feel safe on the campus as gays, lesbians, and bisexuals.

Gay, lesbian, and bisexual students between the ages of 21–23 responded to the survey. Students are juniors and seniors with SAT scores of 1100 or higher and grade point averages of 3.0 or higher. Students have majors in the liberal arts.

All of the students are openly gay on the campus and most are out to their parents and family. None are considered out-of-state students and all live off campus. All of the students responding came out before attending college, and none said that being gay, lesbian, or bisexual affected their choosing Purdue. Furthermore, if information on the climate for gays, lesbians, and bisexuals at Purdue had been available, the majority of the respondents would have made a different choice.

The respondents are involved in the gay, lesbian, and bisexual student group, which has an average membership of 40–45 students and sponsors dances, speakers, and safe-sex education. The group receives no funding from the student government. Students are active in the Varsity Glee Club. They date other Purdue students and state that their dating activity takes place off campus, where they congregate in bars.

All of the students view the lack of student organization as the largest problem at Purdue, with the lack of role models and coming out following second.

Gay men's and lesbians' cultural contributions are not a part of regular courses, nor does the university offer courses on gay, lesbian, and bisexual issues. The university provides free, anonymous HIV testing, but no counseling for those who are HIV+ or have AIDS, or condoms free of charge. The student group provides safe-sex education.

All of the respondents recommend Purdue to other gay, lesbian, and bisexual students.

Rice University • *Houston, Texas*

Students define Rice's position on gay, lesbian, and bisexual issues as noncommittal. Although the university does not have a committee on gay, lesbian, and bisexual issues, sexual orientation is included in its affirmative action policy. In addition, counseling services are available for gay, lesbian, and bisexual students. Housing for cohabitating couples is not available. According to the students, the municipality in which the university is located does not have a civil rights law that includes sexual orientation.

Unanimously, students believe that homophobia is a serious problem on the campus, though none of those responding report being victims of hate crimes. However, all of the students have knowledge of hate crimes committed on the campus, including assault. The university maintains hate-crime statistics.

All of the students believe that Rice takes action in response to hate crimes, and all agree that the university's security force is supportive. All of the students feel safe on the campus as gays, lesbians, and bisexuals.

Gay, lesbian, and bisexual students between the ages of 19–22 responded to the survey. Students are sophomores and juniors with SAT scores of 1100 or higher and grade point averages of 3.5 or higher. Students have majors in the liberal arts and mathematical economic analysis.

All of the students are openly gay on the campus as well as to their parents and families. Most are considered out-of-state students and all live in residence halls. None of the students responding came out before attending college, and none said that being gay, lesbian, or bisexual affected their choosing Rice. However, if information on the climate for gays, lesbians, and bisexuals at Rice had been available, all of the respondents would have made a different choice.

The respondents are involved in the gay, lesbian, and bisexual student group, which has an average membership of 25 students and sponsors speakers, safe-sex education, and Pride and National Coming Out Day activities. The group receives no funding from the student government. Students are also active in other organizations such as the University Court, the speech and debate team, and career advisers. The students date other Rice students and state that some of their dating activity takes place on the campus. Off campus, students congregate in bars and private homes and apartments.

All of the students view coming out as the largest problem at Rice, with the lack of role models and student organization following second.

Although gay men's and lesbians' cultural contributions are not a part of regular courses, the university does offer courses on gay, lesbian, and bisexual issues in the social sciences. The university provides free, confidential HIV testing and condoms free of charge. Counseling is not available for those who are HIV+ or have AIDS. Both the Health Center and the student group provide safe-sex education.

All of the respondents recommend Rice to other gay, lesbian, and bisexual students, although one student claims that "it is hard to say. Compared to some other schools, Rice has a long way to go. However, the university does have an anti-discrimination clause and attitudes are such that I see a good chance for more progress."

Rochester Institute of Technology • *Rochester, New York*

The students responding do not know Rochester's position on gay, lesbian, and bisexual issues. Although the Institute does not have a committee on gay, lesbian, and bisexual issues, sexual orientation is included in its affirmative action statement. Respondents do not know whether Rochester provides counseling services for gay, lesbian, and bisexual students. Housing for cohabitating couples is not available. According to the students, the municipality in which the Institute is located has a civil rights law that includes sexual orientation.

Unanimously, students believe that homophobia is a serious problem on the campus. Those responding report being victims of harassment and vandalism. Moreover, all of the students have knowledge of hate crimes committed on the campus. Students do not know whether the Institute maintains hate-crime statistics.

Most of the students believe that Rochester does nothing in response to these incidents. In addition, all of the respondents state that they do not feel supported by the Institute's security force. Consequently, none of the students feel safe on the campus as gays, lesbians, and bisexuals.

Gay, lesbian, and bisexual students between the ages of 19–21 responded to the survey. Students are sophomores and juniors with SAT scores of 899 or higher and grade point averages of 2.0 and higher. Students declaring majors are studying accounting.

All of the students surveyed are openly gay on the campus as well as to their parents and families. The majority are considered out-of-state students and all live off campus. None of the students responding came out before attending college, and said that being gay, lesbian, or bisexual affected their choosing Rochester. However, if information on the climate for gays, lesbians, and bisexuals at Rochester been available, all of the respondents would have made a different choice.

The respondents are involved in a new gay, lesbian, and bisexual student group, which has an initial membership of 10 students and sponsors safe-sex education and Pride and National Coming Out Day activities. The group receives funding from the student government. The students responding state that they tend not to date other Rochester students. Off campus, students congregate in bars.

All of the students view coming out as the largest problem at Rochester, with lack of role models and student organization following second.

Although gay men's and lesbians' cultural contributions are not a part of some regular courses, the Institute does offer courses on gay, lesbian, and bisexual issues in women's studies and the liberal arts. It provides free, anonymous HIV testing, but students do not know if counseling is available for those who are HIV+ or have AIDS or if condoms are provided free of charge. Both the Health Center and the student group provide safe-sex education.

All of the respondents recommend Rochester Institute to other gay, lesbian, and bisexual students.

Rutgers University • *Newark, New Jersey*

Students define Rutgers's position on gay, lesbian, and bisexual issues as somewhere between proactive and noncommittal. The university has a committee on gay, lesbian, and bisexual issues, and sexual orientation is included in the university's affirmative action policy. In addition, counseling services are available for gay, lesbian, and bisexual students, as is housing for cohabitating couples. According to the students, the municipality in which the university is located has a civil rights law that includes sexual orientation.

Unanimously, students believe that homophobia is a serious problem on the campus. Those responding report being victims of harassment. Moreover, all of the students have knowledge of hate crimes committed on the campus. The university maintains hate-crime statistics.

All of the students believe that Rutgers takes action in response to hate crimes and agree that the university's security force is supportive. All of the students feel safe on the campus as gays, lesbians, and bisexuals.

Gay, lesbian, and bisexual students between the ages of 20–22 responded to the survey. Students are juniors and seniors with SAT scores of 900 or higher and grade point averages of 3.5 or higher. Students have majors in the liberal arts and business administration.

Most of the students are openly gay on the campus. Those who are not cite fear of reprisal as the primary reason. All, however, are out to their parents and families. Half are considered out-of-state students and all live off campus, some with their families. All of the students responding came out before attending college, and none said that being gay, lesbian, or bisexual affected their choosing Rutgers. If information on the climate for gays, lesbians, and bisexuals at Rutgers had been available, half of the respondents would have chosen to go elsewhere.

The respondents are involved in the gay, lesbian, and bisexual student group, which has an average membership of 25–30 students and sponsors speakers, safe-sex education, and Pride and National Coming Out Day activities. The group receives funding from the student government. Students are also active in the student government. They date other Rutgers students and state that their dating activity takes place on the campus. Off campus, students congregate in bars, religious organizations, and private homes and apartments.

All of the students view the lack of role models as the largest problem at Rutgers, with the lack of student organization and substance abuse following second.

Although gay men's and lesbians' cultural contributions are not a part of regular courses, the university does offer courses on gay, lesbian, and bisexual issues in the social sciences. The university does not provide free, anonymous HIV testing; however, counseling for those who are HIV+ or have AIDS is available, and condoms are free of charge. Both the Health Center and the student group provide safe-sex education for the campus.

All of the respondents recommend Rutgers to other gay, lesbian, and bisexual students.

St. John's University • *Collegeville, Minnesota*

Students define St. John's position on gay, lesbian, and bisexual issues as reactive. Although the university does not have a committee on gay, lesbian, and bisexual issues, sexual orientation is included in its affirmative action policy. In addition, counseling services are available for gay, lesbian, and bisexual students. Students do not know if housing for cohabiting couples is available. According to the students, the municipality in which the university is located does not have a civil rights law that includes sexual orientation.

Students are divided on whether homophobia is a serious problem on the campus. None of those responding report being victims of hate crimes. However, all of the students have knowledge of hate crimes committed on the campus, including assault. The university maintains hate-crime statistics.

All of students believe that St. John's takes action in response to hate crimes and most agree that the University's security force is supportive. Half of the students feel safe on the campus as gays, lesbians, and bisexuals.

Gay, lesbian, and bisexual students between the ages of 19–21 responded to the survey. Students are sophomores and juniors with SAT scores of 900 or higher and grade point averages of 2.5 or higher. Students have majors in the liberal arts.

All of the students are openly gay on the campus as well as to their parents and families. Half are considered out-of-state students and all live in residence halls. None of the students responding came out before attending college, and none said that being gay, lesbian, or bisexual affected their choosing St. John's. Furthermore, if information on the climate for gays, lesbians, and bisexuals at St. John's had been available, the respondents' choices would not have been different.

The respondents are involved in the two gay, lesbian, and bisexual student groups, which have average memberships of 15–50 students and sponsors speakers, safe-sex education, and Pride and National Coming Out Day activities. The group receives funding from the student government and Counseling and Career Services. In addition, students are active in other organizations such as Men's Chorus, Greek life, and student government. Most students date other St. John's students and state that their dating activity takes place on the campus. Off campus, students congregate in bars and coffeehouses.

All of the students view coming out as the largest problem at St. John's, with the lack of role models following second.

Although gay men's and lesbians' cultural contributions are a part of some regular courses, the university does not offer courses on gay, lesbian, and bisexual issues. The university does not provide free, anonymous HIV testing or condoms. However, counseling is available for those who are HIV+ or have AIDS. Both the Health Center and the student group provide safe-sex education.

Half of the respondents recommend St. John's to other gay, lesbian, and bisexual students. One student comments: "I was the first gay student to come out publicly in the student newspaper—December 12, 1991. Our campus has changed a lot since then."

St. Lawrence University • *Canton, New York*

Students define St. Lawrence's position on gay, lesbian, and bisexual issues as noncommittal. Students do not know if the university has a committee on gay, lesbian, and bisexual issues, but sexual orientation is included in its affirmative action policy. St. Lawrence provides counseling services for gay, lesbian, and bisexual students. None of the students know if housing for cohabitating couples is available, nor do they know if the municipality in which the university is located has a civil rights law that includes sexual orientation.

Unanimously, students believe that homophobia is a serious problem on the campus. Two thirds of those responding report being victims of verbal abuse and hate mail. Moreover, all the students have knowledge of hate crimes committed on the campus, including assault. Both the university and the student group maintain hate-crime statistics.

One third of the students believe that St. Lawrence takes action in response to these incidents, and most feel supported by the university's security force. The remaining students do not know the administration's position. Most of the students feel safe on the campus as gays, lesbians, and bisexuals; one third of the students feel safe sometimes.

Gay, lesbian, and bisexual students between the ages of 21–23 responded to the survey. Students are seniors with SAT scores of 1100 or higher and grade point averages of 3.5 and higher. All have majors in the liberal arts.

All of the students are openly gay on the campus but few are out to parents and family members. None are considered out-of-state students, and all live in residence halls. All of the students responding came out before attending college, and none said that being gay, lesbian, or bisexual affected their choosing St. Lawrence. Furthermore, if information on the climate for gays, lesbians, and bisexuals at St. Lawrence had been available, the respondents would not have made a different choice.

The respondents are involved in the gay, lesbian, and bisexual student group, which has an average membership of 5–10 students and sponsors speakers, safe-sex education, and Pride and National Coming Out Day activities. The group does not receive funding from the student government. All of the students responding state that they date other St. Lawrence students and that their dating activity takes place on campus. Off campus, students congregate in bars.

All of the students view coming out as the largest problem at St. Lawrence, with the lack of role models and alcohol abuse following second.

Gay men's and lesbians' cultural contributions are not a part of regular courses, nor are courses offered on gay, lesbian, and bisexual issues. The university does, however, provide free, anonymous HIV testing, condoms, and counseling for those who are HIV+ or have AIDS. Both the Health Center and the student group provide safe-sex education.

All of the respondents recommend St. Lawrence to other gay, lesbian, and bisexual students who are "very out and active."

St. Olaf College • *St. Paul, Minnesota*

Students define St. Olaf's position on gay, lesbian, and bisexual issues as noncommittal. The college does not have a committee on gay, lesbian, and bisexual issues, and sexual orientation is not included in its affirmative action policy. However, counseling services are available for gay, lesbian, and bisexual students. Housing for cohabitating couples is not available. According to the students, the municipality in which the college is located does not have a civil rights law that includes sexual orientation.

Unanimously, students believe that homophobia is a serious problem on the campus. Half of those responding report being victims of verbal abuse. Moreover, all of the students have knowledge of hate crimes committed on the campus. No one maintains hate-crime statistics.

All of the students believe that St. Olaf takes action in response to hate crimes. Students are ambivalent concerning the security force's support. All of the students feel safe on the campus as gays, lesbians, and bisexuals.

Gay, lesbian, and bisexual students between the ages of 20–23 responded to the survey. Students are juniors and seniors with SAT scores of 900 or higher and grade point averages of 2.5 or higher. Students have majors in fine arts, political science, environmental planning, and women's studies.

All of the students are openly gay on the campus as well as to their parents and families. Most are considered out-of-state students and live in residence halls. Some students live off campus with their families. Few of the students responding came out before attending college, and none said that being gay, lesbian, or bisexual affected their choosing St. Olaf. Furthermore, if information on the climate for gays, lesbians, and bisexuals at St. Olaf had been available, three quarters of the respondents would have made a different choice.

The respondents are involved in the gay, lesbian, and bisexual student group, which has an average membership of 90 students and sponsors dances, speakers, safe-sex education, and Pride and National Coming Out Day activities. The group receives funding from the student government. In addition, students are active in student government. The students tend not to date other St. Olaf students. Off campus, students congregate in bars.

All of the students view the lack of role models as the largest problem at St. Olaf, with coming out and alcohol abuse following second.

Although gay men's and lesbians' cultural contributions are a part of some regular courses, the college does not offer courses on gay, lesbian, and bisexual issues. It does not provide free, anonymous HIV testing, counseling for those who are HIV+ or have AIDS, or condoms free of charge. Both the Health Center and the student group provide safe-sex education.

All of the respondents recommend St. Olaf to other gay, lesbian, and bisexual students. "St. Olaf is a good place to be because it gives queerfolks something to work for."

Salem State College • *Salem, Massachusetts*

Students define Salem State's position on gay, lesbian, and bisexual issues as noncommittal. The college does not have a committee on gay, lesbian, and bisexual issues, and sexual orientation is not included in its affirmative action policy. Counseling services are available for gay, lesbian, and bisexual students, but housing for cohabiting couples is not. Students do not know if the municipality in which the college is located has a civil rights law that includes sexual orientation.

Unanimously, students believe strongly that homophobia is a serious problem on the campus. Those responding report being victims of verbal abuse, hate mail, and harassment. Moreover, all of the students have knowledge of hate crimes committed on the campus, including assault. No one maintains hate-crime statistics.

All of the students believe that Salem State does nothing in response to hate crimes, and all agree that the college's security force is not supportive. Students do not feel safe on the campus as gays, lesbians, and bisexuals.

Gay, lesbian, and bisexual students between the ages of 22–24 responded to the survey. Students are seniors with SAT scores of 900

or higher and grade point averages of 2.0 or higher. Students have majors in the liberal arts.

All of the students are openly gay on the campus but not to their parents and families. None are considered out-of-state students and all live off campus. All of the students responding came out before attending college, and none said that being gay, lesbian, or bisexual affected their choosing Salem State. However, if information on the climate for gays, lesbians, and bisexuals at Salem State had been available, all of the respondents would have made a different choice.

The respondents are involved in the gay, lesbian, and bisexual student group, which has an average membership of 6 students and sponsors safe-sex education. The group receives no funding from the student government. The students date other Salem State students and indicate that their dating activity takes place off campus, where they congregate in bars.

All of the students view the lack of role models as the largest problem at Salem State, with the lack of student organization and alcohol abuse following second.

Gay men's and lesbians' cultural contributions are not a part of regular courses, nor does the college offer courses on gay, lesbian, and bisexual issues. The college does not provide free, anonymous HIV testing, but short-term counseling is available for those who are HIV+ or have AIDS. Condoms are provided free of charge. Both the Health Center and the student group provide safe-sex education.

None of the respondents recommend Salem State to other gay, lesbian, and bisexual students.

Salisbury State University • *Salisbury, Maryland*

Students define Salisbury's position on gay, lesbian, and bisexual issues as noncommittal. Although the university does not have a committee on gay, lesbian, and bisexual issues, sexual orientation is included in its affirmative action statement, and counseling services are available for gay, lesbian, and bisexual students. Housing for cohabitating couples is not available. According to the students, the municipality in which the university is located does not have a civil rights law that includes sexual orientation.

Unanimously, students believe that homophobia is a serious problem on the campus. Those responding report being victims of verbal abuse and threats. Moreover, all of the students have knowledge of hate crimes committed on the campus, including assault. No one maintains hate-crime statistics.

The majority of the students believe that Salisbury takes action in response to these incidents and feel supported by the university's security force. Consequently, all of the students feel safe on the campus as gays, lesbians, and bisexuals.

Gay, lesbian, and bisexual students between the ages of 20–24 responded to the survey. Students are juniors seniors with SAT scores of 1100 or higher and grade point averages of 2.0 and higher. Students have majors in the liberal arts.

All of the students surveyed are openly gay on the campus as well as to their parents and families. None are considered out-of-state students and all live off campus. All of the students responding came out before attending college, and none said that being gay, lesbian, or bisexual affected their choosing Salisbury. However, if information on the climate for gays, lesbians, and bisexuals at Salisbury had been available, all of the respondents would have made a different choice.

The respondents are involved in the gay, lesbian, and bisexual student group, which has an average membership of 10 students and sponsors speakers and safe-sex education. The group receives no funding from the student government. Students tend not to date other Salisbury students. Off campus, students congregate in bars and religious organizations.

All of the students view the lack of role models as the largest problem at Salisbury, with coming out and the lack of student organization following second.

Gay men's and lesbians' cultural contributions are not a part of regular courses, nor does the university offer courses on gay, lesbian, and bisexual issues. It does not provide free, anonymous HIV testing but refers students to an off-campus testing site. Counseling is not available for those who are HIV+ or have AIDS, but condoms are provided free of charge. Both the Health Center and the student group provide safe-sex education.

All of the respondents recommend Salisbury to other gay, lesbian, and bisexual students.

San Diego State University • *San Diego, California*

Students define San Diego State's position on gay, lesbian, and bisexual issues as proactive. The university has a committee on gay, lesbian, and bisexual issues (Recruitment/Retention Committee), and sexual orientation is included in the University's affirmative action policy. San Diego State provides counseling services for gay, lesbian, and bisexual students. Students do not know if housing for cohabitating couples is available. According to the students, the municipality in which the university is located has a civil rights law that includes sexual orientation.

Unanimously, students believe that homophobia is a serious problem on the campus. Those responding report being victims of verbal abuse, harassment, and vandalism. Moreover, all the students have knowledge of hate crimes committed on the campus, including hate mail and assault. Both the university and the student group maintain hate-crime statistics.

Most of the students believe that San Diego State takes action in response to these incidents, and most feel supported by the university's security force. Most of the students feel safe on the campus as gays, lesbians, and bisexuals.

Gay, lesbian, and bisexual students between the ages of 26–40 responded to the survey. Students are seniors with SAT scores of 900 or higher and grade point averages ranging from 2.5 to 3.0. All have majors in the liberal arts and sciences.

All of the students are openly gay on the campus as well as to their parents and families. None are considered out-of-state students and all live off campus with life partners. Fifty percent of the students responding came out before attending college, and none said that being gay, lesbian, or bisexual affected their choosing San Diego State. Furthermore, if information on the climate for gays, lesbians, and bisexuals at San Diego State had been available, the respondents' choices would not have been different.

The respondents are involved in the gay, lesbian, and bisexual student group, which has an average membership of 50–150 students and sponsors dances, speakers, safe-sex education, and Pride and National Coming Out Day activities. The group receives funding from the student government. Students are also active in other organizations such as the Biology Field Club, the Women's Resource, and Greek-letter organizations. The students responding indicate that their life partners attend San Diego State as well. Off campus, students congregate in bars, religious organizations, and various sports groups.

All of the students view coming out as the largest problem at San Diego State, with the lack of role models and alcohol abuse following second.

Although gay men's and lesbians' cultural contributions are not a part of regular courses, the university does offer courses on gay, lesbian, and bisexual issues in women's studies, education, and the social sciences. The university provides free, anonymous HIV testing, and condoms for a nominal charge. None of the students know whether the university offers counseling for those who are HIV+ or have AIDS. Both the Health Center and the student group provide safe-sex education.

Half of the respondents recommend San Diego State to other gay, lesbian, and bisexual students who are out and politically active. One student states that the university "is conservative and homophobic and strong in Greek support. There are many challenges here at SDSU; for those gays willing to challenge their personal abilities, I would recommend this college."

San Jose State University • *San Jose, California*

Students define San Jose State's position on gay, lesbian, and bisexual issues as noncommittal. Although the university does not have a committee on gay, lesbian, and bisexual issues, sexual orientation is included in its affirmative action policy. San Jose State provides counseling services for gay, lesbian, and bisexual students; however, housing for cohabitating couples is not available. According to the students, the municipality in which the university is located does not have a civil rights law that includes sexual orientation.

Unanimously, students believe that homophobia is a serious problem on the campus. Those responding report being victims of verbal abuse, harassment, and vandalism. Moreover, all the students have knowledge of hate crimes committed on the campus, including hate mail and assault. No one maintains hate-crime statistics.

All of the students believe that San Jose State takes action in response to these incidents; however, none feel supported by the university's security force. Nevertheless, all of the students feel safe on the campus as gays, lesbians, and bisexuals.

Gay and lesbian students between the ages of 19–24 responded to the survey. Students are sophomores, juniors, and seniors with SAT scores of 1100 or higher and grade point averages ranging from 2.5 to 3.5 and higher. All have majors in the liberal arts.

All of the students are openly gay on the campus as well as to their parents and families. None are considered out-of-state students. Twenty-five percent live in residence halls while the remainder live in off-campus apartments. All of the students responding came out before attending college, and none said that being gay, lesbian, or bisexual affected their choosing San Jose State. Furthermore, if information on the climate for gays, lesbians, and bisexuals at San Jose State had been available, the respondents' choices would not have been different.

The respondents are involved in the gay, lesbian, and bisexual student group, which has an average membership of 100–300 students and sponsors dances, speakers, safe-sex education, and Pride Day activities. The group receives funding from the student government. Students are also active in other organizations such as the Student Health Advisory Committee, the Students United for Accessible Education, and the San Jose State University AIDS Education Task Force. The students date other San Jose State students and indicate that their dating activity takes place on the campus. Off campus, students congregate in bars and at the community center.

All of the students view coming out as the largest problem at San Jose State, with the lack of role models and student organization following second.

Although gay men's and lesbians' cultural contributions are not a part of regular courses, the university does offers courses on gay, lesbian, and bisexual issues in the sociology department. The university does not provide free, anonymous HIV testing, but it does provide condoms for a nominal charge and offers counseling and referrals to local agencies for those who are HIV+ or have AIDS. Both the Health Center and the student group provide safe-sex education for the campus.

The majority of the respondents recommend San Jose State to other gay, lesbian, and bisexual students.

Santa Clara University, School of Law •
Santa Clara, California

Students define Santa Clara's position on gay, lesbian, and bisexual issues as noncommittal. The university does not have a committee on gay, lesbian, and bisexual issues, but sexual orientation is included in its affirmative action statement, and counseling services are available for gay, lesbian, and bisexual students. Students do not know if housing for cohabitating couples is available. According to the students, the municipality in which the university is located does not have a civil rights law that includes sexual orientation.

Unanimously, students believe strongly that homophobia is a serious problem on the campus. Those responding report being victims of hate mail and religious zealots. Moreover, most of the students have knowledge of hate crimes committed on the campus. Students do not know who, if anyone, maintains hate-crime statistics.

All of the students believe that Santa Clara takes action in response to hate crimes and strongly agree that the university's security force is supportive. Consequently, all of the students feel safe on the campus as gays, lesbians, and bisexuals.

Gay, lesbian, and bisexual students between the ages of 25–41 responded to the survey. Students are graduates with SAT scores of 900 or higher and grade point averages of 2.0 and higher.

All of the students surveyed are openly gay on the campus as well as to their parents and families. None are considered out-of-state students and all live off campus, some with life partners. Most of the students responding came out before attending college, and few said that being gay, lesbian, or bisexual affected their choosing Santa Clara. Furthermore, if information on the climate for gays, lesbians, and bisexuals at Santa Clara had been available, the respondents' choices would not have been different.

The respondents are involved in the gay, lesbian, and bisexual student group, which has an average membership of 7 students and sponsors dances, speakers, and safe-sex education. The group receives funding from the student government. Most students date other Santa

Clara students. Some students have life partners who do not attend Santa Clara. Off campus, students congregate in bars.

All of the students view coming out as the largest problem at Santa Clara, with the lack of role models and student organization following second.

Gay men's and lesbians' cultural contributions are a part of some regular courses (depending on the professor), and the university offers courses on gay, lesbian, and bisexual issues in English and the social sciences. Students do not know if the university provides free, anonymous HIV testing or condoms. However, counseling is available for those who are HIV+ or have AIDS. The Health Center, Campus Ministry (in a positive way), and the student group provide safe-sex education.

Most of the respondents do not recommend Santa Clara to other gay, lesbian, and bisexual students because it is "still too conservative. The administration is more liberal than the students. So is the faculty."

Santa Monica College • *Santa Monica, California*

Most students define Santa Monica's position on gay, lesbian, and bisexual issues as proactive. Although the college does not have a committee on gay, lesbian, and bisexual issues, sexual orientation is included in its affirmative action statement, and counseling services are available for gay, lesbian, and bisexual students. Students do not know if housing for cohabitating couples is available. According to the students, the municipality in which the college is located has a civil rights law that includes sexual orientation.

Half of the students do not believe that homophobia is a serious problem on the campus. Those responding report being victims of verbal abuse and harassment. Fifty percent of the students have knowledge of hate crimes committed on the campus. Students do not know who, if anyone, maintains hate-crime statistics.

All of the students believe that Santa Monica takes action in response to hate crimes and agree that the college's security force is supportive. Consequently, all of the students feel safe on the campus as gays, lesbians, and bisexuals.

Gay, lesbian, and bisexual students between the ages of 24–25

responded to the survey. Students are sophomores with SAT scores of 900 or higher and grade point averages of 3.5 and higher.

All of the students surveyed are openly gay on the campus as well as to their parents and families. None are considered out-of-state students and all live off campus, some with life partners. Most of the students responding came out before attending college, and some said that being gay, lesbian, or bisexual affected their choosing Santa Monica. Furthermore, if information on the climate for gays, lesbians, and bisexuals at Santa Monica had been available, half of the respondents would have made a different choice.

The respondents are involved in the gay, lesbian, and bisexual student group, which has an average membership of 50–60 students and sponsors speakers, safe-sex education, and Pride and National Coming Out Day activities. The group receives funding from the student government. Students tend not to date other Santa Monica students. Off campus, students congregate in bars, the community center, religious organizations, and private homes and apartments.

All of the students view the lack of role models as the largest problem at Santa Monica, with alcohol abuse and coming out following second.

Gay men's and lesbians' cultural contributions are not a part of regular courses, nor does the college offer courses on gay, lesbian, and bisexual issues. It does provide free, anonymous HIV testing, condoms, and counseling for those who are HIV+ or have AIDS. Both the Health Center and the student group provide safe-sex education.

All of the respondents recommend Santa Monica to other gay, lesbian, and bisexual students.

Sarah Lawrence College • *Bronxville, New York*

Students define Sarah Lawrence College's position on gay, lesbian, and bisexual issues as proactive, the result of some prodding. The college does not have a committee on gay, lesbian, and bisexual issues, and students do not know if sexual orientation is included in its affirmative action statement. Counseling services are available for gay, lesbian, and bisexual students, but housing for cohabitating couples is not. Students do not know if the municipality in which the college is located has a civil rights law that includes sexual orientation.

None of the students believe that homophobia is a serious problem on the campus, though 50 percent of those responding report being victims of verbal abuse and all of the students have knowledge of hate crimes committed on the campus. Respondents do not know who, if anyone, maintains hate-crime statistics.

The majority of the students believe that Sarah Lawrence College takes action in response to these incidents, but are divided on whether they feel supported by the college's security force. However, all of the students feel safe on the campus as gays, lesbians, and bisexuals.

Gay, lesbian, and bisexual students between the ages of 19–22 responded to the survey. Students are sophomores with SAT scores of 1100 or higher and estimated grade point averages of 3.5 and higher (Sarah Lawrence does not have grades). Students have majors in theater, women's studies, and the liberal arts.

All of the students surveyed are openly gay on the campus as well as to their parents and families. All are considered out-of-state students and live in residence halls. All of the students responding came out before attending college and said that being gay, lesbian, or bisexual affected their choosing Sarah Lawrence. However, if information on the climate for gays, lesbians, and bisexuals at Sarah Lawrence had been available, half of the respondents would have made a different choice.

The respondents are involved in the gay, lesbian, and bisexual student group, which has an average membership of 35 students and sponsors dances, speakers, safe-sex education and Pride and National Coming Out Day activities. In addition, some students are active in athletics. The group receives no funding from the student government. Fifty percent of the students date other Sarah Lawrence students and state that their dating activity takes place on campus. Off campus, students congregate in bars.

All of the students view coming out as the largest problem at Sarah Lawrence, with alcohol abuse and the lack of role models following second.

Gay men's and lesbians' cultural contributions are a part of regular courses, and the college offers courses on gay, lesbian, and bisexual issues in the English department. The college does not provides free, anonymous HIV testing but counseling is available for those who are HIV+ or have AIDS. Condoms are not provided. Both the Health Center and the student group provide safe-sex education.

All of the respondents recommend Sarah Lawrence to other gay, lesbian, and bisexual students "because it is safe and comfortable, though the community is fragmented."

Skidmore College • *Saratoga Springs, New York*

Students define Skidmore's position on gay, lesbian, and bisexual issues as noncommittal. The college does not have a committee on gay, lesbian, and bisexual issues, but sexual orientation is included in its affirmative action statement, and counseling services are available for gay, lesbian, and bisexual students. Housing for cohabitating couples is not available. Students do not know if the municipality in which the college is located has a civil rights law that includes sexual orientation.

Unanimously, students believe that homophobia is not a serious problem on the campus. Half of those responding report being victims of vandalism. In addition, most of the students have knowledge of hate crimes committed on the campus with the exception of assault. Students do not know who, if anyone, maintains hate-crime statistics.

None of the students know how Skidmore reacts to hate crimes, and half agree that the college's security force is supportive. Consequently, all of the students feel safe on the campus as gays, lesbians, and bisexuals.

Gay, lesbian, and bisexual students between the ages of 20–21 responded to the survey. Students are juniors with SAT scores of 1100 or higher and grade point averages of 2.5 and higher. Students have majors in the liberal arts.

Half of the students surveyed are openly gay on the campus as well as to their parents and families. Most are considered out-of-state students and all live in residence halls. Most of the students responding came out before attending college, and none said that being gay, lesbian, or bisexual affected their choosing Skidmore. Furthermore, if information on the climate for gays, lesbians, and bisexuals at Skidmore had been available, the respondents' choices would not have been different.

The respondents are involved in the gay, lesbian, and bisexual student group, which has an average membership of 5–10 students and sponsors safe-sex education. The group receives funding from the student government. In addition, students are active in singing groups. Students date other Skidmore students and state that their dating activity takes place on the campus. Some students have life partners also attending Skidmore. Off campus, students congregate in bars.

All of the students view coming out as the largest problem at Skidmore, with the lack of role models and student organization following second.

Although gay men's and lesbians' cultural contributions are not a part of regular courses, the college offers courses on gay, lesbian, and bisexual issues in English, the social sciences, liberal studies, and government. The college does not provide free, anonymous HIV testing or condoms. However, counseling is available or those who are HIV+ or have AIDS. Both the college and the student group provide safe-sex education.

All of the respondents recommend Skidmore to other gay, lesbian, and bisexual students.

Smith College • *Northampton, Massachusetts*

Students define Smith's position on gay, lesbian, and bisexual issues somewhere between proactive and noncommittal. The college has a committee on gay, lesbian, and bisexual issues, and sexual orientation is included in the college's affirmative action policy. In addition, counseling services are available, but not specifically geared toward lesbian and bisexual students. Housing for cohabitating couples is not available. According to the students, the municipality in which the college is located has a civil rights law that includes sexual orientation.

The majority of students believe that homophobia is a serious problem on the campus. Sixty percent of those responding report being victims of verbal abuse and harassment. Moreover, all of the students have knowledge of hate crimes committed on the campus. The college maintains hate-crime statistics.

Seventy percent of the students believe that Smith takes action in response to hate crimes, and all agree that the college's security force is supportive. Eighty-five percent feel safe on the campus as lesbians and bisexuals.

Lesbian and bisexual students between the ages of 19–21 responded to the survey. Students are sophomores, juniors, and seniors with SAT scores of 900 or higher and grade point averages of 3.0 or higher. Students have majors in economics, health, biology, women's studies, Latin American studies, and art.

Eighty percent of the students are openly lesbian on the campus, and all are out to their parents and families. Ninety percent are considered out-of-state students, and all live in residence halls. Seventy percent of the students responding came out before attending college, and 40 percent said that being lesbian or bisexual affected their choosing Smith. Furthermore, if information on the climate for lesbians and bisexuals at Smith had been available, half of the respondents would have made a different choice.

The respondents are involved in the lesbian and bisexual student group, which has an average membership of 100+ students and sponsors speakers, safe-sex education, and Pride and National Coming Out Day activities. The group receives funding from the student government. In addition, students are active in the Plant Club, the Rugby Club, the Latina Organization, and athletic teams. The students date other Smith students and state that their dating activity takes place on the campus. Off campus, students congregate in bars.

All of the students view coming out as the largest problem at Smith, with the lack of role models following second.

Lesbians' cultural contributions are a part of some regular courses. The college also offers courses on gay, lesbian, and bisexual issues in English, history, women's studies, and the social sciences. The college provides anonymous HIV testing for a nominal fee. Students do not know if counseling is available for those who are HIV+ or have AIDS. Condoms are provided. Both the Health Center and the student group provide safe-sex education for the campus.

All of the respondents recommend Smith to other lesbian and bisexual students, with students commenting that "Smith is one the best campuses for lesbians and bisexuals. Although unorganized and apathetic, the campus has a large lesbian and bisexual community."

Southern Illinois University, Carbondale • *Carbondale, Illinois*

Students define Carbondale's position on gay, lesbian, and bisexual issues as proactive. The university has a committee on gay, lesbian, and bisexual issues, and sexual orientation is included in the university's affirmative action policy. In addition, counseling services are available for gay, lesbian, and bisexual students. Students do not know if housing for cohabitating couples is available. According to the students, the municipality in which the university is located does not have a civil rights law that includes sexual orientation.

Unanimously, students believe that homophobia is not a serious problem on the campus. None of those responding report being victims of hate crimes. However, all of the students have knowledge of hate crimes committed on the campus. The university maintains hate-crime statistics.

Students do not know how Carbondale reacts to hate crimes. All agree that the university's security force is not supportive, yet all students feel safe on the campus as gays, lesbians, and bisexuals.

Gay, lesbian, and bisexual students between the ages of 22–31 responded to the survey. Students are seniors with SAT scores of 1100 or higher and grade point averages of 3.0 or higher. Students have majors in the liberal arts and social work.

All of the students are openly gay on the campus as well as to their parents and family. Most are considered out-of-state students and all live off campus, some with life partners. All of the students responding came out before attending college, and none said that being gay, lesbian, or bisexual affected their choosing Carbondale. Furthermore, if information on the climate for gays, lesbians, and bisexuals at Carbondale had been available, the respondents' choices would not have been different.

The respondents are involved in the gay, lesbian, and bisexual student group, which has an average membership of 10–20 students and sponsors dances, speakers, safe-sex education, and Pride and National Coming Out Day activities. The group receives funding from the student government. The students date other Carbondale students and state that their dating activity takes place off campus, where they congregate in bars.

All of the students view the lack of student organization as the largest problem at Carbondale, with coming out and substance abuse following second.

Although gay men's and lesbians' cultural contributions are a part of regular courses, the university does not offer courses on gay, lesbian, and bisexual issues. It does provide free, anonymous HIV testing and counseling for those who are HIV+ or have AIDS. Students do not know if condoms are provided free of charge. The student group provides safe-sex education.

However, none of the respondents recommend Carbondale to other gay, lesbian, and bisexual students.

State University of New York, Albany • *Albany, New York*

Students define SUNY Albany's position on gay, lesbian, and bisexual issues as proactive. The university has a committee on gay, lesbian, and bisexual issues and counseling services are available for gay, lesbian, and bisexual students. Students do not know if sexual orientation is included in the university's affirmative action policy. Housing for cohabiting couples is not available. Students do not know if the municipality in which the university is located has a civil rights law that includes sexual orientation.

Unanimously, students believe strongly that homophobia is a serious problem on the campus. Those responding report being victims of verbal abuse. Moreover, all of the students have knowledge of hate crimes committed on the campus. The student group maintains hate-crime statistics.

Students do not know how SUNY Albany reacts to hate crimes and are ambivalent concerning the security force's support. All of the students feel safe on the campus as gays, lesbians, and bisexuals.

Gay, lesbian, and bisexual students between the ages of 20–23 responded to the survey. Students are seniors with SAT scores of 899 or higher and grade point averages of 3.0 or higher. Students have majors in the liberal arts.

All of the students are openly gay on the campus as well as to their parents and family. None are considered out-of-state students and all live off campus. None of the students responding came out before attending college, and none said that being gay, lesbian, or bisexual affected their choosing SUNY Albany. Furthermore, if information on the climate for gays, lesbians, and bisexuals at SUNY Albany had been available, the respondents' choices would not have been different.

The respondents are involved in the gay, lesbian, and bisexual student group, which has an average membership of 15 students and sponsors dances, speakers, safe-sex education, and Pride and National Coming Out Day activities. The group receives funding from the student government. In addition, students are active in Earthbound NY. The students date other SUNY Albany students and state that their dating activity takes place off campus, where they congregate in bars, the community center, and in private homes and apartments.

All of the students view coming out as the largest problem at SUNY Albany, with the lack of role models and alcohol abuse following second.

Gay men's and lesbians' cultural contributions are not a part of regular courses, nor does the university offer courses on gay, lesbian, and bisexual issues, HIV testing, or condoms. Students do not know if counseling is available for those who are HIV+ or have AIDS. Both the Health Center and the student group provide safe-sex education.

All of the respondents recommend SUNY Albany to other gay, lesbian, and bisexual students.

State University of New York, Binghamton •
Binghamton, New York

Students define SUNY Binghamton's position on gay, lesbian, and bisexual issues as proactive. The university has a committee on gay, lesbian, and bisexual issues, and sexual orientation is included in the university's affirmative action policy. In addition, counseling services are available for gay, lesbian, and bisexual students, as is housing for cohabitating couples. According to the students, the municipality in which the university is located does not have a civil rights law that includes sexual orientation.

Unanimously, students believe that homophobia is a serious problem on the campus, though none of those responding report being victims of hate crimes. However, all of the students have knowledge of hate crimes committed on the campus, including assault. Both the university and the student group maintain hate-crime statistics.

Most of the students believe that SUNY Binghamton takes action in response to hate crimes, but students are divided concerning support of the university's security force. All of the students feel safe on the campus as gays, lesbians, and bisexuals.

Gay, lesbian, and bisexual students between the ages of 21–24 responded to the survey. Students are juniors, seniors, and graduate students with SAT scores of 1100 or higher and grade point averages of 3.0 or higher. Students have majors in the liberal arts.

All of the students are openly gay on the campus as well as to their parents and families. Graduates are considered out-of-state students and all students live off campus, some with their families. Half of the students responding came out before attending college, and none said that being gay, lesbian, or bisexual affected their choosing SUNY Binghamton. Furthermore, if information on the climate for gays, lesbians, and bisexuals at SUNY Binghamton had been available, the respondents' choices would not have been different.

The respondents are involved in the gay, lesbian, and bisexual student group, which has an average membership of 8 students and sponsors speakers and safe-sex education. The group receives funding from the student government. The students tend not to date other SUNY Binghamton students. Off campus, students congregate in bars and at the community center.

All of the students view coming out as the largest problem at SUNY Binghamton, with the lack of role models and student organization following second.

Gay men's and lesbians' cultural contributions are a part of regular courses. The university also offers courses on gay, lesbian, and bisexual issues in history, philosophy, women's studies, and gay studies. The university does not provide free, anonymous HIV testing. Students do not know if counseling is available for those who are HIV+ or have AIDS. Condoms are provided free of charge. The student group provides safe-sex education.

All of the respondents recommend SUNY Binghamton to other gay, lesbian, and bisexual students.

State University of New York, Buffalo • *Buffalo, New York*

Students define SUNY Buffalo's position on gay, lesbian, and bisexual issues as noncommittal. Although the university does not have a committee on gay, lesbian, and bisexual issues, sexual orientation is included in its affirmative action policy. SUNY Buffalo provides counseling services for gay, lesbian, and bisexual students. Housing for cohabitating couples is not available. According to the students, the municipality in which the university is located does not have a civil rights law that includes sexual orientation.

Unanimously, students strongly agree that homophobia is a serious problem on the campus. Those responding report being victims of hate mail, verbal abuse, harassment, and vandalism. Moreover, all of the students have knowledge of hate crimes committed on the campus, including assault. The student group maintains hate-crime statistics.

Students believe that SUNY Buffalo does nothing in response to these incidents, and they do not feel supported by the university's security force. Furthermore, none of the students feel safe on the campus as gays, lesbians, and bisexuals.

Gay, lesbian, and bisexual students between the ages of 20–23 responded to the survey. Students are juniors and seniors with SAT scores of 1100 or higher and grade point averages of 3.5 and higher. All have majors in the liberal arts.

All of the students, to some extent, are openly gay on the campus. Most are out to some family members; slightly more than half are out to their parents. None are considered out-of-state students and all live off campus, half with their families. All of the students responding came out before attending college, and none said that being gay, lesbian, or bisexual affected their choosing SUNY Buffalo.

The respondents are involved in the gay, lesbian, and bisexual student group, which has an average membership of 20 students and sponsors activities for National Coming Out Day. The group receives funding from the student government. In addition, students are active in other organizations such as the Student Government and the Pro Choice Student group. The students do not date other SUNY Buffalo students. Off campus, students congregate in bars.

All of the students view coming out as the largest problem at

SUNY Buffalo, with the lack of student organization and role models following second. The primary weakness of the student group at Buffalo, according to students, is that many students are only marginally open about their sexual orientation.

Gay men's and lesbians' cultural contributions are not a part of regular courses, nor does the university offer courses on gay, lesbian, and bisexual issues. The university does not provide free, anonymous HIV testing or counseling services for those with AIDS or HIV, but it does provide condoms and safe-sex education.

None of the respondents recommend SUNY Buffalo to other gay, lesbian, and bisexual students, with one student commenting that "SUNY Buffalo is a bad school for gays primarily because the Buffalo community is one of the least active, most persecuted and self-hating communities in the country. If the Buffalo community were stronger, the atmosphere would be more supportive of people who are coming out."

State University of New York, Cortland • *Cortland, New York*

Students define SUNY Cortland's position on gay, lesbian, and bisexual issues as proactive. The university does not have a committee on gay, lesbian, and bisexual issues, but sexual orientation is included in its affirmative action policy. Counseling services are available for gay, lesbian, and bisexual students. Housing for cohabitating couples is not available. Students do not know if the municipality in which the university is located has a civil rights law that includes sexual orientation.

Unanimously, students believe strongly that homophobia is a serious problem on the campus. Most of those responding report being victims of harassment and verbal abuse. Moreover, all of the students have knowledge of hate crimes committed on the campus. The university maintains hate-crime statistics.

All of students believe that SUNY Cortland takes action in response to hate crimes and agree that the university's security force is supportive. However, most of the students do not feel safe on the campus as gays, lesbians, and bisexuals.

Gay, lesbian, and bisexual students between the ages of 20–25 responded to the survey. Students are sophomores, juniors, and seniors with SAT scores of 900 or higher and grade point averages of 2.0 or higher. Students have majors in liberal studies, English, psychology, and sociology.

Eighty percent of the students are openly gay on the campus, and all are out to their parents and families. None are considered out-of-state students. Students live predominantly off campus, but some live in residence halls. Most of the students responding came out before attending college, and none said that being gay, lesbian, or bisexual affected their choosing SUNY Cortland. If information on the climate for gays, lesbians, and bisexuals at SUNY Cortland had been available, 40 percent of the respondents would have made a different choice.

The respondents are involved in the gay, lesbian, and bisexual student group, which has an average membership of 15–20 students and sponsors speakers and safe-sex education. The group receives funding from the student government. In addition, students are active in the Black Student Union and athletics. The students tend not to date other SUNY Cortland students. Off campus, students congregate in bars.

All of the students view coming out as the largest problem at SUNY Cortland, with the lack of role models and alcohol abuse following second.

Although gay men's and lesbians' cultural contributions are not a part of regular courses, the university does offer courses on gay, lesbian, and bisexual issues in women's studies and in the interdisciplinary program. The university provides free, anonymous HIV testing, counseling for those who are HIV+ or have AIDS, and condoms free of charge. Both the Health Center and the student group provide safe-sex education.

Eighty percent of the respondents recommend SUNY Cortland to other gay, lesbian, and bisexual students.

State University of New York, New Paltz •
New Paltz, New York

Students define SUNY New Paltz's position on gay, lesbian, and bisexual issues as proactive. The university does not have a committee on gay, lesbian, and bisexual issues nor is sexual orientation included in its affirmative action statement. However, counseling services are available for gay, lesbian, and bisexual students. Students do not know if housing for cohabitating couples is available. According to the students, the municipality in which the university is located has a pending civil rights law that includes sexual orientation.

Unanimously, students believe that homophobia is a serious problem on the campus. Those responding report being victims of harassment and assault. Moreover, all of the students have knowledge of hate crimes committed on the campus. No one knows who maintains hate-crime statistics.

All of the students believe that SUNY New Paltz takes action in response to these incidents, but none of the respondents feel supported by the university's security force. Consequently, students do not really feel safe on the campus as gays, lesbians, and bisexuals.

Gay, lesbian, and bisexual students between the ages of 21–24 responded to the survey. Students are juniors and seniors with SAT scores of 899 or higher and grade point averages of 2.0 and higher. Students have majors in the liberal arts and mass communications.

All of the students surveyed are openly gay on the campus as well as to their parents and families. None considered out-of-state students. Two thirds of the students live in residence halls and the remaining students live off campus. One third of the students responding came out before attending college, but none said that being gay, lesbian, or bisexual affected their choosing SUNY New Paltz. However, if information on the climate for gays, lesbians, and bisexuals at SUNY New Paltz had been available, all of the respondents would have made a different choice.

The respondents are involved in the gay, lesbian, and bisexual student group, which has an average membership of 15–20 students and sponsors dances, speakers, safe-sex education, and Pride and National Coming Out Day activities. In addition, students are resident assistants, peer educators, and athletes. The students date other SUNY New Paltz students and state that their dating activity takes place on campus. Off campus, students congregate in bars, diners, and private apartments.

All of the students view the apathy in the student organization as the largest problem at SUNY New Paltz, with alcohol abuse and the lack of role models following second.

Gay men's and lesbians' cultural contributions are not a part of regular courses, but the university does offer courses on gay, lesbian, and bisexual issues in women's studies. The university does not provide free, anonymous HIV testing or counseling for those who are HIV+ or have AIDS; it does not provide condoms. The student group provides safe-sex education, and some classes also address the issue.

All of the respondents recommend SUNY New Paltz to other gay, lesbian, and bisexual students.

State University of New York, Plattsburgh •
Plattsburgh, New York

Students define SUNY Plattsburgh's position on gay, lesbian, and bisexual issues somewhere between proactive and noncommittal. The university does not have a committee on gay, lesbian, and bisexual issues, nor is sexual orientation included in its affirmative action policy (except in housing). However, counseling services are available for gay, lesbian, and bisexual students; housing for cohabitating couples is not available. According to the students, the municipality in which the university is located has a civil rights law that includes sexual orientation.

Unanimously, students believe that homophobia is a serious problem on the campus. Most of those responding report being victims of verbal abuse. Moreover, all of the students have knowledge of hate crimes committed on the campus. The university maintains hate-crime statistics.

All of students believe that SUNY Plattsburgh takes action in response to hate crimes and agree that the university's security force is supportive. All of the students feel safe most of the time on the campus as gays, lesbians, and bisexuals.

Gay, lesbian, and bisexual students between the ages of 19–25 responded to the survey. Students are freshmen, sophomores, and seniors with SAT scores of 900 or higher and grade point averages of 2.5 or higher. Students have majors in the liberal arts.

All of the students are openly gay on the campus as well as to their parents and families. None are considered out-of-state students. Students live both in residence halls and off campus. Most of the students responding came out before attending college, and none said that being gay, lesbian, or bisexual affected their choosing SUNY Plattsburgh. But if information on the climate for gays, lesbians, and bisexuals at SUNY Plattsburgh had been available, most of the respondents would have made a different choice.

The respondents are involved in the gay, lesbian, and bisexual student group, which has an average membership of 20 students and sponsors dances, speakers, safe-sex education, and Pride and National Coming Out Day activities. The group receives funding from the student government. In addition, students are active in theater groups. The students date other SUNY Plattsburgh students and state that some of their dating activity takes place on the campus. Off campus, students congregate in bars.

All of the students view coming out as the largest problem at SUNY Plattsburgh, with the lack of role models and alcohol abuse following second.

Gay men's and lesbians' cultural contributions are a part of some regular courses. The university also offers courses on gay, lesbian, and bisexual issues in English, women's studies, and the social sciences. The university provides free, anonymous HIV testing, counseling for those who are HIV+ or have AIDS, and condoms free of charge. Both the Health Center and the student group provide safe-sex education.

Two thirds of the respondents recommend SUNY Plattsburgh to other gay, lesbian, and bisexual students, with reservation.

Suffolk College • *Selden, New York*

Students define Suffolk's position on gay, lesbian, and bisexual issues as noncommittal. Although the college does not have a committee on gay, lesbian, and bisexual issues, sexual orientation is included in its affirmative action policy. In addition, counseling services are available for gay, lesbian, and bisexual students. Students do not know if housing for cohabitating couples is available or if the municipality in which the college is located has a civil rights law that includes sexual orientation.

Unanimously, students believe strongly that homophobia is a serious problem on the campus. Those responding report being victims

of harassment. Moreover, all of the students have knowledge of hate crimes committed on the campus. No one maintains hate-crime statistics.

Students do not know how Suffolk reacts to hate crimes. All agree that the college's security force is not supportive, and none of the students feel safe on the campus as gays, lesbians, and bisexuals.

Gay, lesbian, and bisexual students between the ages of 23–25 responded to the survey. Students are seniors and graduate students with SAT scores of 900 or higher and grade point averages of 2.0 or higher. Students have majors in the liberal arts and travel and tourism.

All of the students are openly gay on the campus but not to their parents and families. None are considered out-of-state students and all live off campus. None of the students responding came out before attending college, and none said that being gay, lesbian, or bisexual affected their choosing Suffolk. Furthermore, if information on the climate for gays, lesbians, and bisexuals at Suffolk had been available, all of the respondents would have made a different choice.

The respondents are involved in the gay, lesbian, and bisexual student group, which has an average membership of 10 students and sponsors dances, speakers, and Pride and National Coming Out Day activities. The group receives funding from the student government. The students tend not to date other Suffolk students. Off campus, students congregate in bars.

All of the students view coming out as the largest problem at Suffolk, with the lack of role models and student organization following second.

Gay men's and lesbians' cultural contributions are not a part of regular courses, nor does the college offer courses on gay, lesbian, and bisexual issues. The college does not provide free, anonymous HIV testing. Students do not know if counseling is available for those who are HIV+ or have AIDS, if condoms are provided, or who, if anyone, provides safe-sex education.

None of the respondents recommend Suffolk to other gay, lesbian, and bisexual students.

Susquehanna University • *Selinsgrove, Pennsylvania*

Students define Susquehanna's position on gay, lesbian, and bisexual issues as noncommittal. The university does not have a committee on gay, lesbian, and bisexual issues, sexual orientation is not included in its affirmative action policy, and counseling services are not available for gay, lesbian, and bisexual students. Students do not know if housing for cohabitating couples is available or if the municipality in which the university is located has a civil rights law that includes sexual orientation.

Unanimously, students believe that homophobia is a serious problem on the campus. None of those responding report being victims of hate crimes, but all of the students have knowledge of hate crimes committed on the campus. Students do not know who, if anyone, maintains hate-crime statistics.

Students do not know how Susquehanna reacts to hate crimes. All agree that the university's security force is not supportive, and none of the students feel safe on the campus as gays, lesbians, and bisexuals.

Gay, lesbian, and bisexual students between the ages of 18–20 responded to the survey. Students are freshmen and sophomores with SAT scores of 1100 or higher and grade point averages of 3.5 or higher. Students have majors in the liberal arts.

All of the students are openly gay or in the process of coming out on the campus. None are out to their parents and families. All are considered out-of-state students and live in residence halls. All of the students responding came out before attending college, and none said that being gay, lesbian, or bisexual affected their choosing Susquehanna. Furthermore, if information on the climate for gays, lesbians, and bisexuals at Susquehanna had been available, the respondents' choices would not have been different.

The respondents are involved in the gay, lesbian, and bisexual student group, which has an average membership of 6 students. The group receives no funding from the student government. In addition, students are active in the Student Association for Cultural Awareness. The students tend not to date other Susquehanna students.

All of the students view coming out as the largest problem at Susquehanna, with the lack of role models following second.

Gay men's and lesbians' cultural contributions are not a part of

regular courses, nor does the university offer courses on gay, lesbian, and bisexual issues. Students do not know if the university provides free, anonymous HIV testing or counseling for those who are HIV+ or have AIDS. Condoms are available for a nominal fee.

All of the respondents recommend Susquehanna to other gay, lesbian, and bisexual students.

Swarthmore College • *Swarthmore, Pennsylvania*

Students define Swarthmore's position on gay, lesbian, and bisexual issues as proactive. The college has a committee on gay, lesbian, and bisexual issues, and sexual orientation is included in the college's affirmative action policy. In addition, counseling services are available for gay, lesbian, and bisexual students. Students do not know if housing for cohabitating couples is available or if the municipality in which the college is located has a civil rights law that includes sexual orientation.

Unanimously, students believe that homophobia is a serious problem on the campus. Those responding report being victims of harassment. Moreover, all of the students have knowledge of hate crimes committed on the campus. The college maintains hate-crime statistics.

Students do not know how Swarthmore reacts to hate crimes. All of the respondents, however, agree that the college's security force is supportive. All of the students feel safe on the campus as gays, lesbians, and bisexuals.

Gay, lesbian, and bisexual students between the ages of 19–21 responded to the survey. Students are sophomores and juniors with SAT scores of 1100 or higher and grade point averages of 3.5 or higher. Students have majors in the liberal arts.

All of the students are openly gay on the campus as well as to their parents and families. All are considered out-of-state students and live in residence halls. None of the students responding came out before attending college, and none said that being gay, lesbian, or bisexual affected their choosing Swarthmore. But if information on the climate for gays, lesbians, and bisexuals at Swarthmore had been available, most of the respondents would have made a different choice.

The respondents are involved in the gay, lesbian, and bisexual student group, which has an average membership of 20–30 students

and sponsors dances, speakers, safe-sex education, and Pride and National Coming Out Day activities. The group receives funding from the student government. The students date other Swarthmore students and state that their dating activity takes place on the campus. Some students have life partners attending the school. Off campus, students congregate in bars.

All of the students view coming out as the largest problem at Swarthmore, with the lack of role models following second.

Although gay men's and lesbians' cultural contributions are not a part of regular courses, the college does offer courses on gay, lesbian, and bisexual issues in English and the social sciences. The college provides free, anonymous HIV testing, counseling for those who are HIV+ or have AIDS, and condoms free of charge. Both the Health Center and the student group provide safe-sex education.

All of the respondents recommend Swarthmore to other gay, lesbian, and bisexual students.

Syracuse University • *Syracuse, New York*

Students define Syracuse's position on gay, lesbian, and bisexual issues as both proactive and noncommittal. Although the university does not have a committee on gay, lesbian, and bisexual issues, sexual orientation is included in its affirmative action statement, and counseling services are available for gay, lesbian, and bisexual students. Housing for cohabitating couples is not available. Students do not know if the municipality in which the university is located has a civil rights law that includes sexual orientation.

Unanimously, the undergraduate students believe that homophobia is not a serious problem on the campus; graduate students do see it as a problem. Those responding report being victims of verbal abuse, harassment, and vandalism. Moreover, 60 percent of the students have knowledge of hate crimes committed on the campus, including assault. Both the university and the student group maintain hate-crime statistics.

One third of the students believe that Syracuse takes action in response to these incidents, but the majority of the respondents state that they do not feel supported by the university's security force.

Most of the students feel somewhat safe on the campus as gays, lesbians, and bisexuals.

Gay, lesbian, and bisexual students between the ages of 18–36 responded to the survey. Students are freshmen, juniors, seniors, and graduate students with SAT scores of 1100 or higher and grade point averages of 2.0 and higher (graduate students have GPAS of 3.0 or higher). Students have majors in journalism, computer graphics, psychology, education, environmental science, and communications.

All of the students surveyed are openly gay on the campus as well as to their parents and families. Two thirds are considered out-of-state students; some live in residence halls but most live off campus, a few with life partners. All of the students responding came out before attending college, and one third said that being gay, lesbian, or bisexual affected their choosing Syracuse. If information on the climate for gays, lesbians, and bisexuals at Syracuse been available, a third of the respondents would have made a different choice.

The respondents are involved in the gay, lesbian, and bisexual student group, which has an average membership of 50 students and sponsors dances, speakers, safe-sex education, and Pride and National Coming Out Day activities. The group receives funding from the student government. In addition, students are active in other organizations such as Students Concerned About Rape Education, Paradigm, and Review and Archive magazines. The students date other Syracuse students but state that their dating activity takes place off campus, where they congregate in bars, parks, and book stores.

All of the students view coming out as the largest problem at Syracuse, with the lack of role models and student organization following second.

Although gay men's and lesbians' cultural contributions are not a part of regular courses, the university does offer courses on gay, lesbian, and bisexual issues in English and women's studies. The university provides free, confidential HIV testing and condoms free of charge. Students do not know if counseling is available for those who are HIV+ or have AIDS. Both the Health Center and the student group provide safe-sex education.

One third of the respondents recommend Syracuse to other gay, lesbian, and bisexual students; the remainder recommend the school with some reservations. The majority of graduate students do not recommend Syracuse.

Tallahassee Community College • *Tallahassee, Florida*

Students define Tallahassee's position on gay, lesbian, and bisexual issues as negative. The college does not have a committee on gay, lesbian, and bisexual issues nor is sexual orientation included in its affirmative action statement. However, counseling services are available for gay, lesbian, and bisexual students. Housing for cohabitating couples is not available. According to the students, the municipality in which the college is located does not have a civil rights law that includes sexual orientation.

Unanimously, students believe strongly that homophobia is a serious problem on the campus. Those responding report being victims of hate mail, verbal abuse, vandalism, and harassment. Moreover, all of the students have knowledge of hate crimes committed on the campus, including assault. Both the college and the student group maintain hate-crime statistics.

All of the students believe that Tallahassee takes action in response to these incidents (though some say that the action is very weak), but none of the respondents feel supported by the college's security force. Consequently, students do not feel safe on the Tallahassee campus as gays, lesbians, and bisexuals.

Gay, lesbian, and bisexual students between the ages of 18–20 responded to the survey. Students are freshmen and sophomores with SAT scores of 1100 or higher and grade point averages of 3.5 and higher. Students have majors in the liberal arts.

All of the students surveyed are openly gay on the campus as well as to their parents and families. None are considered out-of-state students and all live off campus. All of the students responding came out before attending college, but none said that being gay, lesbian, or bisexual affected their choosing Tallahassee. Furthermore, if information on the climate for gays, lesbians, and bisexuals at Tallahassee had been available, the respondents' choices would not have been different.

The respondents are involved in the gay, lesbian, and bisexual

student group, which has an average membership of 15 students and sponsors dances, speakers, safe-sex education, and Pride and National Coming Out Day activities. The students tend not to date other Tallahassee students. Off campus, students congregate in bars and at other social networks.

All of the students view alcohol abuse as the largest problem at Tallahassee, with coming out and the lack of role models following second.

Gay men's and lesbians' cultural contributions are not a part of regular courses, nor does the college offer courses on gay, lesbian, and bisexual issues. The college does provide free, anonymous HIV testing and condoms free of charge. Students do not know if counseling is available for those who are HIV+ or have AIDS. Both the Health Center and the student group provide safe-sex education.

All of the respondents recommend Tallahassee to other gay, lesbian, and bisexual students.

Temple University • *Philadelphia, Pennsylvania*

Students define Temple's position on gay, lesbian, and bisexual issues as noncommittal. Although the university does not have a committee on gay, lesbian, and bisexual issues, sexual orientation is included in its affirmative action policy. In addition, counseling services are available for gay, lesbian, and bisexual students. Students do not know if housing for cohabitating couples is available. According to the students, the municipality in which the university is located does not have a civil rights law that includes sexual orientation.

Unanimously, students believe that homophobia is a serious problem on the campus. Those responding report being victims of hate mail. Moreover, all of the students have knowledge of hate crimes committed on the campus. Students do not know who, if anyone, maintains hate-crime statistics.

All of students believe that Temple takes action in response to hate crimes, and all agree that the university's security force is supportive. All of the students feel safe on the campus as gays, lesbians, and bisexuals.

Gay, lesbian, and bisexual students between the ages of 23–28 responded to the survey. Students are seniors and graduate students with SAT scores of 900 or higher and grade point averages of 3.0 or higher. Students have majors in the liberal arts.

All of the students are openly gay on the campus as well as to their parents and families. All are considered out-of-state students and live off campus. None of the students responding came out before attending college, and none said that being gay, lesbian, or bisexual affected their choosing Temple. Furthermore, if information on the climate for gays, lesbians, and bisexuals at Temple been available, none of the respondents' choices would have been different.

The respondents are involved in the gay, lesbian, and bisexual student group, which has an average membership of 30–50 students and sponsors dances, speakers, safe-sex education, and Pride and National Coming Out Day activities. The group receives funding from the student government. The students tend not to date other Temple students. Off campus, students congregate in bars and at other local colleges.

All of the students view the lack of role models as the largest problem at Temple, with substance abuse following second.

Gay men's and lesbians' cultural contributions are a part of some regular courses. The university also offers courses on gay, lesbian, and bisexual issues in English, women's studies, history, and the social sciences. The university provides free, anonymous HIV testing, and condoms free of charge. Students do not know if counseling is available for those who are HIV+ or have AIDS. The student group provides safe-sex education for itself.

All of the respondents recommend Temple to other gay, lesbian, and bisexual students.

Texas A&M University • *College Station, Texas*

Students define Texas A&M's position on gay, lesbian, and bisexual issues as noncommittal. The university does not have a committee on gay, lesbian, and bisexual issues, nor is sexual orientation included in its affirmative action policy. However, counseling services are available for gay, lesbian, and bisexual students. Students do not know if housing for cohabiting couples is available. According to the students, the municipality in which the university is located does not have a civil rights law that includes sexual orientation.

Unanimously, students believe that homophobia is a serious problem on the campus. Half of those responding report being victims of harassment and verbal abuse. Moreover, all of the students have knowledge of hate crimes committed on the campus, including assault. No one knows who, if anyone, maintains hate-crime statistics.

All of students believe that Texas A&M takes action in response to hate crimes and agree that the university's security force is supportive. All of the students feel safe on the campus as gays, lesbians, and bisexuals.

Gay, lesbian, and bisexual students between the ages of 19–22 responded to the survey. Students are sophomores, juniors, and seniors with SAT scores of 1100 or higher and grade point averages of 2.5 or higher. Students have majors in computer and biomedical engineering.

Most of the students are openly gay on the campus. Those who are not cite fear of reprisal as the primary reason. All of the students, however, are out to their parents and families. None are considered out-of-state students and all live off campus, some with life partners. Half of the students responding came out before attending college, and none said that being gay, lesbian, or bisexual affected their choosing Texas A&M. Furthermore, if information on the climate for gays, lesbians, and bisexuals at Texas A&M had been available, the respondents' choices would not have been different.

The respondents are involved in the gay, lesbian, and bisexual student group, which has an average membership of 75–100 students and sponsors dances, speakers, safe-sex education, and Pride and National Coming Out Day activities. The group receives funding from the student government. In addition, students are active in other organizations such as the Student Program Council and the women engineers' organization. Most students date other Texas A&M students and state that their dating activity takes place on the campus. Off campus, students congregate in bars and cafes.

All of the students view coming out as the largest problem at Texas A&M, with the lack of role models and alcohol abuse following second.

Although gay men's and lesbians' cultural contributions are not a part of regular courses, the university does offer courses on gay, lesbian, and bisexual issues in English. The university provides free, anonymous HIV testing and counseling for those who are HIV+ or have AIDS. Students do not know if condoms are provided. Both the Health Center and the student group provide safe-sex education.

All of the respondents recommend Texas A&M to other gay, lesbian, and bisexual students.

Texas Tech University • *Lubbock, Texas*

Most students define Texas Tech's position on gay, lesbian, and bisexual issues as negative, with some saying the university is non-committal. The university does not have a committee on gay, lesbian, and bisexual issues, nor is sexual orientation included in its affirmative action policy. In addition, counseling services are not available for gay, lesbian, and bisexual students, nor is housing for cohabitating couples. According to the students, the municipality in which the university is located does not have a civil rights law that includes sexual orientation.

Unanimously, students believe strongly that homophobia is a serious problem on the campus. The majority of those responding report being victims of harassment, vandalism, and verbal abuse. Moreover, all of the students have knowledge of hate crimes committed on the campus, including assault. Students do not know who, if anyone, maintains hate-crime statistics.

All of students believe that Texas Tech takes action in response to hate crimes, but none agree that the university's security force is supportive. Consequently, 75 percent of the students do not feel safe on the campus as gays, lesbians, and bisexuals.

Gay, lesbian, and bisexual students between the ages of 22–28 responded to the survey. Students are seniors and graduate students with SAT scores of 1100 or higher and grade point averages of 3.5 or higher.

The majority of the students are openly gay on the campus. Those who are not cite fear of reprisal as the primary reason. Most are out to their parents and families. None are considered out-of-state students and all live off campus. Few of the students responding came out before attending college, and none said that being gay, lesbian, or bisexual affected their choosing Texas Tech. If information on the climate for gays, lesbians, and bisexuals at Texas Tech had been available, one third of the respondents would have made a different choice.

The respondents are involved in the gay, lesbian, and bisexual student group, which has an average membership of 10–25 students and sponsors speakers, safe-sex education, and Pride and National Coming Out Day activities. The group receives funding from the student government. In addition, students are active in athletics. The students date other Texas Tech students and state that some of their dating activity takes place on the campus. Off campus, students congregate in bars and at the community center.

All of the students view coming out as the largest problem at Texas Tech, with the lack of role models following second.

Gay men's and lesbians' cultural contributions are not a part of regular courses, nor does the university offer courses on gay, lesbian, and bisexual issues. However, the university provides free, anonymous HIV testing, counseling for those who are HIV+ or have AIDS, and condoms free of charge. Both the Health Center and the student group provide safe-sex education.

Half of the respondents recommend Texas Tech to other gay, lesbian, and bisexual students.

Towson State University • *Towson, Maryland*

Students define Towson State's position on gay, lesbian, and bisexual issues as proactive. The university has a committee on gay, lesbian, and bisexual issues, and sexual orientation has recently been included in the university's affirmative action policy. Counseling services are available specifically for gays, lesbians, and bisexuals. Housing is not available for cohabiting couples. According to the students, the municipality in which the university is located does not have a civil rights law that includes sexual orientation.

Unanimously, students believe that homophobia is a serious problem on the campus. Those responding report being victims of verbal abuse, harassment, hate mail, and vandalism. Moreover, all of the students have knowledge of hate crimes committed on the campus, including assault. The university maintains hate-crime statistics.

All of the students believe that Towson takes action in response to hate crimes, and all believe that the university's security force is supportive. However, less than three quarters of the students feel safe on the campus as gays, lesbians, and bisexuals.

Gay, lesbian, and bisexual students between the ages of 19–28 responded to the survey. Students are sophomores, juniors, seniors, and graduate students with SAT scores of 1100 or higher and grade point averages of 3.0 and higher. Students have majors in the liberal arts.

All of the students are openly gay on the campus as well as to their parents and families. None are considered out-of-state students and live both in residence halls and in off-campus apartments and houses. Three quarters of the students came out before attending college, and none said that being gay, lesbian, or bisexual affected their choosing Towson. Furthermore, if information on the climate for gay, lesbians, and bisexuals at Towson had been available, the respondents' choices would not have been different.

The respondents are involved in the gay, lesbian, and bisexual student group, which has an average membership of 30 students and sponsors speakers, safe-sex education, and Pride and National Coming Out Day activities. The group receives funding from the student government. In addition, students are active in Greek life, the literary magazine, the progressive student union, theater, and athletics. The students date other Towson students and state that some of their dating activity takes place on the campus. Off campus, students congregate in bars and private homes and apartments.

All of the students view coming out as the largest problem at Towson, with the lack of role models and student organization following second.

Gay men's and lesbians' cultural contributions are a part of some regular courses, depending on the professor. In addition, the university offers courses on gay, lesbian, and bisexual issues in English, art history, and history. The university provides free, anonymous HIV testing, counseling for those who are HIV+ or have AIDS, and condoms free of charge. Both the Health Center and the student group provide safe-sex education.

All of the respondents recommend Towson to other gay, lesbian, and bisexual students.

Trinity College • *Hartford, Connecticut*

Students define Trinity's position on gay, lesbian, and bisexual issues as noncommittal. Although the college does not have a committee on gay, lesbian, and bisexual issues, sexual orientation is included in its affirmative action policy. Counseling services are not available for gay, lesbian, and bisexual students, nor is housing for cohabitating couples. According to the students, the municipality in which the college is located has a civil rights law that includes sexual orientation.

Unanimously, students believe strongly that homophobia is a serious problem on the campus. Those responding report being victims of harassment, ostracism, and verbal abuse. Moreover, all of the students have knowledge of hate crimes committed on the campus, including assault. The Women's Center maintains hate-crime statistics.

All of the students believe that Trinity does nothing in response to hate crimes. All agree that the college's security force is not supportive. Consequently, none of the students feel safe on the campus as gays, lesbians, and bisexuals.

Gay, lesbian, and bisexual students between the ages of 19–23 responded to the survey. Students are sophomores, juniors, and seniors with SAT scores of 900 or higher and grade point averages of 2.5 or higher. Students have majors in American studies, English, and women's studies.

All of the students are openly gay on the campus as well as to their parents and families. All are considered out-of-state students and live both in residence halls and off campus. None of the students responding came out before attending college, and none said that being gay, lesbian, or bisexual affected their choosing Trinity. If information on the climate for gays, lesbians, and bisexuals at Trinity had been available, half of the respondents would have made a different choice.

The respondents are involved in the gay, lesbian, and bisexual student group, which has an average membership of 5–8 students and sponsors dances, speakers, safe-sex education, and Pride and National Coming Out Day activities. The group receives funding from the student government. In addition, students are active in the women's center, Pan-African Alliance, and various academic committees. The students date other Trinity students and state that their dating activity takes place on the campus. Off campus, students congregate in bars.

All of the students view coming out as the largest problem at Trinity with the lack of role models and student organization following second.

Gay men's and lesbians' cultural contributions are not a part of regular courses, nor does the college offer courses on gay, lesbian, and bisexual issues. The college does not provide free, anonymous HIV testing or counseling for those who are HIV+ or have AIDS. Condoms are provided free of charge. Both the Health Center and the student group provide safe-sex education.

None of the respondents recommend Trinity to other gay, lesbian, and bisexual students. One student comments: "The School thrives on the 'Ole Boy Network,' the frats, alcohol abuse, sexual assault, racism, homophobia, ethnocentrism, and ignorance. Being what is termed 'a very small, mini Ivy League,' it aspires to greatness, but settles for mediocrity. Being gay is enough of a burden sometimes. But being gay on campus—out, that is—is a nightmare."

Tufts University • *Medford, Massachusetts*

Students define Tufts' position on gay, lesbian, and bisexual issues as noncommittal. The university has a committee on gay, lesbian, and bisexual issues, and sexual orientation is included in the university's affirmative action policy. In addition, counseling services are available for gay, lesbian, and bisexual students. Housing for cohabitating couples is not available. According to the students, the municipality in which the university is located has a civil rights law that includes sexual orientation.

Unanimously, students believe that homophobia is a serious problem on the campus. Those responding report being victims of harassment, vandalism, assault, and verbal abuse. Moreover, all of the students have knowledge of hate crimes committed on the campus. The student group maintains hate-crime statistics.

All of students believe that Tufts takes action in response to hate crimes. Students are divided concerning the security force's support. Three quarters of the students do not feel safe on the campus as gays, lesbians, and bisexuals.

Gay, lesbian, and bisexual students between the ages of 19–25 responded to the survey. Students are sophomores, juniors, and graduate students with SAT scores of 900 or higher and grade point averages of 2.0 or higher (graduate students have GPAs of 3.5 or higher). Students have majors in social psychology, women's studies, sociology, and art history.

All of the students are openly gay on the campus as well as to their parents and families. Most are considered out-of-state students and live in residence halls. Three quarters of the students responding came out before attending college, and none said that being gay, lesbian, or bisexual affected their choosing Tufts. Furthermore, if information on the climate for gays, lesbians, and bisexuals at Tufts had been available, the respondents' choices would not have been different.

The respondents are involved in the gay, lesbian, and bisexual student group, which has an average membership of 20–70 students and sponsors dances, speakers, safe-sex education, and Pride and National Coming Out Day activities. The group receives funding from the student government. In addition, students are active in other organizations such as the Student Senate, Tufts Democrats, and campus women's groups. One quarter of the students date other Tufts students and state that their dating activity takes place on the campus. Off campus, students congregate in bars.

All of the students view alcohol abuse as the largest problem at Tufts, with coming out following second.

Although gay men's and lesbians' cultural contributions are not a part of regular courses, the university does offer courses on gay, lesbian, and bisexual issues in English, history, women's studies, and the social sciences. The university does not provide free, anonymous HIV testing or condoms. However, counseling is available for those who are HIV+ or have AIDS. The student group provides safe-sex education.

Three quarters of the respondents recommend Tufts to other gay, lesbian, and bisexual students.

Union College • *Schenectady, New York*

Students define Union's position on gay, lesbian, and bisexual issues as noncommittal. The college does not have a committee on gay, lesbian, and bisexual issues, nor is sexual orientation included in its affirmative action policy. Students do not know if counseling services are available for gay, lesbian, and bisexual students. Housing for cohabitating couples is not available. According to the students, the municipality in which the college is located does not have a civil rights law that includes sexual orientation.

Unanimously, students believe that homophobia is a serious problem on the campus. Although none of those responding report being victims of hate crimes, all of the students have knowledge of hate crimes committed on the campus. No one maintains hate-crime statistics.

Some of the students believe that Union takes action in response to hate crimes. None, however, agree that the college's security force is supportive. The majority of the students do not feel safe on the campus as gays, lesbians, and bisexuals.

Gay, lesbian, and bisexual students between the ages of 20–22 responded to the survey. Students are freshmen, juniors, and seniors with SAT scores of 1100 or higher and grade point averages of 3.0 or higher. Students have majors in pre-medicine, biology, and sociology.

None of the students are openly gay on the campus and cite fear of reprisal as the primary reason. However, all are out to their parents and families. All are considered out-of-state students and live both off campus and in residence halls. Most of the students responding came out before attending college, and none said that being gay, lesbian, or bisexual affected their choosing Union. However, if information on the climate for gays, lesbians, and bisexuals at Union had been available, all of the respondents would have made a different choice.

The respondents are involved in the gay, lesbian, and bisexual student group, which has an average membership of 7 students and sponsors safe-sex education. The group receives funding from the student government. In addition, students are active in the Asian Student Union. The students tend not to date other Union students. Off campus, students congregate in bars and the community center.

All of the students view coming out as the largest problem at Union, with the lack of role models and student organization following second.

Gay men's and lesbians' cultural contributions are not a part of regular courses, nor does the college offer courses on gay, lesbian, and bisexual issues. The college does not provide free, anonymous HIV testing, but it does provide counseling for those who are HIV+ or have AIDS. Condoms are available free of charge. Both the Health Center and the student group provide safe-sex education.

None of the respondents recommend Union to other gay, lesbian, and bisexual students. However, one student comments: "I only came to Union because of the seven-year accelerated medical program. If I were to do it all over again, I think I would still attend Union knowing I'm gay, but it would only be because of the medical program. So if a gay student were interested in such a program, Union is a good school. The environment is neither overtly homophobic nor gay-supportive. Thus, most gay people would not be harassed."

University of Alabama • *Tuscaloosa, Alabama*

Students define Alabama's position on gay, lesbian, and bisexual issues as proactive. The university does not have a committee on gay, lesbian, and bisexual issues, nor is sexual orientation included in its affirmative action policy. However, counseling services are available for gay, lesbian, and bisexual students. Housing for cohabitating couples is not available. According to the students, the municipality in which the university is located does not have a civil rights law that includes sexual orientation.

Unanimously, students believe strongly that homophobia is a serious problem on the campus. Half of those responding report being victims of verbal abuse. Moreover, all of the students have knowledge of hate crimes committed on the campus. No one maintains hate-crime statistics.

All of students believe that Alabama takes action in response to hate crimes, and agree that the university's security force is supportive. All of the students feel safe on the campus as gays, lesbians, and bisexuals.

Gay, lesbian, and bisexual students between the ages of 22–29

responded to the survey. Students are seniors and graduate students with SAT scores of 900 or higher and grade point averages of 2.0 or higher (graduate students average 3.5 or higher). Students have majors in telecommunications, film, English, biology, and marketing.

Most of the students are openly gay on the campus and all are out to their parents and families. None are considered out-of-state students and all live off campus. All of the students responding came out before attending college, and none said that being gay, lesbian, or bisexual affected their choosing Alabama. If information on the climate for gays, lesbians, and bisexuals at Alabama had been available, half of the respondents would have made a different choice.

The respondents are involved in the gay, lesbian, and bisexual student group, which has an average membership of 30–50 students and sponsors speakers, safe-sex education, and Pride and National Coming Out Day activities. The group receives funding from the student government. In addition, students are active in Students for Choice. The students date other Alabama students and state that their dating activity takes place on the campus. Off campus, students congregate in bars.

All of the students view coming out as the largest problem at Alabama, with the lack of role models and alcohol abuse following second.

Although gay men's and lesbians' cultural contributions are not a part of regular courses, the university does offer courses on gay, lesbian, and bisexual issues in English. The university does not provide free, anonymous HIV testing; however, counseling is available for those who are HIV+ or have AIDS, and condoms are provided free of charge. Both the Health Center and the student group provide safe-sex education.

None of the respondents recommend Alabama to other gay, lesbian, and bisexual students, stating that "there are better colleges that are more suited to gay students."

University of Arizona • *Tucson, Arizona*

Students define Arizona's position on gay, lesbian, and bisexual issues as noncommittal. Although the university does not have a committee on gay, lesbian, and bisexual issues, sexual orientation is included in its affirmative action policy. In addition, counseling services are available for gay, lesbian, and bisexual students, as is housing for cohabitating couples. According to the students, the municipality in which the university is located has a civil rights law that includes sexual orientation.

Unanimously, students believe strongly that homophobia is a serious problem on the campus. Those responding report being victims of verbal abuse. Moreover, all of the students have knowledge of hate crimes committed on the campus, including assault. No one maintains hate-crime statistics.

Students believe that Arizona does nothing in response to hate crimes, and all agree that the university's security force is not supportive. None of the students feel safe on the campus as gays, lesbians, and bisexuals.

Gay, lesbian, and bisexual students between the ages of 20–22 responded to the survey. Students are juniors and seniors with SAT scores of 1100 or higher and grade point averages of 2.5 or higher. Students have majors in the liberal arts.

All of the students are openly gay on the campus as well as to their parents and families. None are considered out-of-state students and all live off campus. All of the students responding came out before attending college, and none said that being gay, lesbian, or bisexual affected their choosing Arizona. If information on the climate for gays, lesbians, and bisexuals at Arizona had been available, most of the respondents would have made a different choice.

The respondents are involved in the gay, lesbian, and bisexual student group, which has an average membership of 34 students and sponsors dances, speakers, safe-sex education, and Pride and National Coming Out Day activities. The group receives funding from the student government. The students date other Arizona students and state that their dating activity takes place on the campus. Some have life partners attending the university. Off campus, students congregate in bars and at the community center.

All of the students view the lack of student organization as the largest problem at Arizona, with the lack of role models and coming out following second.

Although gay men's and lesbians' cultural contributions are not a part of regular courses, the university does offer courses on gay, lesbian, and bisexual issues in English and women's studies. The university does not provide free, anonymous HIV testing, counseling for those who are HIV+ or have AIDS, or condoms free of charge. Both the Health Center and the student group provide safe-sex education.

All of the respondents recommend Arizona to other gay, lesbian, and bisexual students.

University of California, Berkeley • *Berkeley, California*

Those students responding do not know UC Berkeley's position on gay, lesbian, and bisexual issues. They also do not know if the university has a committee on gay, lesbian, and bisexual issues, or if sexual orientation is included in its affirmative action policy. However, counseling services are available for gay, lesbian, and bisexual students. Housing for cohabitating couples is not available. Students do not know if the municipality in which the university is located has a civil rights law that includes sexual orientation.

Unanimously, students believe that homophobia is a serious problem on the campus. None of those responding report being victims of hate crimes, but all of the students have knowledge of hate crimes committed on the campus. Students do not know who, if anyone, maintains hate-crime statistics.

None of the students know how the university reacts to hate crimes, but all agree that the university's security force is supportive. All of the students feel safe on the campus as gays, lesbians, and bisexuals.

Gay, lesbian, and bisexual students between the ages of 19–36 responded to the survey. Students are sophomores, juniors, seniors, and graduate students with SAT scores of 1100 or higher and grade point averages of 3.5 or higher. Students have majors in the liberal arts, integrative biology, and zoology.

Most of the students are openly gay on the campus. Those who are not cite fear of reprisal as the primary reason. All of the students, however, are out to their parents and families. None are considered out-of-state students and all live off campus, some with life partners. All of the students responding came out before attending college, and none said that being gay, lesbian, or bisexual affected their choosing

Berkeley. Furthermore, if information on the climate for gays, lesbians, and bisexuals at Berkeley been available, the respondents' choices would not have been different.

The respondents are involved in the gay, lesbian, and bisexual student group, which sponsors dances, speakers, safe-sex education, and Pride and National Coming Out Day activities. The group receives no funding from the student government. The students tend not to date other Berkeley students. Off campus, students congregate in bars.

All of the students view the lack of role models as the largest problem at Berkeley, with coming out and alcohol abuse following second.

Although gay men's and lesbians' cultural contributions are not a part of regular courses, the university does offer courses on gay, lesbian, and bisexual issues in women's studies. The university provides free, anonymous HIV testing, counseling for those who are HIV+ or have AIDS, and condoms free of charge. Both the Health Center and the student group provide safe-sex education.

All of the respondents recommend Berkeley to other gay, lesbian, and bisexual students.

University of California, Berkeley, School of Law •
Berkeley, California

Students define UC Berkeley Law School's position on gay, lesbian, and bisexual issues as proactive, although some say it is noncommittal. Although the university does not have a committee on gay, lesbian, and bisexual issues, sexual orientation is included in its affirmative action policy. In addition, counseling services are available for gay, lesbian, and bisexual students. Housing for cohabitating couples is not available. According to the students, the municipality in which the university is located has a civil rights law that includes sexual orientation.

Students are divided in the belief that homophobia is a serious problem on the campus. Fifty percent of those responding report being victims of verbal abuse and vandalism. Moreover, all of the students have knowledge of hate crimes committed on the campus, including assault. Students do not know who, if anyone, maintains hate-crime statistics.

All of the students believe that Berkeley does nothing in response to hate crimes, and all agree that the university's security force is not supportive. Most of the time, however, students feel safe on the campus as gays, lesbians, and bisexuals.

Gay, lesbian, and bisexual students between the ages of 24–26 responded to the survey. Students are all Juris Doctor candidates with SAT scores of 1100 or higher and grade point averages of 3.0 or higher.

All of the students are openly gay on the campus as well as to their parents and families. None are considered out-of-state students and all live off campus, some with life partners. All of the students responding came out before attending college, and half said that being gay, lesbian, or bisexual affected their choosing Berkeley. If information on the climate for gays, lesbians, and bisexuals at Berkeley had been available, the respondents' choices would not have been different.

The respondents are involved in the gay, lesbian, and bisexual student group, which has an average membership of 45–50 students and sponsors speakers, safe-sex education, and Pride and National Coming Out Day activities. The group receives funding from the student government. In addition, students are active in other organizations such as the Boalt Hall Fund for Diversity, the Women's Law Journal, the Admissions Committee, and the Law Journal. Fifty percent of the students date other Berkeley students and state that their dating activity takes place on the campus. Off campus, students congregate in bars and political organizations.

All of the students view the lack of role models as the largest problem at Berkeley.

Although gay men's and lesbians' cultural contributions are not a part of regular courses, the university does offer courses on gay, lesbian, and bisexual issues in law. The university does not provide free, anonymous HIV testing or condoms. Counseling, however, is available for those who are HIV+ or have AIDS. Both the Health Center and the student group provide safe-sex education.

All of the respondents recommend UC Law School at Berkeley to other gay, lesbian, and bisexual students.

University of California, Davis, School of Law •
Davis, California

Students define UC Davis Law School's position on gay, lesbian, and bisexual issues as noncommittal. Although the University has a committee on gay, lesbian, and bisexual issues, sexual orientation is not included in the university's affirmative action policy. Students do not know if counseling services are available for gay, lesbian, and bisexual students. Housing for cohabitating couples is not available. According to the students, the municipality in which the university is located has a civil rights law that includes sexual orientation.

Unanimously, students do not believe that homophobia is a serious problem on the campus. None of those responding report being victims of hate crimes. However, all of the students have knowledge of hate crimes committed on the campus. Students do not know who, if anyone, maintains hate-crime statistics.

All of students believe that UC Davis takes action in response to hate crimes and agree that the university's security force is supportive. All of the students feel safe on the campus as gays, lesbians, and bisexuals.

Gay, lesbian, and bisexual students between the ages of 24–29 responded to the survey. Students are Juris Doctor candidates with grade point averages of 2.5 or higher.

All of the students are openly gay on the campus as well as to their parents and families. None are considered out-of-state students and all live off campus. All of the students responding came out before attending college, and said that being gay, lesbian, or bisexual affected their choosing UC Davis. Furthermore, if information on the climate for gays, lesbians, and bisexuals at UC Davis had been available, the respondents' choices would not have been different.

The respondents are involved in the gay, lesbian, and bisexual student group, which has an average membership of 15 students and sponsors speakers, safe-sex education, and Pride and National Coming Out Day activities. The group receives funding from the student government. In addition, students are active in various law associations. The students tend not to date other UC Davis students. Off campus, students congregate in bars.

All of the students view the lack of role models as the largest problem at UC Davis, with coming out and the lack of student organization following second.

Although gay men's and lesbians' cultural contributions are not a part of regular courses, the university does offer courses on gay, lesbian, and bisexual issues in women's studies. The university provides free, anonymous HIV testing and counseling for those who are HIV+ or have AIDS, but it does not provide condoms. Both the Health Center and the student group provide safe-sex education.

All of the respondents recommend UC Davis to other gay, lesbian, and bisexual students.

University of California, Irvine • *Irvine, California*

Students define UC Irvine's position on gay, lesbian, and bisexual issues as noncommittal. Although the university has a committee on gay, lesbian, and bisexual issues, sexual orientation is not included in the university's affirmative action statement. UC Irvine provides counseling services for gay, lesbian, and bisexual students; however, housing for cohabitating couples is not available. According to the students, the municipality in which the university is located does not have a civil rights law that includes sexual orientation.

Unanimously, students believe that homophobia is a serious problem on the campus. Fifty percent of those responding report being victims of hate mail, vandalism, and verbal abuse. Moreover, all of the students have knowledge of hate crimes committed on the campus, including assault and harassment. Both the university and the student group maintain hate-crime statistics.

Fifty percent of the students do not know how the administration reacts to incidents of hate crimes, while 25 percent believe the university is supportive and 25 percent believe the university does nothing in response. Students divide evenly on their view of the university's security force: half are not sure how supportive security officers are and half perceive the department to be unsupportive. The students are also split evenly on the safety of the Irvine campus.

Gay, lesbian, and bisexual students between the ages of 19–24 responded to the survey. Students are freshmen, juniors, and sophomores with SAT scores of 900 or higher and grade point averages of

3.0 and higher. Students have majors in sociology, criminology, legal studies, women's studies, and literature.

Half of the students surveyed are openly gay on the campus; those who are not state fear of reprisal as the reason. All of the students are out to some family members, half are out to their parents. Twenty-five percent are considered out-of-state students, with half living in residence halls and half living off campus. Seventy-five percent of the students responding came out before attending college, and none said that being gay, lesbian, or bisexual affected their choosing UC Irvine. However, if information on the climate for gays, lesbians, and bisexuals at UC Irvine had been available, 75 percent would have made a different choice.

The respondents are involved in the gay, lesbian, and bisexual student group, which has an average membership of 100 students and sponsors dances, speakers, safe-sex education, and Pride and National Coming Out Day activities. The group receives funding from the student government. The majority of the respondents do not date other UC Irvine students; however, those who do indicate that their dating activity takes place off campus. A few have life partners attending the university. Off campus, students congregate in bars and at the community center.

All of the students view the lack of student organization as the largest problem at UC Irvine, with coming out and the lack of role models following second.

Although gay men's and lesbians' cultural contributions are not a part of regular courses, the university does offer courses on gay, lesbian, and bisexual issues in English, history, art, women's studies, and the social sciences. The university does not provide free, anonymous HIV testing, but it does provide condoms and counseling for those who are HIV+ or have AIDS. Both the university and the student group provide safe-sex education.

Seventy-five of the respondents recommend UC Irvine to other gay, lesbian, and bisexual students.

University of California, Los Angeles • *Los Angeles, California*

Students define UCLA's position on gay, lesbian, and bisexual issues as noncommittal. The university has a committee on gay, lesbian, and bisexual issues, but sexual orientation is not included in the university's affirmative action policy. Counseling services are available for gay, lesbian, and bisexual students, but housing for cohabitating couples is not. According to the students, the municipality in which the university is located has a civil rights law that includes sexual orientation.

Unanimously, students believe that homophobia is a serious problem on the campus. Those responding report being victims of verbal abuse and harassment. Moreover, all of the students have knowledge of hate crimes committed on the campus, including assault. The student group maintains hate-crime statistics.

Two thirds of students believe that UCLA takes action in response to hate crimes; the remaining students believe the administration does nothing. None of the students feel supported by the university's security force. All of the students feel somewhat safe on the campus as gays, lesbians, and bisexuals.

Gay, lesbian, and bisexual students between the ages of 18–21 responded to the survey. Students are freshmen, sophomores, and seniors with SAT scores of 1100 or higher and grade point averages of 3.0 or higher. Students have majors in English, communication studies, women's studies, and sociology.

All of the students are openly gay on the campus and most are out to their parents and families. None are considered out-of-state students and most live in residence halls. All of the students responding came out before attending college, and most said that being gay, lesbian, or bisexual affected their choosing UCLA. If information on the climate for gays, lesbians, and bisexuals at UCLA had been available, two thirds of the respondents would have made a different choice.

The respondents are involved in the gay, lesbian, and bisexual student group, which has an average membership of 20–50 students and sponsors dances, speakers, safe-sex education, and Pride and National Coming Out Day activities. The group receives funding from the student government. In addition, students are active in political groups and student government. The students date other UCLA students and state that their dating activity takes place on the campus. Off campus, students congregate in bars, the community center, and at other off-campus organizations.

All of the students view coming out as the largest problem at UCLA, with the lack of role models and student organization following second.

Although gay men's and lesbians' cultural contributions are not a part of regular courses, the university does offer courses on gay, lesbian, and bisexual issues in English, women's studies, and psychology. The university provides free, anonymous HIV testing (a donation is requested), counseling for those who are HIV+ or have AIDS, and condoms and dental dams. Both the Health Center and the student group provide safe-sex education.

All of the respondents recommend UCLA to other gay, lesbian, and bisexual students.

University of California, San Diego • *San Diego, California*

Students define UC San Diego's position on gay, lesbian, and bisexual issues as noncommittal. Although the university does not have a committee on gay, lesbian, and bisexual issues, sexual orientation is included in its affirmative action policy. In addition, counseling services are available for gay, lesbian, and bisexual students. Housing for cohabitating couples is not available. According to the students, the municipality in which the university is located has a civil rights law that includes sexual orientation.

Unanimously, students believe that homophobia is a serious problem on the campus. The majority of those responding report being victims of hate mail, harassment, vandalism, and verbal abuse. Moreover, all of the students have knowledge of hate crimes committed on the campus, including assault. Both the university and the student group maintain hate-crime statistics.

Most of the students believe that UC San Diego does nothing in response to hate crimes. All, however, agree that the university's security force is supportive. All of the students feel safe on the campus as gays, lesbians, and bisexuals.

Gay, lesbian, and bisexual students between the ages of 20–24 responded to the survey. Students are juniors and seniors with SAT scores of 1100 or higher and grade point averages of 2.5 or higher. Students have majors in English, animal physiology, and computer science.

All of the students are openly gay on the campus and most are out to their parents and families. None are considered out-of-state students and all live off campus, some with their families and some with life partners. Few of the students responding came out before attending college, and none said that being gay, lesbian, or bisexual affected their choosing UC San Diego. Furthermore, if information on the climate for gays, lesbians, and bisexuals at UC San Diego had been available, one third of the respondents would have made a different choice.

The respondents are involved in the gay, lesbian, and bisexual student group, which has an average membership of 40 students and sponsors dances, speakers, safe-sex education, and Pride and National Coming Out Day activities. The group receives funding from the student government. In addition, students are active in peer education and counseling. Most of the students date other UC San Diego students and state that their dating activity takes place on the campus. Off campus, students congregate in bars and at the community center.

All of the students view the lack of role models as the largest problem at UC San Diego, with coming out and alcohol abuse following second.

Gay men's and lesbians' cultural contributions are not a part of regular courses, but the university offers courses on gay, lesbian, and bisexual issues in English, women's studies, and the social sciences. The university provides free, anonymous HIV testing, counseling for those who are HIV+ or have AIDS, and condoms free of charge. Both the Health Center and the student group provide safe-sex education.

All of the respondents recommend UC San Diego to other gay, lesbian, and bisexual students.

University of California, Santa Cruz • *Santa Cruz, California*

Students define UC Santa Cruz's position on gay, lesbian, and bisexual issues as proactive. The university has a committee on gay, lesbian, and bisexual issues, and sexual orientation is included in the university's affirmative action policy. In addition, counseling services are available for gay, lesbian, and bisexual students. Housing for cohabitating couples is currently being debated. According to the students, the municipality in which the university is located has a civil rights law that includes sexual orientation.

Unanimously, students believe that homophobia is not a serious problem on the campus, although those responding report being victims of verbal abuse and have knowledge of hate crimes committed on the campus, including assault. Both the university and the student group maintain hate-crime statistics.

All of students believe that UC Santa Cruz takes action in response to hate crimes and strongly agree that the university's security force is supportive. All of the students feel safe on the campus as gays, lesbians, and bisexuals, saying that "it's very easy to be out here."

Gay, lesbian, and bisexual students between the ages of 19–21 responded to the survey. Students are sophomores, juniors, and seniors with SAT scores of 1100 or higher. Students have majors in the liberal arts and sciences.

All of the students are openly gay on the campus as well as to their parents and families. None are considered out-of-state students and all live in university housing. None of the students responding came out before attending college, and none said that being gay, lesbian, or bisexual affected their choosing UC Santa Cruz. Furthermore, if information on the climate for gays, lesbians, and bisexuals at UC Santa Cruz had been available, none of the respondents would have made a different choice.

The respondents are involved in the gay, lesbian, and bisexual student group, which has an average membership of 50 students and sponsors dances, speakers, safe-sex education, and Pride and National Coming Out Day activities. The group receives funding from the student government. The students date other UC Santa Cruz students and state that their dating activity takes place on the campus. Off campus, students congregate in bars, the community center, religious organizations, and coffeehouses.

All of the students view substance abuse as the largest problem at UC Santa Cruz, with coming out and alcohol abuse following second.

Gay men's and lesbians' cultural contributions are a part of regular courses. The university also offers courses on gay, lesbian, and bisexual issues in English, history, art, education, theater, women's studies, and the social sciences. The university provides free, anonymous HIV testing, counseling for those who are HIV+ or have AIDS, and condoms free of charge. Both the Health Center and the student group provide safe-sex education.

All of the respondents enthusiastically recommend UC Santa Cruz to other gay, lesbian, and bisexual students.

University of Cincinnati • *Cincinnati, Ohio*

Students define Cincinnati's position on gay, lesbian, and bisexual issues as noncommittal. Although the university does not have a committee on gay, lesbian, and bisexual issues, sexual orientation is included in its affirmative action policy. In addition, counseling services are available for gay, lesbian, and bisexual students, as is housing for cohabitating couples. According to the students, the municipality in which the university is located has a civil rights law that includes sexual orientation.

Unanimously, students believe strongly that homophobia is a serious problem on the campus. Those responding report being victims of harassment and verbal abuse. Moreover, all of the students have knowledge of hate crimes committed on the campus, including assault. The student group maintains hate-crime statistics.

All of the students believe that Cincinnati does nothing in response to hate crimes. All agree that the university's security force is not supportive. Most of the students do not feel safe on the campus as gays, lesbians, and bisexuals.

Gay, lesbian, and bisexual students between the ages of 18–21 responded to the survey. Students are freshmen, sophomores, and juniors with SAT scores of 900 or higher and grade point averages of 3.0 or higher. Students declaring majors are studying the liberal arts and music.

All of the students are openly gay on the campus as well as to their parents and families. Most are considered out-of-state students and all live off campus. Half of the students responding came out before attending college, and none said that being gay, lesbian, or bisexual affected their choosing Cincinnati. Furthermore, if information on the climate for gays, lesbians, and bisexuals at Cincinnati had been available, the respondents' choices would not have been different.

The respondents are involved in the gay, lesbian, and bisexual student group, which has an average membership of 20–30 students

and sponsors dances, speakers, safe-sex education, and Pride and National Coming Out Day activities. The group receives funding from the student government. The students date other Cincinnati students and state that their dating activity takes place on the campus. Off campus, students congregate in bars.

All of the students view coming out as the largest problem at Cincinnati, with the lack of role models and alcohol abuse following second.

Although gay men's and lesbians' cultural contributions are not a part of regular courses, the university does offer courses on gay, lesbian, and bisexual issues in women's studies. The university does not provide free, anonymous HIV testing or counseling for those who are HIV+ or have AIDS. Condoms are available free of charge. Both the Health Center and the student group provide safe-sex education.

Half of the respondents recommend Cincinnati to other gay, lesbian, and bisexual students.

University of Colorado, Denver • *Denver, Colorado*

Students define Colorado's position on gay, lesbian, and bisexual issues as negative. The university does not have a committee on gay, lesbian, and bisexual issues, nor is sexual orientation included in its affirmative action policy. However, counseling services are available for gay, lesbian, and bisexual students. Housing for cohabitating couples is not available. According to the students, the municipality in which the university is located has a civil rights law that includes sexual orientation. That law, with the recent legislation passed in the state, has been rendered unenforceable.

Unanimously, students do not believe that homophobia is a serious problem on the campus. None of those responding report being victims of hate crimes. However, all of the students have knowledge of hate crimes committed on the campus. No one maintains hate-crime statistics.

All of the students believe that Colorado takes action in response to hate crimes and agree that the University's security force is supportive. All of the students feel safe on the campus as gays, lesbians, and bisexuals.

Gay, lesbian, and bisexual students between the ages of 18–22

responded to the survey. Students are freshmen, sophomores, and juniors with SAT scores of 1100 or higher and grade point averages of 3.5 or higher. Students have majors in the liberal arts.

All of the students are openly gay on the campus as well as to their parents and families. None are considered out-of-state students and all live off campus, some with their families. All of the students responding came out before attending college, and none said that being gay, lesbian, or bisexual affected their choosing Colorado. Furthermore, if information on the climate for gays, lesbians, and bisexuals at Colorado had been available, the respondents' choices would not have been different.

The respondents are involved in the gay, lesbian, and bisexual student group, which has an average membership of 50 students and sponsors speakers, safe-sex education, and Pride and National Coming Out Day activities. The group receives funding from the student government. In addition, students are active in the feminist alliance. The students tend not to date other Colorado students. Off campus, students congregate in bars, the community center, and cafes.

All of the students view alcohol abuse as the largest problem at Colorado, with coming out and other substance abuse following second.

Gay men's and lesbians' cultural contributions are not a part of regular courses, nor does the university offer courses on gay, lesbian, and bisexual issues. The university provides free, anonymous HIV testing and counseling for those who are HIV+ or have AIDS. Students do not know if condoms are provided. Both the Health Center and the student group provide safe-sex education.

All of the respondents recommend Colorado to other gay, lesbian, and bisexual students.

University of Connecticut • *Storrs, Connecticut*

Students define UConn's position on gay, lesbian, and bisexual issues as noncommittal. Although the university does not have a committee on gay, lesbian, and bisexual issues, sexual orientation is included in its affirmative action policy. In addition, counseling services are available for gay, lesbian, and bisexual students. Students do not know if housing for cohabitating couples is available. According to the students, the municipality in which the university is located has a civil rights law that includes sexual orientation.

Unanimously, students believe that homophobia is a serious problem on the campus, though none of those responding report being victims of hate crimes. Moreover, few of the students have knowledge of hate crimes committed on the campus. No one maintains hate-crime statistics.

All of the students believe that UConn takes action in response to hate crimes and agree that the university's security force is supportive. However, the majority of the students do not feel safe on the campus as gays, lesbians, and bisexuals.

Gay, lesbian, and bisexual students between the ages of 20–22 responded to the survey. Students are juniors and seniors with SAT scores of 1100 or higher and grade point averages of 3.0 or higher. Students have majors in the liberal arts and business administration.

All of the students are openly gay on the campus as well as to their parents and families. None are considered out-of-state students and all live off campus, some with their families. None of the students responding came out before attending college, and none said that being gay, lesbian, or bisexual affected their choosing UConn. If information on the climate for gays, lesbians, and bisexuals at UConn had been available, most of the respondents would have made a different choice.

The respondents are involved in the gay, lesbian, and bisexual student group, which has an average membership of 45 students and sponsors dances, speakers, and safe-sex education. The group receives funding from the student government. The students date other UConn students and state that their dating activity takes place on the campus. Off campus, students congregate in bars.

All of the students view coming out as the largest problem at UConn.

Gay men's and lesbians' cultural contributions are not a part of regular courses, nor does the university offer courses on gay, lesbian, and bisexual issues. The university does not provide free, anonymous HIV testing or counseling for those who are HIV+ or have AIDS. Condoms, however, are provided free of charge. Both the Health Center and the student group provide safe-sex education for the campus.

None of the respondents recommend UConn to other gay, lesbian, and bisexual students if "being comfortably gay is the issue."

University of Connecticut, School of Social Work •
West Hartford, Connecticut

Students define UConn's position on gay, lesbian, and bisexual issues as proactive. Although the university does not have a committee on gay, lesbian, and bisexual issues, sexual orientation is included in its affirmative action statement, and counseling services are available for gay, lesbian, and bisexual students. Housing for cohabitating couples is not available. According to the students, the municipality in which the university is located has a civil rights law that includes sexual orientation.

Unanimously, students believe that homophobia is not a serious problem on the campus. None of those responding report being victims of hate crimes, but half of the students have knowledge of hate crimes committed on the campus, including assault. Both the university and the student group maintain hate-crime statistics.

Students believe that the university takes actions in response to hate crimes, and all agree that the university's security force is supportive. Consequently, all of the students feel safe on the UConn campus as gays, lesbians, and bisexuals.

Gay, lesbian, and bisexual students between the ages of 24–26 responded to the survey. Students are graduates with SAT scores of 900 or higher and grade point averages of 3.5 and higher.

All of the students surveyed are openly gay on the campus as well as to some family members. None are considered out-of-state students and all live off campus, some with life partners. None of the students responding came out before attending college, and none said that being gay, lesbian, or bisexual affected their choosing UConn. Furthermore, if information on the climate for gays, lesbians, and bisexuals at UConn had been available, the respondents' choices would not have been different.

The respondents are involved in the gay, lesbian, and bisexual student group, which has an average membership of 20 students and sponsors dances, speakers, safe-sex education, and Pride and National Coming Out Day activities. The group receives funding from the student government. Students tend not to date other UConn students. Off campus, students congregate in bars, the community center, and religious organizations.

All of the students view coming out as the largest problem at UConn, with the lack of role models and ineffective student organization following second.

Gay men's and lesbians' cultural contributions are a part of regular courses, and the university offers courses on gay, lesbian, and bisexual issues in social work. Students state that the school does not have a health center but counseling is available for those who are HIV+ or have AIDS. The student group provides safe-sex education.

All of the respondents recommend UConn's School of Social Work to other gay, lesbian, and bisexual students and remind students that "the UConn School of Social Work is not part of the main campus in Storrs. It is part of a small regional campus."

University of Delaware • *Newark, Delaware*

Students responding vary widely in defining Delaware's position on gay, lesbian, and bisexual issues as proactive and noncommittal. The university has a committee on gay, lesbian, and bisexual issues; sexual orientation is included in the university's affirmative action statement; and counseling services are available for gay, lesbian, and bisexual students. Housing for cohabiting couples is not available. According to the students, the municipality in which the university is located has a civil rights law that includes sexual orientation.

Unanimously, students strongly believe that homophobia is a serious problem on the campus. Those responding report being victims of harassment. Moreover, all of the students have knowledge of hate crimes committed on the campus, including assault. Both the university and the student group maintain hate-crime statistics.

All of the students believe that Delaware takes action in response to these incidents, and all feel supported by the university's security force. However, students do not really feel safe on the campus as gays, lesbians, and bisexuals.

Gay, lesbian, and bisexual students between the ages of 22–23 responded to the survey. Students are seniors with SAT scores of 900

or higher and grade point averages of 2.5 and higher. Students have majors in the liberal arts.

All of the students surveyed are openly gay on the campus as well as to their parents and families. None are considered out-of-state students and all live off campus. None of the students responding came out before attending college, and none said that being gay, lesbian, or bisexual affected their choosing Delaware. However, if information on the climate for gays, lesbians, and bisexuals at Delaware had been available, all of the respondents would have made a different choice.

The respondents are involved in the gay, lesbian, and bisexual student group, which has an average membership of 25 students and sponsors dances, speakers, safe-sex education, and Pride and National Coming Out Day activities. The students date other Delaware students and state that their dating activity takes place on the campus. A minority of the students have life partners attending the university. Off campus, students congregate in bars.

All of the students view coming out as the largest problem at Delaware, with alcohol abuse and the lack of role models following second.

Gay men's and lesbians' cultural contributions are not a part of regular courses, but the university does offers courses on gay, lesbian, and bisexual issues in English and women's studies. The university provides free, anonymous HIV testing and counseling for those who are HIV+ or have AIDS. Condoms are not provided. Both the Health Center and the student group provide safe-sex education.

All of the respondents recommend Delaware to other gay, lesbian, and bisexual students, some with reservations.

University of Hawaii, Manoa • *Honolulu, Hawaii*

Students define Hawaii's position on gay, lesbian, and bisexual issues as noncommittal, but most students do not know the administration's position. The university does not have a committee on gay, lesbian, and bisexual issues; however, sexual orientation is included in its affirmative action statement, and counseling services are available for gay, lesbian, and bisexual students. Housing for cohabitating couples is not available. Students do not know if the municipality in which the university is located has a civil rights law that includes sexual orientation.

The majority of the students believe that homophobia is a serious problem on the campus. Twenty-five percent of those responding report being victims of vandalism. Most of the students have knowledge of hate crimes committed on the campus with the exception of assault. Students do not know who, if anyone, maintains hate-crime statistics.

Most of the students believe that Hawaii does nothing in response to hate crimes; the remaining students do not know how the administration reacts. The majority also do not feel supported by the university's security force. However, most of the students feel safe on the Hawaii campus as gays, lesbians, and bisexuals.

Gay, lesbian, and bisexual students between the ages of 20–34 responded to the survey. Students are freshmen, juniors, seniors, and graduate students with SAT scores of 1100 or higher and grade point averages of 3.5 and higher. Students have majors in zoology, English as a second language, mass communication, theater, education, physics, pre-med, and English.

The majority of the students surveyed are not openly gay on the campus; those who aren't cite fear of reprisal as the primary reason. The majority, however, are out to their parents and families. None are considered out-of-state students and all live off campus, some with their families and some with life partners. Eighty percent of the students responding came out before attending college, and 10 percent said that being gay, lesbian, or bisexual affected their choosing Hawaii. Furthermore, if information on the climate for gays, lesbians, and bisexuals at Hawaii had been available, few of the respondents would have made different choices.

The respondents are involved in the gay, lesbian, and bisexual student group, which has an average membership of 20–50 students and sponsors speakers and safe-sex education. The group receives no funding from the student government. A minority of the students date other Hawaii students, with their dating activity taking place off campus, where they congregate in bars, clubs, country and western dance groups, and private homes and apartments.

All of the students view coming out as the largest problem at

Hawaii, with the lack of student organization and role models following second.

Although gay men's and lesbians' cultural contributions are not a part of regular courses, the university offers courses on gay, lesbian, and bisexual issues in the social sciences and history. The university provides free, anonymous HIV testing, counseling for those who are HIV+ or have AIDS, and condoms free of charge. Peer educators provide safe-sex education.

Half of the respondents recommend Hawaii to other gay, lesbian, and bisexual students.

University of Idaho • *Moscow, Idaho*

Students define Idaho's position on gay, lesbian, and bisexual issues somewhere between negative and noncommittal. The university does not have a committee on gay, lesbian, and bisexual issues, nor is sexual orientation included in its affirmative action policy. However, counseling services are available for gay, lesbian, and bisexual students. Students do not know if housing for cohabiting couples is available. According to the students, the municipality in which the university is located does not have a civil rights law that includes sexual orientation.

Unanimously, students believe that homophobia is a serious problem on the campus. Half of those responding report being victims of verbal abuse. Moreover, all of the students have knowledge of hate crimes committed on the campus, including assault. Students do not know who, if anyone, maintains hate-crime statistics.

Students do not know how Idaho reacts to hate crimes. All agree that the university's security force is supportive, and all of the students feel safe on the campus as gays, lesbians, and bisexuals.

Gay, lesbian, and bisexual students between the ages of 23–25 responded to the survey. Students are seniors with SAT scores of 1100 or higher and grade point averages of 3.0 or higher. Students have majors in the liberal arts and music.

Most of the students are openly gay on the campus as well as to their parents and families. Those who are not out cite discrimination within their academic department as the primary reason. Some are considered out-of-state students and all live off campus. Half of the students responding came out before attending college, and none said that being gay, lesbian, or bisexual affected their choosing Idaho. Furthermore, if information on the climate for gays, lesbians, and bisexuals at Idaho had been available, half of the respondents would have made a different choice.

The respondents are involved in the gay, lesbian, and bisexual student group, which has an average membership of 15–30 students and sponsors dances, speakers, safe-sex education, and Pride and National Coming Out Day activities. The group receives funding from the student government. The students date other Idaho students and state that their dating activity takes place on the campus. Off campus, students congregate in bars and private homes and apartments.

All of the students view coming out as the largest problem at Idaho, with the lack of role models and student organization following second.

Gay men's and lesbians' cultural contributions are not a part of regular courses, nor does the university offer courses on gay, lesbian, and bisexual issues. The university does not provide free, anonymous HIV testing or counseling for those who are HIV+ or have AIDS. Condoms are provided free of charge. Both the Health Center and the student group provide safe-sex education for the campus.

All of the respondents recommend Idaho to other gay, lesbian, and bisexual students. "While policies do not provide protection from discrimination based on sexual orientation, the campus overall is accepting. Many in the GLBA also attend classes at Washington State University and attend support groups there as well."

University of Illinois, Urbana-Champaign •
Champaign, Illinois

Students define Urbana-Champaign's position on gay, lesbian, and bisexual issues as noncommittal. The university does not have a committee on gay, lesbian, and bisexual issues, nor is sexual orientation included in its affirmative action policy. However, counseling services are available for gay, lesbian, and bisexual students. Housing for cohabitating couples is not available. According to the students, the municipality in which the university is located has a civil rights law that includes sexual orientation.

Fifty percent of the students believe that homophobia is a serious problem on the campus. Those responding report being victims of verbal abuse. Moreover, all of the students have knowledge of hate crimes committed on the campus, including assault. Students do not know who, if anyone, maintains hate-crime statistics.

All of the students believe that Urbana-Champaign does nothing in response to hate crimes, but half agree that the university's security force is supportive. Still, none of the students feel safe on the campus as gays, lesbians, and bisexuals.

Gay, lesbian, and bisexual students between the ages of 18–22 responded to the survey. Students are freshmen and juniors with ACT scores of 27 or higher and grade point averages of 2.0 or higher. Students have majors in the liberal arts, aviation, and economics.

None of the students are openly gay on the campus, citing fear of reprisal and their military status as the primary reasons. Most, however, are out to their parents and families. None are considered out-of-state students and half live in residence halls. Most of the students responding came out before attending college, and none said that being gay, lesbian, or bisexual affected their choosing Urbana-Champaign. Furthermore, if information on the climate for gays, lesbians, and bisexuals at Urbana-Champaign had been available, 50 percent of the respondents would have made a different choice.

The respondents are involved in the gay, lesbian, and bisexual student group, which has an average membership of 20 students and sponsors dances, speakers, safe-sex education, and Pride and National Coming Out Day activities. The group receives funding from the student government. Students date other Urbana-Champaign students and state that their dating activity takes place on the campus. Some have life partners attending the school. Off campus, students congregate in bars.

All of the students view coming out as the largest problem at Urbana-Champaign, with the lack of role models and alcohol abuse following second.

Gay men's and lesbians' cultural contributions are a part of some regular courses; the university also offers courses on gay, lesbian, and bisexual issues in English. The university provides free, anonymous

HIV testing, counseling for those who are HIV+ or have AIDS, and condoms. Both the Health Center and the student group provide safe-sex education.

Half of the respondents recommend Urbana-Champaign to other gay, lesbian, and bisexual students.

University of Iowa • *Iowa City, Iowa*

Students define Iowa's position on gay, lesbian, and bisexual issues as proactive, although some say it is merely "lip service." Although the university does not have a committee on gay, lesbian, and bisexual issues, sexual orientation is included in its affirmative action policy. In addition, counseling services are available for gay, lesbian, and bisexual students. Housing for cohabitating couples is not available. According to the students, the municipality in which the university is located has a civil rights law that includes sexual orientation.

Unanimously, students believe that homophobia is a serious problem on the campus. None of those responding report being victims of verbal abuse, but all of the students have knowledge of hate crimes committed on the campus. The student group maintains hate-crime statistics.

All of the students believe that Iowa takes action in response to hate crimes. None, however, agree that the university's security force is supportive. All of the students feel safe on the campus as gays, lesbians, and bisexuals.

Gay, lesbian, and bisexual students between the ages of 20–28 responded to the survey. Students are juniors, seniors, and graduate students with SAT scores of 900 or higher and grade point averages of 3.5 or higher. Students have majors in the liberal arts and social work.

All of the students are openly gay on the campus as well as to their parents and families. None are considered out-of-state students and all live off campus. All of the students responding came out before attending college, and none said that being gay, lesbian, or bisexual affected their choosing Iowa. However, if information on the climate for gays, lesbians, and bisexuals at Iowa had been available, all of the respondents would have made a different choice.

The respondents are involved in the gay, lesbian, and bisexual student group, which has an average membership of 24 students and

sponsors dances, speakers, safe-sex education, and Pride and National Coming Out Day activities. The group receives funding from the student government. The students date other Iowa students and state that their dating activity takes place off campus, where they congregate in bars.

All of the students view the lack of student organization as the largest problem at Iowa, with coming out and alcohol abuse following second.

Although gay men's and lesbians' cultural contributions are not a part of regular courses, the university does offer courses on gay, lesbian, and bisexual issues in women's studies and the social sciences. The university provides free, anonymous HIV testing, counseling for those who are HIV+ or have AIDS, and condoms free of charge. Both the Health Center and the student group provide safe-sex education for the campus.

All of the respondents recommend Iowa to other gay, lesbian, and bisexual students.

University of Massachusetts, Boston • *Boston, Massachusetts*

Of the students responding, 60 percent define UMass's position on gay, lesbian, and bisexual issues as proactive while 40 percent define it as noncommittal. The university has a committee on gay, lesbian, and bisexual issues, and sexual orientation is included in the university's affirmative action statement. Students do not know if counseling services are provided for gay, lesbian, and bisexual students, or if housing for cohabitating couples is available. According to the students, the municipality in which the university is located has a civil rights law that includes sexual orientation.

Eighty percent of the students do not believe that homophobia is a serious problem on the campus, but 60 percent of those responding report being victims of verbal abuse, assault, and harassment. Moreover, all of the students have knowledge of hate crimes committed on the campus. The university maintains hate-crime statistics.

Forty percent of the students believe that UMass takes action in response to these incidents, and 80 percent feel supported by the university's security force. Consequently, all of the students feel safe on the UMass campus as gays, lesbians, and bisexuals.

Gay, lesbian, and bisexual students between the ages of 21–41 responded to the survey. Students are freshmen, juniors, and seniors with SAT scores of 899 or higher and grade point averages of 2.5 and higher. Students have majors in social psychology, sociology, psychology, and theater.

All of the students surveyed are openly gay on the campus as well as to their parents and families. Very few are considered out-of-state students and all live off campus, some with their families and some with life partners. Eighty percent of the students responding came out before attending college, and 40 percent said that being gay, lesbian, or bisexual affected their choosing UMass. However, if information on the climate for gays, lesbians, and bisexuals at UMass had been available, the respondents' choices would not have been different.

The respondents are involved in the gay, lesbian, and bisexual student group, which has an average membership of 15–50 students and sponsors dances, speakers, safe-sex education, and Pride and National Coming Out Day activities. The group receives funding from the student government. Twenty percent of the respondents consider themselves cross dressers. One fifth of the students state that they date other UMass students, but their dating activity takes place off campus, where they congregate in bars and at the community center.

All of the students view coming out as the largest problem at UMass, with the lack of role models and alcohol abuse following second.

Gay men's and lesbians' cultural contributions are a part of some regular courses, and the university offers courses on gay, lesbian, and bisexual issues in history, English, art, women's studies, and the social sciences. Students do not know if the university provides free, anonymous HIV testing or counseling for those who are HIV+ or have AIDS. Condoms are provided free of charge. Both the Health Center and the student group provide safe-sex education for the campus.

All of the respondents recommend UMass to other gay, lesbian, and bisexual students.

University of Massachusetts, Dartmouth •
North Dartmouth, Massachusetts

Students define UMass at Dartmouth's position on gay, lesbian, and bisexual issues as proactive. The university has a committee on gay, lesbian, and bisexual issues, and sexual orientation is included in the university's affirmative action policy. In addition, counseling services are available for gay, lesbian, and bisexual students. Students do not know if housing for cohabitating couples is available. According to the students, the municipality in which the university is located has a civil rights law that includes sexual orientation.

Unanimously, students believe that homophobia is a serious problem on the campus. Those responding report being victims of verbal abuse. Moreover, all of the students have knowledge of hate crimes committed on the campus. Students do not know who, if anyone, maintains hate-crime statistics.

Students do not know how UMass, Dartmouth, reacts to hate crimes. Students are ambivalent concerning the university security force's support, but all of the students feel safe on the campus as gays, lesbians, and bisexuals.

Gay, lesbian, and bisexual students between the ages of 21–27 responded to the survey. Students are sophomores and juniors with SAT scores of 900 or higher and grade point averages of 2.5 or higher. Students have majors in the liberal arts, business, and chemistry.

Most of the students are openly gay on the campus and all are out to their parents and families. Those who are not out on the campus cite business reasons. None are considered out-of-state students and all live off campus, some with their families. All of the students responding came out before attending college, and none said that being gay, lesbian, or bisexual affected their choosing UMass, Dartmouth. Furthermore, if information on the climate for gays, lesbians, and bisexuals at UMass, Dartmouth, had been available, half of the respondents would have made a different choice.

The respondents are involved in the gay, lesbian, and bisexual student group, which has an average membership of 125 students and sponsors dances, speakers, safe-sex education, and Pride and National Coming Out Day activities. The group receives funding from the student government. The students date other UMass, Dartmouth, students and state that their dating activity takes place off of the campus, where they congregate in bars.

All of the students view coming out as the largest problem at UMass, Dartmouth, with the lack of role models and alcohol abuse following second.

Gay men's and lesbians' cultural contributions are not a part of regular courses, nor does the university offer courses on gay, lesbian, and bisexual issues. Students do not know if the university provides free, anonymous HIV testing or counseling for those who are HIV+ or have AIDS. Condoms are available free of charge. Both the Health Center and the student group provide safe-sex education.

All of the respondents recommend UMass, Dartmouth, to other gay, lesbian, and bisexual students.

University of Maine, Farmington • *Farmington, Maine*

Students define Farmington's position on gay, lesbian, and bisexual issues somewhere between proactive and noncommittal. The university has a committee on gay, lesbian, and bisexual issues, and sexual orientation is included in the university's affirmative action policy. In addition, counseling services are available for gay, lesbian, and bisexual students. Housing for cohabitating couples is not available. According to the students, the municipality in which the university is located does not have a civil rights law that includes sexual orientation.

Unanimously, students believe strongly that homophobia is a serious problem on the campus. Those responding report being victims of harassment, vandalism, and verbal abuse. Moreover, all of the students have knowledge of hate crimes committed on the campus, including assault. Both the university and the student group maintain hate-crime statistics.

All of the students believe that Farmington takes action in response to hate crimes, and all agree that the university's security force is supportive. All of the students feel safe on the campus as gays, lesbians, and bisexuals.

Gay, lesbian, and bisexual students between the ages of 19–23 responded to the survey. Students are sophomores, juniors, and seniors with SAT scores of 900 or higher and grade point averages of 3.0 or higher. Students have majors in the liberal arts and education.

All of the students are openly gay on the campus as well as to their parents and families. None are considered out-of-state students and all live off campus, some with life partners. None of the students responding came out before attending college, and none said that being gay, lesbian, or bisexual affected their choosing Farmington. Furthermore, if information on the climate for gays, lesbians, and bisexuals at Farmington had been available, the respondents' choices would not have been different.

The respondents are involved in the gay, lesbian, and bisexual student group, which has an average membership of 5–10 students and sponsors speakers, safe-sex education, and Pride and National Coming Out Day activities. The group receives funding from the student government. Students are also active in the student newspaper. The students date other Farmington students and state that some of their dating activity takes place on the campus. Off campus, students congregate in bars and private homes and apartments.

All of the students view the lack of role models as the largest problem at Farmington, with the lack of student organization and coming out following second.

Gay men's and lesbians' cultural contributions are not a part of regular courses, nor does the university offer courses on gay, lesbian, and bisexual issues. The university does not provide free, anonymous HIV testing or counseling for those who are HIV+ or have AIDS. Condoms are provided for a nominal fee. Both the Health Center and the student group provide safe-sex education.

All of the respondents recommend Farmington to other gay, lesbian, and bisexual students. Students seem to view the administration as fairly supportive and are most critical of the president.

University of Maine, Orono • *Orono, Maine*

Students define Orono's position on gay, lesbian, and bisexual issues as proactive. The university has a committee on gay, lesbian, and bisexual issues, and sexual orientation is included in the university's affirmative action policy. In addition, counseling services are available for gay, lesbian, and bisexual students. Housing for cohabitating couples is not available. According to the students, the municipality in which the university is located does not have a civil rights law that includes sexual orientation.

Unanimously, students believe that homophobia is a serious problem on the campus. Those responding report being victims of harassment, vandalism, and verbal abuse. Moreover, all of the students have knowledge of hate crimes committed on the campus, including assault. No one maintains hate-crime statistics.

All of the students believe that Orono takes action in response to hate crimes and agree that the university's security force is supportive. However, none of the students feel safe on the campus as gays, lesbians, and bisexuals.

Gay, lesbian, and bisexual students between the ages of 19–21 responded to the survey. Students are juniors and seniors with SAT scores of 900 or higher and grade point averages of 3.0 or higher. Students have majors in the liberal arts.

Most of the students are openly gay on the campus. Those who are not cite fear of reprisal as the primary reason. None of the students are out to their parents and families. Half are considered out-of-state students and all live in residence halls. None of the students responding came out before attending college, and none said that being gay, lesbian, or bisexual affected their choosing Orono. Furthermore, if information on the climate for gays, lesbians, and bisexuals at Orono had been available, half of the respondents would have made a different choice.

The respondents are involved in the gay, lesbian, and bisexual student group, which has an average membership of 45 students and sponsors dances, speakers, safe-sex education, and Pride and National Coming Out Day activities. The group receives funding from the student government. Additionally, students are active in Greek life. Most students date other Orono students and state that their dating activity takes place off campus, where they congregate in bars.

All of the students view coming out as the largest problem at Orono, with the lack of role models and student organization following second.

Gay men's and lesbians' cultural contributions are not a part of regular courses, nor does the university offer courses on gay, lesbian, and bisexual issues. The university does not provide free, anonymous

HIV testing or counseling for those who are HIV+ or have AIDS. Condoms are provided free of charge. Both the Health Center and the student group provide safe-sex education.

Half of the respondents recommend Orono to other gay, lesbian, and bisexual students.

University of Miami • *Coral Gables, Florida*

Students define Miami's position on gay, lesbian, and bisexual issues as proactive. Although the university has a committee on gay, lesbian, and bisexual issues, sexual orientation is not included in the university's affirmative action policy. Counseling services, however, are available for gay, lesbian, and bisexual students. Housing for cohabiting couples is not available. According to the students, the municipality in which the university is located does not have a civil rights law that includes sexual orientation.

Unanimously, students believe that homophobia is a serious problem on the campus. None of those responding report being victims of hate crimes, but all of the students have knowledge of hate crimes committed on the campus. The student group maintains hate-crime statistics.

Students do not know how Miami reacts to hate crimes. All agree that the university's security force is not supportive. Yet all of the students feel safe on the campus as gays, lesbians, and bisexuals.

Gay, lesbian, and bisexual students between the ages of 20–22 responded to the survey. Students are juniors and seniors with SAT scores of 900 or higher and grade point averages of 2.5 or higher. Students have majors in the liberal arts and broadcast journalism.

All of the students are openly gay on the campus as well as to their parents and families. None are considered out-of-state students and all live in residence halls. None of the students responding came out before attending college, and none said that being gay, lesbian, or bisexual affected their choosing Miami. Furthermore, if information on the climate for gays, lesbians, and bisexuals at Miami had been available, none of the respondents' choices would have been different.

The respondents are involved in the gay, lesbian, and bisexual student group, which has an average membership of 35 students and sponsors dances, speakers, safe-sex education, and Pride and National Coming Out Day activities. The group receives no funding from the student government. The students date other Miami students and state that their dating activity takes place on the campus. Off campus, students congregate in bars.

All of the students view alcohol abuse as the largest problem at Miami, with other substance abuse and the lack of student organization following second.

Gay men's and lesbians' cultural contributions are not a part of regular courses, nor does the university offer courses on gay, lesbian, and bisexual issues. The university provides free, anonymous HIV testing, counseling for those who are HIV+ or have AIDS, and condoms free of charge. Both the Health Center and the student group provide safe-sex education.

All of the respondents recommend Miami to other gay, lesbian, and bisexual students.

University of Minnesota • *Minneapolis, Minnesota*

Students vary defining Minnesota's position on gay, lesbian, and bisexual issues as proactive and noncommittal. The university has a committee on gay, lesbian, and bisexual issues; sexual orientation is included in the university's affirmative action statement; counseling services are available for gay, lesbian, and bisexual students; and housing for cohabitating couples is available. According to the students, the municipality in which the university is located has a civil rights law that includes sexual orientation.

Students divide evenly on whether they believe homophobia is a serious problem on the campus. One quarter of those responding report being victims of verbal abuse and harassment. However, all of the students have knowledge of hate crimes committed on the campus, including assault. Both the university and the student group maintain hate-crime statistics.

Three quarters of the students believe that Minnesota takes action in response to these incidents, but they do not feel supported by the university's security force. All of the students feel relatively safe on the Minnesota campus as gays, lesbians, and bisexuals.

Gay, lesbian, and bisexual students between the ages of 20–38 responded to the survey. Students are sophomores, juniors, and graduate students with SAT scores of 899 or higher and grade point averages of 2.5 and higher. Graduate students have SAT scores of 1100 or higher and grade point averages of 3.5 or higher. Students have majors in art, human relationships, industrial relations, and journalism.

All of the students surveyed are openly gay on the campus and most are out to their parents and families. Those who are not are undergraduates. Most are not considered out-of-state students and all live off campus, some undergraduates with their families. All of the students responding came out before attending college, and half said that being gay, lesbian, or bisexual affected their choosing Minnesota. However, if information on the climate for gays, lesbians, and bisexuals at Minnesota been available, half of the undergraduate respondents would have chosen to go elsewhere.

The respondents are involved in the gay, lesbian, and bisexual student group, which will have an average membership of 30–50 students and sponsors dances, speakers, safe-sex education, and Pride and National Coming Out Day activities. The group receives funding from the student government. The students date other Minnesota students, with the majority of their dating activity taking place on campus. Off campus, students congregate in bars, religious organizations, and at the community center.

All of the students say that alcohol abuse as the largest problem at Minnesota, with lack of role models and coming out following second.

Gay men's and lesbians' cultural contributions are a part of some regular courses, and the university also offers courses on gay, lesbian, and bisexual issues in English, art, and women's studies. The university provides free, anonymous HIV testing, condoms free of charge, and counseling for those who are HIV+ or have AIDS. Both the Health Center and the student group provide safe-sex education.

All of the respondents recommend Minnesota to other gay, lesbian, and bisexual students.

University of Missouri, Columbia • *Columbia, Missouri*

Of the students responding, half define Missouri's position on gay, lesbian, and bisexual issues as proactive, and half define it as noncommittal. Although the university does not have a committee on gay, lesbian, and bisexual issues, sexual orientation is included in its affirmative action policy. In addition, counseling services are available for gay, lesbian, and bisexual students. Students do not know if housing for cohabitating couples is available. According to the students, the municipality in which the university is located does not have a civil rights law that includes sexual orientation.

Unanimously, students believe that homophobia is a serious problem on the campus. Those responding report being victims of verbal abuse and harassment. Moreover, all of the students have knowledge of hate crimes committed on the campus, including assault. Students do not know who, if anyone, maintains hate-crime statistics.

All of the students believe that Missouri takes action in response to hate crimes. Seventy-five percent agree that the university's security force is supportive. Consequently, most students feel safe on the campus as gays, lesbians, and bisexuals.

Gay, lesbian, and bisexual students between the ages of 19–23 responded to the survey. Students are sophomores, juniors, and seniors with SAT scores of 900 or higher and grade point averages of 2.5 or higher. Students have majors in music education, performance, art, political science, and engineering.

All of the students are openly gay on the campus as well as to their parents and families. Twenty-five percent are considered out-of-state students and all live off campus, some with their families. Seventy-five percent of the students responding came out before attending college, and some of those said that being gay, lesbian, or bisexual affected their choosing Missouri. If information on the climate for gays, lesbians, and bisexuals at Missouri had been available, half of the respondents would have chosen to go elsewhere.

The respondents are involved in the gay, lesbian, and bisexual student group, which has an average membership of 45 students and sponsors dances, speakers, safe-sex education, and Pride and National Coming Out Day activities. The group receives funding from the student government. Students are also active in other organizations such as Peace Studies, the American Society of Mechanical Engineers, the Materials Society, Greek-letter organizations, and athletics. The students date other Missouri students and most state that their dating activity takes place on the campus. Off campus, students congregate in bars and religious organizations.

All of the students view the lack of role models and coming out as the largest problems at Missouri.

Although gay men's and lesbians' cultural contributions are not a part of regular courses, the university does offer courses on gay, lesbian, and bisexual issues in history and women's studies. The university provides free, anonymous HIV testing, counseling for those who are HIV+ or have AIDS, and condoms free of charge. Both the Health Center and the student group provide safe-sex education.

All of the respondents recommend Missouri to other gay, lesbian, and bisexual students.

University of New Hampshire • *Durham, New Hampshire*

Students define New Hampshire's position on gay, lesbian, and bisexual issues somewhere between proactive and noncommittal. The university has a committee on gay, lesbian, and bisexual issues, and sexual orientation is included in the university's affirmative action policy. In addition, counseling services are available for gay, lesbian, and bisexual students. Housing for cohabitating couples is not available except for those who are residence hall directors. According to the students, the municipality in which the university is located does not have a civil rights law that includes sexual orientation.

Unanimously, students believe that homophobia is a serious problem on the campus. Those responding report being victims of verbal abuse, harassment, vandalism, and assault. Moreover, all of the students have knowledge of hate crimes committed on the campus. No one maintains hate-crime statistics.

All of students believe that New Hampshire takes action in response to hate crimes, and all agree that the university's security force is supportive. Seventy-five percent of the students feel safe on the campus as gays, lesbians, and bisexuals.

Gay, lesbian, and bisexual students between the ages of 21–28 responded to the survey. Students are sophomores, seniors, and graduate students with SAT scores of 900 or higher and grade point averages of 2.0 or higher. Students have majors in the liberal arts, electrical engineering, and education.

All of the students are openly gay on the campus as well as to their parents and families. None are considered out-of-state students and all live off campus, some with their families and some with life partners. Twenty-five percent of the students responding came out before attending college, and none said that being gay, lesbian, or bisexual affected their choosing New Hampshire. But if information on the climate for gays, lesbians, and bisexuals at New Hampshire had been available, 75 percent of the respondents would have chosen to go elsewhere.

The respondents are involved in the gay, lesbian, and bisexual student group, which has an average membership of 20–50 students and sponsors dances, speakers, safe-sex education, and Pride and National Coming Out Day activities. The group receives funding from the student government. The students date other New Hampshire students and state that some of their dating activity takes place on the campus. Off campus, students congregate in bars, the community center, religious organizations, coffeehouses, sports leagues, and private homes and apartments.

All of the students view the lack of role models as the largest problem at New Hampshire, with coming out and alcohol abuse following second.

Although gay men's and lesbians' cultural contributions are not a part of regular courses, the university does offer courses on gay, lesbian, and bisexual issues in English. The university provides anonymous but not free HIV testing, counseling for those who are HIV+ or have AIDS, and condoms free of charge. Both the Health Center and the student group provide safe-sex education.

Fifty percent of the respondents recommend New Hampshire to other gay, lesbian, and bisexual students.

University of North Carolina, Chapel Hill •
Chapel Hill, North Carolina

Students define UNC Chapel Hill's position on gay, lesbian, and bisexual issues as noncommittal. Although the university does not have a committee on gay, lesbian, and bisexual issues, sexual orientation is included in its affirmative action policy. In addition, counseling services are available for gay, lesbian, and bisexual students. Housing for cohabitating couples is not available. According to the students, the municipality in which the university is located has a civil rights law that includes sexual orientation.

Unanimously, students believe that homophobia is a serious problem on the campus. Half of those responding report being victims of verbal abuse, hate mail, and harassment. Moreover, all of the students have knowledge of hate crimes committed on the campus, including assault. Both the university and the student group maintain hate-crime statistics.

All of the students believe that Chapel Hill takes action in response to hate crimes, and that the university's security force is supportive. All of the students feel safe on the campus as gays, lesbians, and bisexuals.

Gay, lesbian, and bisexual students between the ages of 19–30 responded to the survey. Students are seniors and graduate students with SAT scores of 1100 or higher and grade point averages of 2.5 or higher. Students have majors in math education, English education, African-American studies, broadcast journalism, and sociology.

All of the students are openly gay on the campus and most are out to their parents and families. Very few are considered out-of-state students and all live off campus. Three quarters of the students responding came out before attending college, and half said that being gay, lesbian, or bisexual affected their choosing Chapel Hill. If information on the climate for gays, lesbians, and bisexuals at Chapel Hill had been available, the respondents' choices would not have been different.

The respondents are involved in the gay, lesbian, and bisexual student group, which has an average membership of 50–100 students and sponsors dances, speakers, safe-sex education, and Pride and National Coming Out Day activities. The group receives funding from the student government. The students date other Chapel Hill students and state that their dating activity takes place on the campus. Off campus, students congregate in bars and religious organizations.

All of the students view coming out as the largest problem at Chapel Hill, with the lack of role models following second.

Gay men's and lesbians' cultural contributions are a part of regular courses. The university also offers courses on gay, lesbian, and bisexual issues in English, women's studies, religious studies, classics, and the social sciences. Students do not know if the university provides free, anonymous HIV testing, counseling for those who are HIV+ or have AIDS, or condoms. Both the Health Center and the student group provide safe-sex education.

Seventy-five percent of the respondents recommend UNC Chapel Hill to other gay, lesbian, and bisexual students. Some recommend the school but with reservation: "Though UNC-CH's policy is pro-gay, the administration does not act upon it; ROTC, which discriminates against gays and lesbians, remains on campus. Few professors mention lesbian and gay issues and those that do often use condescending attitudes. Lesbians, gays, and bisexuals often ignore each other on campus (especially the out ones) for fear."

University of North Carolina, Greensboro •
Greensboro, North Carolina

Students define UNC Greensboro's position on gay, lesbian, and bisexual issues as noncommittal. Although the university does not have a committee on gay, lesbian, and bisexual issues, sexual orientation is included in its affirmative action policy. In addition, counseling services are available for gay, lesbian, and bisexual students. Housing for cohabitating couples is not available. According to the students, the municipality in which the university is located does not have a civil rights law that includes sexual orientation.

The majority of students believe that homophobia is a serious problem on the campus. Half of those responding report being victims of harassment and verbal abuse. Moreover, most of the students have knowledge of hate crimes committed on the campus, including assault. Students do not know who, if anyone, maintains hate-crime statistics.

Most students believe that UNC Greensboro takes action in response to hate crimes, although a lot do not know how the administration reacts. Most also agree that the university's security force is supportive. Eighty percent of the students feel safe on the campus as gays, lesbians, and bisexuals.

Gay, lesbian, and bisexual students between the ages of 19–25

responded to the survey. Students are freshmen, sophomores, juniors, and seniors with SAT scores of 900 or higher and grade point averages of 2.0 or higher. Students have majors in the liberal arts.

Seventy percent of the students are openly gay on the campus. Those who are not cite fear of reprisal as the primary reason. Less than half are out to their parents and families. None are considered out-of-state students. Students live both in residence halls and off campus, some with life partners and some with their families. Seventy-five percent of the students responding came out before attending college, and 34 percent said that being gay, lesbian, or bisexual affected their choosing UNC Greensboro. If information on the climate for gays, lesbians, and bisexuals at UNC Greensboro been available, 60 percent of the respondents would have gone elsewhere.

The respondents are involved in the gay, lesbian, and bisexual student group, which has an average membership of 30–50 students and sponsors dances, speakers, and safe-sex education. The group receives funding from the student government. In addition, students are active in the Outdoor Activity Club, College Democrats, International Students Association, orchestra, the Campus Activity Board, and Greek life. Most students date other UNC Greensboro students and state that some of their dating activity takes place on the campus. Off campus, students congregate in bars.

All of the students view coming out as the largest problem at UNC Greensboro, with the lack of role models and alcohol abuse following second.

Gay men's and lesbians' cultural contributions are not a part of regular courses, nor does the university offer courses on gay, lesbian, and bisexual issues. The university provides free, anonymous HIV testing, counseling for those who are HIV+ or have AIDS, and condoms free of charge. Both the Health Center and the student group provide safe-sex education.

Ninety-two percent of the respondents recommend UNC Greensboro to other gay, lesbian, and bisexual students.

University of North Florida • *Jacksonville, Florida*

Students define North Florida's position on gay, lesbian, and bisexual issues as somewhere between proactive and noncommittal. The university does not have a committee on gay, lesbian, and bisexual issues, nor is sexual orientation included in its affirmative action statement. North Florida does, however, provide counseling services for gay, lesbian, and bisexual students. Students do not know if housing for cohabitating couples is available. According to the students, the municipality in which the university is located does not have a civil rights law that includes sexual orientation.

Unanimously, students believe that homophobia is a serious problem on the campus. All of those responding report being victims of harassment. Moreover, all of the students have knowledge of hate crimes committed on the campus. The university maintains hate-crime statistics.

None of the students know how the North Florida administration reacts to hate crimes, but most do not feel supported by the university's security force. All students feel safe on the North Florida campus as gays, lesbians, and bisexuals, although some feel it would not be safe to be openly gay.

Gay, lesbian, and bisexual students between the ages of 23–42 responded to the survey. Students are juniors, seniors, and graduate students with SAT scores of 900 or higher and grade point averages of 2.5 and higher. Students have majors predominantly in computer science, political science, and education.

Two thirds of the students surveyed are openly gay on the campus; those who are not cite fear of reprisal as the primary reason. The majority are out to their parents but all are out to other family members. None of respondents are considered out-of-state students and all live off campus, some with their families. One third of the students responding came out before attending college and none said that being gay, lesbian, or bisexual affected their choosing North Florida. Furthermore, if information on the climate for gays, lesbians, and bisexuals at North Florida had been available, the respondents' choices would not have been different.

The respondents are starting a gay, lesbian, and bisexual student group that will have an initial membership of 15 students and will sponsor health education and support groups; the group hopes to receive funding from the student government. In addition, students are active in other organizations such as Students Against Rape and in the student government. One third of the students responding state that they date other North Florida students and that their dating activity typically takes place on campus. Off campus, students congregate in bars and religious organizations.

All of the students view the lack of role models and student organization as the largest problem at North Florida, with coming out following second.

Gay men's and lesbians' cultural contributions are not a part of regular courses, but the university does offer courses on gay, lesbian, and bisexual issues in the women's studies department. Students do not know if the university provides free, anonymous HIV testing or if counseling is available for those who are HIV+ or have AIDS. The university does, however, provide condoms free of charge. Both the Health Center and student groups provide safe-sex education.

Two thirds of the respondents recommend North Florida to other gay, lesbian, and bisexual students.

University of Oklahoma • *Norman, Oklahoma*

Students define Oklahoma's position on gay, lesbian, and bisexual issues as noncommittal. The university does not have a committee on gay, lesbian, and bisexual issues, and sexual orientation is not included in its affirmative action policy. In addition, counseling services are not provided for gay, lesbian, and bisexual students, nor is housing available for cohabiting couples. According to the students, the municipality in which the university is located does not have a civil rights law that includes sexual orientation.

Unanimously, students believe that homophobia is a serious problem on the campus. Those responding report being victims of harassment, hate mail, vandalism, and verbal abuse. Moreover, all of the students have knowledge of hate crimes committed on the campus, including assault. The student group maintains hate-crime statistics.

All of the students believe that Oklahoma does nothing in response to hate crimes, and all agree that the school's security force is not supportive. All of the students, however, feel safe on the campus as gays, lesbians, and bisexuals.

Gay, lesbian, and bisexual students between the ages of 22–23 responded to the survey. Students are seniors with SAT scores of 900

or higher and grade point averages of 3.0 or higher. Students have majors in the liberal arts.

All of the students are openly gay on the campus as well as to their parents and families. None are considered out-of-state students and all live off campus. All of the students responding came out before attending college, and none said that being gay, lesbian, or bisexual affected their choosing Oklahoma. If information on the climate for gays, lesbians, and bisexuals at Oklahoma had been available, all of the respondents would have chosen to go elsewhere.

The respondents are involved in the gay, lesbian, and bisexual student group, which has an average membership of 50 students and sponsors dances, speakers, safe-sex education, and Pride and National Coming Out Day activities. The group receives funding from the student government. The students date other Oklahoma students and state that their dating activity takes place off campus, where they congregate in bars.

All of the students view the lack of role models as the largest problem at Oklahoma, with coming out and substance abuse following second.

Although gay men's and lesbians' cultural contributions are not a part of regular courses, the university does offer courses on gay, lesbian, and bisexual issues in women's studies and human relations. The university does not provide free, anonymous HIV testing, counseling for those who are HIV+ or have AIDS, or condoms free of charge. Both the Health Center and the student group provide safe-sex education.

All of the respondents recommend Oklahoma to other gay, lesbian, and bisexual students.

University of the Pacific • *Stockton, California*

Students define University of the Pacific's position on gay, lesbian, and bisexual issues as noncommittal. Although the university does not have a committee on gay, lesbian, and bisexual issues, sexual orientation is included in its affirmative action statement, and counseling services are available for gay, lesbian, and bisexual students. Students do not know if housing for cohabitating couples is available, or if the municipality in which the university is located has a civil rights law that includes sexual orientation.

Unanimously, students believe strongly that homophobia is a serious problem on the campus. None of those responding report being victims of hate crimes, but all of the students have knowledge of hate crimes committed on the campus. Students do know who, if anyone, maintains hate-crime statistics.

Students do not know how the university reacts to hate crimes, but all agree that the university's security force is supportive. Consequently, all of the students feel safe on the campus as gays, lesbians, and bisexuals.

Gay, lesbian, and bisexual students between the ages of 22–29 responded to the survey. Students are seniors and graduate students with SAT scores of 1100 or higher and grade point averages of 3.5 and higher. Students have majors in the liberal arts and multicultural education.

All of the students surveyed are openly gay on the campus as well as to some family members. Most are considered out-of-state students and all live off campus. All of the students responding came out before attending college, and none said that being gay, lesbian, or bisexual affected their choosing Pacific. Furthermore, if information on the climate for gays, lesbians, and bisexuals at the University of the Pacific had been available, the respondents' choices would not have been different.

The respondents are involved in the gay, lesbian, and bisexual student group, which has an average membership of 30 students and sponsors dances, speakers, safe-sex education, and Pride and National Coming Out Day activities. The group receives funding from the student government. Students tend not to date other university students but some dating activity does take place on the campus. Off campus, students congregate in bars and cafes.

All of the students view the lack of role models as the largest problem at the university, with alcohol abuse and coming out following second.

Gay men's and lesbians' cultural contributions are not a part of regular courses, nor does the university offer courses on gay, lesbian, and bisexual issues. In addition, the university does not provide free, anonymous HIV testing, condoms, or counseling for those who are HIV+ or have AIDS. The student group provides safe-sex education.

All of the respondents recommend the University of the Pacific to other gay, lesbian, and bisexual students.

University of Pennsylvania • *Philadelphia, Pennsylvania*

Students define Penn's position on gay, lesbian, and bisexual issues as proactive. The university has a committee on gay, lesbian, and bisexual issues; sexual orientation is included in the university's affirmative action statement; and counseling services are available for gay, lesbian, and bisexual students. Graduate housing for cohabitating couples is available. According to the students, the municipality in which the university is located has a civil rights law that includes sexual orientation.

Unanimously, students strongly believe that homophobia is a serious problem on the campus. Those responding report being victims of verbal abuse, hate mail, harassment, and vandalism. Moreover, all of the students have knowledge of hate crimes committed on the campus, including assault. The university maintains hate-crime statistics.

All of the students believe that Penn takes action in response to these incidents. Some of the students point out that the university has taken a stand against ROTC discrimination. The majority of the respondents state that they feel supported by the university's security force. Consequently, most of the students feel safe on the Penn campus as gays, lesbians, and bisexuals.

Gay, lesbian, and bisexual students between the ages of 21–27 responded to the survey. Students are juniors, seniors, and graduate students with SAT scores of 1100 or higher and grade point averages of 3.5 and higher. Students have majors in business, nursing, social work, and psychology.

All of the students surveyed are openly gay on the campus as well as to their parents and families. Seventy-five percent are considered out-of-state students and all live off campus, some with life partners. Twenty-five percent of the students responding came out before attending college, and said that being gay, lesbian, or bisexual affected their choosing Penn. If information on the climate for gays, lesbians, and bisexuals at Penn had been available, the majority of the respondents' choices would not have been different.

The respondents are involved in the gay, lesbian, and bisexual student group, which has an average membership of 25–60 students and sponsors dances, speakers, safe-sex education, and Pride and National Coming Out Day activities. The group receives funding from the student government. The students date other Penn students and state that their dating activity takes place on the Penn campus. Off campus, students congregate in bars and at the community center.

All of the students view coming out as the largest problem at Penn, with the lack of role models and alcohol abuse following second.

Gay men's and lesbians' cultural contributions are a part of some regular courses, and the university also offers courses on gay, lesbian, and bisexual issues in history, women's studies, education, the social sciences, and communication. The university provides free, anonymous HIV testing, and counseling is available for those who are HIV+ or have AIDS. Condoms are available for a nominal charge. Both the Health Center and the student group provide safe-sex education.

All of the respondents recommend Penn to other gay, lesbian, and bisexual students. Students state that some classes are outstanding in the treatment of gay, lesbian, and bisexual issues. One student warns: "Beware of student apathy . . . this can be frustrating."

University of Pittsburgh • *Pittsburgh, Pennsylvania*

Students define Pittsburgh's position on gay, lesbian, and bisexual issues as noncommittal. Although the university does not have a committee on gay, lesbian, and bisexual issues, sexual orientation is included in its affirmative action policy. Counseling services are not provided for gay, lesbian, and bisexual students, nor is housing available for cohabitating couples. According to the students, the municipality in which the university is located does not have a civil rights law that includes sexual orientation.

Unanimously, students believe that homophobia is a serious problem on the campus. Those responding report being victims of verbal abuse. Moreover, all of the students have knowledge of hate crimes committed on the campus, including assault. Both the university and the student group maintain hate-crime statistics.

All of the students believe that Pittsburgh takes action in response to hate crimes, but that the university's security force is not supportive. All feel safe on the campus as gays, lesbians, and bisexuals.

Gay, lesbian, and bisexual students between the ages of 20–22 responded to the survey. Students are juniors with SAT scores of 1100 or higher and grade point averages of 2.0 or higher. Students have majors in the liberal arts.

All of the students are openly gay on the campus as well as to their parents and families. None are considered out-of-state students and all live off campus. All of the students responding came out before attending college, and some said that being gay, lesbian, or bisexual affected their choosing Pittsburgh. If information on the climate for gays, lesbians, and bisexuals at Pittsburgh had been available, all of the respondents would have chosen to go elsewhere.

The respondents are involved in the gay, lesbian, and bisexual student group, which has an average membership of 60–70 students and sponsors dances, speakers, safe-sex education, and Pride and National Coming Out Day activities. The group receives funding from the student government. In addition, students are active on the campus radio station. The students tend not to date other Pittsburgh students. Off campus, students congregate in bars.

All of the students view the lack of role models as the largest problem at Pittsburgh, with coming out and alcohol abuse following second.

Gay men's and lesbians' cultural contributions are not a part of regular courses, nor does the university offer courses on gay, lesbian, and bisexual issues. The university does not provide free, anonymous HIV testing or condoms. Counseling, however, is available for those who are HIV+ or have AIDS. The student group provides safe-sex education.

None of the respondents recommend Pittsburgh to other gay, lesbian, and bisexual students.

University of Rochester • *Rochester, New York*

Students define Rochester's position on gay, lesbian, and bisexual issues as noncommittal. Although the university does not have a committee on gay, lesbian, and bisexual issues, sexual orientation is included in its affirmative action policy. In addition, counseling services are available for gay, lesbian, and bisexual students. Housing for cohabitating couples is not available. According to the students, the municipality in which the university is located has a civil rights law that includes sexual orientation.

Unanimously, students believe that homophobia is a serious problem on the campus. Those responding report being victims of verbal abuse and harassment. Moreover, all of the students have knowledge of hate crimes committed on the campus. The student group maintains hate-crime statistics.

All of the students believe that Rochester takes action in response to hate crimes, but none agree that the university's security force is supportive. All of the students feel safe on the campus as gays, lesbians, and bisexuals.

Gay, lesbian, and bisexual students between the ages of 21–23 responded to the survey. Students are seniors with SAT scores of 1100 or higher and grade point averages of 3.0 or higher. Students have majors in the liberal arts and sciences.

All of the students are openly gay on the campus as well as to their parents and families. None are considered out-of-state students and all live off campus, some with life partners. All of the students responding came out before attending college, and none said that being gay, lesbian, or bisexual affected their choosing Rochester. Furthermore, if information on the climate for gays, lesbians, and bisexuals at Rochester had been available, the respondents' choices would not have been different.

The respondents are involved in the gay, lesbian, and bisexual student group, which has an average membership of 40 students and sponsors dances, speakers, safe-sex education, and Pride and National Coming Out Day activities. The group receives funding from the student government. In addition, students are active in athletics. The students tend not to date other Rochester students. Off campus, students congregate in bars.

All of the students view coming out as the largest problem at Rochester, with the lack of role models following second.

Although gay men's and lesbians' cultural contributions are not a part of regular courses, the university does offer courses on gay, lesbian, and bisexual issues in women's studies and philosophy. The university provides free, anonymous HIV testing and counseling for those who are HIV+ or have AIDS. Students do not know if condoms are provided. Both the Health Center and the student group provide safe-sex education.

All of the respondents recommend Rochester to other gay, lesbian, and bisexual students.

University of South Carolina • *Columbia, South Carolina*

Students define USC's position on gay, lesbian, and bisexual issues as noncommittal. The university does not have a committee on gay, lesbian, and bisexual issues, and sexual orientation is not included in its affirmative action policy. However, counseling services are available for gay, lesbian, and bisexual students. Housing for cohabitating couples is not available. According to the students, the municipality in which the university is located does not have a civil rights law that includes sexual orientation.

Unanimously, students believe that homophobia is a serious problem on the campus. Two thirds of those responding report being victims of harassment. Moreover, all of the students have knowledge of hate crimes committed on the campus, including assault. Students do not know who, if anyone, maintains hate-crime statistics.

Most of the students believe that USC takes action in response to hate crimes, but none agree that the university's security force is supportive. All of the students feel somewhat safe on the campus as gays, lesbians, and bisexuals.

Gay, lesbian, and bisexual students between the ages of 19–21 responded to the survey. Students are sophomores and juniors with SAT scores of 900 or higher and grade point averages of 2.5 or higher. Students have majors in elementary education, English, chemistry, and criminal justice.

Most of the students are openly gay on the campus. Those who are not cite fear of reprisal as the primary reason. All, however, are out to their parents and families. None are considered out-of-state students and all live off campus. All of the students responding came out before attending college, and none said that being gay, lesbian, or bisexual affected their choosing USC. Furthermore, if information on the climate for gays, lesbians, and bisexuals at USC had been available, the respondents' choices would not have been different.

The respondents are involved in the gay, lesbian, and bisexual student group, which has an average membership of 80–85 students and sponsors dances, speakers, safe-sex education, and Pride and National Coming Out Day activities. The group receives funding from the student government. In addition, students are active in the Program Union. The students date other USC students and state that some of their dating activity takes place on the campus. Off campus, students congregate in bars.

All of the students view coming out as the largest problem at USC, with the lack of role models and alcohol abuse following second.

Gay men's and lesbians' cultural contributions are not a part of regular courses, nor does the university offer courses on gay, lesbian, and bisexual issues. The university does not provide free, anonymous HIV testing. Students do not know if counseling is available for those who are HIV+ or have AIDS. Condoms, however, are provided free of charge. Both the Health Center and the student group provide safe-sex education.

Two thirds of the respondents do not recommend USC to other gay, lesbian, and bisexual students.

University of South Florida • *Tampa, Florida*

Of the students responding, two thirds define South Florida's position on gay, lesbian, and bisexual issues as proactive while one third view the university as noncommittal. Although the university has a committee on gay, lesbian, and bisexual issues, sexual orientation is not included in the university's affirmative action statement. South Florida does, however, provide counseling services for gay, lesbian, and bisexual students. Housing for cohabitating couples is not available. According to the students, the municipality in which the university is located has a civil rights law that includes sexual orientation.

One third of the students believe that homophobia is a serious problem on the campus, while two thirds do not. The same one third of those responding report being victims of verbal abuse. All of the students have knowledge of hate crimes committed on the campus, including assault. The university maintains hate-crime statistics.

One third of the students believe that South Florida takes action in response to these incidents; the remainder do not know how the administration reacts. All of the respondents feel supported by the university's security force. Consequently, all students feel safe on the South Florida campus as gays, lesbians, and bisexuals.

Gay, lesbian, and bisexual students between the ages of 19–25 responded to the survey. Students are sophomores, juniors, and seniors with SAT scores of 900 or higher and grade point averages of 2.5 and higher. Students have majors predominantly in education, psychology, and microbiology.

All of the students surveyed are openly gay on the campus as well as to their parents and families. None are considered out-of-state students. Two thirds live off campus, some with their families, and one third live in residence halls. One third of the students responding came out before attending college, but none said that being gay, lesbian, or bisexual affected their choosing South Florida. Furthermore, if information on the climate for gays, lesbians, and bisexuals at South Florida had been available, the respondents' choices would not have been different.

The respondents are involved in the gay, lesbian, and bisexual student group, which will have an initial membership of 30–50 students and sponsors dances, speakers, safe-sex education, and Pride and National Coming Out Day activities. The group receives funding from the student government. In addition, students are active in other organizations such as Student Radio and the University Chorus. Two thirds of the students responding state that they date other South Florida students; however, only one third of those state that their dating activity typically takes place on campus. One third have life partners attending the university. Off campus, students congregate in bars and religious organizations.

All of the students view coming out as the largest problem at South Florida, with alcohol and other substance abuse following second.

Although gay men's and lesbians' cultural contributions are a part of some regular courses, the university does not offer courses on gay, lesbian, and bisexual issues. The university does not provide free, anonymous HIV testing, but counseling is available for those who are HIV+ or have AIDS. The university also provides condoms free of charge. The Health Center and student groups provide safe-sex education.

All of the respondents recommend South Florida to other gay, lesbian, and bisexual students. One of the resident students commented that he is openly gay and has "received no harassment and a good amount of encouragement."

University of Southern California • *Los Angeles, California*

Students define USC's position on gay, lesbian, and bisexual issues as noncommittal. The university has a committee on gay, lesbian, and bisexual issues, but sexual orientation is not included in the university's affirmative action policy. Counseling services are provided for gay, lesbian, and bisexual students, but housing for cohabitating couples is not available. According to the students, the municipality in which the university is located has a civil rights law that includes sexual orientation.

Unanimously, students believe that homophobia is a serious problem on the campus, but none of those responding report being victims of hate crimes. Moreover, none of the students have knowledge of hate crimes committed on the campus. Students do not know who, if anyone, maintains hate-crime statistics.

All of the students believe that USC takes action in response to hate crimes, but none agree that the university's security force is supportive. All of the students feel safe on the campus as gays, lesbians, and bisexuals.

Gay, lesbian, and bisexual students between the ages of 22–28 responded to the survey. Students are seniors with SAT scores of 1100 or higher and grade point averages of 3.0 or higher. Students have majors in the liberal arts.

All of the students are openly gay on the campus as well as to their parents and families. None are considered out-of-state students and all live off campus. All of the students responding came out before attending college, and none said that being gay, lesbian, or bisexual affected their choosing USC. If information on the climate for gays, lesbians, and bisexuals at USC had been available, most of the respondents would have gone elsewhere.

The respondents are involved in the gay, lesbian, and bisexual student group, which has an average membership of 30 students and sponsors dances, speakers, safe-sex education, and Pride and National Coming Out Day activities. The group receives funding from the student government. In addition, students are active in the Student Senate. The students date other USC students and state that their dating activity takes place on the campus. Some have life partners attending USC. Off campus, students congregate in bars and local gyms.

All of the students view coming out as the largest problem at USC, with the lack of student organization and alcohol abuse following second.

Although gay men's and lesbians' cultural contributions are not a part of regular courses, the university does offer courses on gay, lesbian, and bisexual issues in English, history, and the social sciences. The university provides anonymous, but not free, HIV testing, and condoms are free of charge. Students do not know if counseling is available for those who are HIV+ or have AIDS. Both the Health Center and the student group provide safe-sex education.

All of the respondents recommend USC to other gay, lesbian, and bisexual students.

University of Southern Maine • *Portland, Maine*

Students vary defining Southern Maine's position on gay, lesbian, and bisexual issues: seventy percent say noncommittal; 20 percent say proactive; and 10 percent say negative. The university has a committee on gay, lesbian, and bisexual issues, and sexual orientation is included in the university's affirmative action policy. In addition, counseling services are available for gay, lesbian, and bisexual students. Housing for cohabitating couples is not available. According to the students, the municipality in which the university is located does not yet have a civil rights law that includes sexual orientation. The issue is currently under debate.

Unanimously, students believe strongly that homophobia is a serious problem on the campus. Those responding report being victims

of harassment, hate mail, vandalism, assault, and verbal abuse. Moreover, all of the students have knowledge of hate crimes committed on the campus. Both the university and the student group maintain hate-crime statistics.

All of the students believe that Southern Maine takes action in response to hate crimes. The majority of students agree that the university's security force is not supportive. Most of the students feel somewhat safe on the campus as gays, lesbians, and bisexuals.

Gay, lesbian, and bisexual students between the ages of 19–25 responded to the survey. Students are freshmen, sophomores, juniors, and seniors with SAT scores of 900 or higher and grade point averages of 2.0 or higher. Students have majors in history, English, women's studies, American studies, music education, art, and philosophy.

Eighty percent of the students are openly gay on the campus. Those who are not cite fear of reprisal as the primary reason. Seventy percent are out to their parents and families. None are considered out-of-state students. Forty percent live in residence halls; the rest live off campus, some with life partners. Forty percent of the students responding came out before attending college, and none said that being gay, lesbian, or bisexual affected their choosing Southern Maine. If information on the climate for gays, lesbians, and bisexuals at Southern Maine had been available, 40 percent of the respondents would have chosen to go elsewhere.

The respondents are involved in the gay, lesbian, and bisexual student group, which has an average membership of 10–20 students and sponsors dances, speakers, safe-sex education, and Pride and National Coming Out Day activities. The group receives funding from the student government. In addition, students are active in other organizations such as the Medieval Society, the Women's Center, the Student Senate, and the History Students' Association. The students date other Southern Maine students and state that some their dating activity takes place on the campus. Off campus, students congregate in bars, ACT-UP meetings, and in private homes and apartments.

All of the students view coming out as the largest problem at Southern Maine, with the lack of role models and alcohol abuse following second.

Although gay men's and lesbians' cultural contributions are not a

part of regular courses, the university does offer courses on gay, lesbian, and bisexual issues in art, history, philosophy, English, women's studies, and the social sciences. The university does not provide free, anonymous HIV testing, but counseling is available for those who are HIV+ or have AIDS. Condoms are free of charge. Both the Health Center and the student group provide safe-sex education.

Seventy percent of the respondents recommend Southern Maine to other gay, lesbian, and bisexual students.

University of Texas, Austin • *Austin, Texas*

Students define Austin's position on gay, lesbian, and bisexual issues as noncommittal. Although the university does not have a committee on gay, lesbian, and bisexual issues, sexual orientation is included in its affirmative action policy. In addition, counseling services are available for gay, lesbian, and bisexual students. Housing for cohabitating couples is not available. According to the students, the municipality in which the university is located has a civil rights law that includes sexual orientation.

Unanimously, students believe that homophobia is a serious problem on the campus. Those responding report being victims of verbal abuse, hate mail, and vandalism. Moreover, all of the students have knowledge of hate crimes committed on the campus. Students do not know who, if anyone, maintains hate-crime statistics.

Students do not know how Austin reacts to hate crimes, but all agree that the university's security force is not supportive. All of the students feel safe on the campus as gays, lesbians, and bisexuals.

Gay, lesbian, and bisexual students between the ages of 20–22 responded to the survey. Students are juniors, seniors, and graduate students with SAT scores of 1100 or higher and grade point averages of 3.5 or higher. Students have majors in the liberal arts.

All of the students are openly gay on the campus and most are out to their parents and families. None are considered out-of-state students and all live off campus. All of the students responding came out before attending college, and none said that being gay, lesbian, or bisexual affected their choosing Austin. Furthermore, if information on the climate for gays, lesbians, and bisexuals at Austin had been available, the respondents' choices would not have been different.

The respondents are involved in the gay, lesbian, and bisexual student group, which has an average membership of 50–100 students and sponsors dances, speakers, safe-sex education, and Pride and National Coming Out Day activities. The group receives funding from the student government. In addition, students are active in the Council of Graduate Students. The students date other Austin students and state that their dating activity takes place on the campus. Off campus, students congregate in bars, book stores, and cafes.

All of the students view the lack of student organization as the largest problem at Austin, with coming out and the lack of role models following second.

Gay men's and lesbians' cultural contributions are a part of regular courses. The university also offers courses on gay, lesbian, and bisexual issues in English. The university does not provide free, anonymous HIV testing or counseling for those who are HIV+ or have AIDS. Condoms, however, are available free of charge. Both the Health Center and the student group provide safe-sex education.

All of the respondents recommend Austin to other gay, lesbian, and bisexual students.

University of Vermont • *Burlington, Vermont*

Students define UVM's position on gay, lesbian, and bisexual issues as proactive. The university has a committee on gay, lesbian, and bisexual issues; sexual orientation is included in the university's affirmative action statement; and counseling services are available for gay, lesbian, and bisexual students. Students do not know if housing for cohabitating couples is available. According to the students, the municipality in which the university is located has a civil rights law that includes sexual orientation.

Seventy-five percent of the students believe that homophobia is a serious problem on the campus. Fifty percent of those responding report being victims of vandalism and harassment. Moreover, all of the students have knowledge of hate crimes committed on the campus, including assault. The university maintains hate-crime statistics.

All of the students believe that UVM takes action in response to these incidents, and all of the respondents state that they feel supported by the university's security force. Consequently, all of the students feel safe on the campus as gays, lesbians, and bisexuals.

Gay, lesbian, and bisexual students between the ages of 20–23 responded to the survey. Students are juniors, seniors, and graduate students with SAT scores of 1100 or higher and grade point averages of 2.5 and higher. Students have majors in mathematics, music theory and composition, history, and environmental studies.

All of the students surveyed are openly gay on the campus as well as to their parents and families. Half are considered out-of-state students and live in residence halls. The remaining students live off campus. Fifty percent of the students responding came out before attending the university, and said that being gay, lesbian, or bisexual affected their choosing UVM. If information on the climate for gays, lesbians, and bisexuals at UVM had been available, the respondents' choices would not have been different.

The respondents are involved in the gay, lesbian, and bisexual student group, which has an average membership of 10–15 students and sponsors dances, speakers, safe-sex education, and Pride and National Coming Out Day activities. The group receives funding from the student government. Twenty-five percent of the respondents are into the leather scene. Additionally, students are active in other organizations such as the Tae Kwan Do Club, Alcohol and Drug Education, music ensembles, the German House, and Sign Language House. The majority of students date other UVM students and state that their dating activity takes place on the Vermont campus. Off campus, students congregate in bars.

All of the students view coming out as the largest problem at UVM, with alcohol abuse and the lack of role models following second.

Although gay men's and lesbians' cultural contributions are not a part of some regular courses, and the university offers courses on gay, lesbian, and bisexual issues in women's studies. The university provides free, anonymous HIV testing, and counseling is available for those who are HIV+ or have AIDS. Condoms are available for a nominal charge. Both the Health Center and the student group provide safe-sex education.

All of the respondents recommend UVM to other gay, lesbian, and bisexual students.

University of Virginia, School of Law • *Charlottesville, Virginia*

Students define UVA Law School's position on gay, lesbian, and bisexual issues somewhere between proactive and noncommittal, depending on the issue. The university does not have a committee on gay, lesbian, and bisexual issues, but sexual orientation is included in its affirmative action policy. In addition, counseling services are available for gay, lesbian, and bisexual students. Housing for cohabitating couples is not available. According to the students, the municipality in which the university is located does not have a civil rights law that includes sexual orientation.

Unanimously, students believe that homophobia is a serious problem on the campus. None of those responding report being victims of verbal abuse, but all of the students have knowledge of hate crimes committed on the campus including assault. Students do not know who, if anyone, maintains hate-crime statistics.

All of students believe that UVA takes action in response to hate crimes and agree that the university's security force is supportive. All of the students feel safe on the campus as gays, lesbians, and bisexuals.

Gay, lesbian, and bisexual students between the ages of 25–27 responded to the survey. Students are Juris Doctor candidates with grade point averages of 3.0 or higher.

All of the students are openly gay on the campus as well as to their parents and families. Most are considered out-of-state students and all live off campus. All of the students responding came out before attending college, and none said that being gay, lesbian, or bisexual affected their choosing UVA. Furthermore, if information on the climate for gays, lesbians, and bisexuals at UVA had been available, the respondents' choices would not have been different.

The respondents are involved in the gay, lesbian, and bisexual student group, which has an average membership of 20 students and sponsors dances, speakers, safe-sex education, and Pride and National Coming Out Day activities. The group receives funding from the student government. In addition, students are active in various law associations. The students date other UVA students and state that their dating activity takes place on the campus. Off campus, students congregate in bars and religious organizations.

All of the students view coming out as the largest problem at UVA, with the lack of role models and student organization following second.

Although gay men's and lesbians' cultural contributions are not a part of regular courses, the university does offer courses on gay, lesbian, and bisexual issues in psychology. Students do not know if the university provides free, anonymous HIV testing, but counseling for those who are HIV+ or have AIDS is available, and condoms are provided free of charge. Both the Health Center and the student group provide safe-sex education.

All of the respondents recommend UVA Law School to other gay, lesbian, and bisexual students.

University of Wisconsin, Eau Claire • *Eau Claire, Wisconsin*

Students define Wisconsin's position on gay, lesbian, and bisexual issues as proactive. Although the university does not have a committee on gay, lesbian, and bisexual issues, sexual orientation is included in its affirmative action policy. In addition, counseling services are available for gay, lesbian, and bisexual students. Housing for cohabitating couples is not available. According to the students, the municipality in which the university is located has a civil rights law that includes sexual orientation.

Unanimously, students believe that homophobia is a serious problem on the campus. Those responding report being victims of harassment and verbal abuse. Moreover, all of the students have knowledge of hate crimes committed on the campus, including assault. Both the university and the student group maintain hate-crime statistics.

All of the students believe that Wisconsin takes action in response to hate crimes and agree that the university's security force is supportive. Two thirds of the students do not feel safe on the campus as gays, lesbians, and bisexuals.

Gay, lesbian, and bisexual students between the ages of 18–20 responded to the survey. Students are freshmen, sophomores, and juniors with SAT scores of 900 or higher and grade point averages of 3.0 or higher. Students have majors in business administration, art, and mathematics.

All of the students are openly gay on the campus, and most are out to their parents and families. Half are considered out-of-state students. Two thirds of the students live in residence halls. All of the students responding came out before attending college, and none said that being gay, lesbian, or bisexual affected their choosing Wisconsin. If information on the climate for gays, lesbians, and bisexuals at Wisconsin had been available, one third of the respondents would have made a different choice.

The respondents are involved in the gay, lesbian, and bisexual student group, which has an average membership of 40–45 students and sponsors dances, speakers, safe-sex education, and Pride and National Coming Out Day activities. The group receives funding from the student government. In addition, students are active in other organizations such as the Student Senate, Art Students' Association, and the Scandinavian Club. Most students date other Wisconsin students and state that their dating activity takes place on the campus. Off campus, students congregate in bars.

All of the students view coming out as the largest problem at Wisconsin, with the lack of role models following second.

Gay men's and lesbians' cultural contributions are not a part of regular courses, nor does the university offer courses on gay, lesbian, and bisexual issues. The university does provide free, anonymous HIV testing and counseling for those who are HIV+ or have AIDS. Condoms are not provided. Both the Health Center and the student group provide safe-sex education.

Two thirds of the respondents recommend Wisconsin to other gay, lesbian, and bisexual students.

Virginia Polytechnic Institute and State University •
Blacksburg, Virginia

Students define Virginia Tech's position on gay, lesbian, and bisexual issues as noncommittal. Although the school does not have a committee on gay, lesbian, and bisexual issues, sexual orientation is included in its affirmative action policy. In addition, counseling services are available for gay, lesbian, and bisexual students, as is graduate housing for cohabitating couples. According to the students, the municipality in which the school is located does not have a civil rights law that includes sexual orientation.

Unanimously, students believe that homophobia is a serious problem on the campus. Those responding report being victims of verbal abuse. Moreover, all of the students have knowledge of hate crimes committed on the campus, including assault. Both the school and the student group maintain hate-crime statistics.

All of the students believe that Virginia Tech takes action in response to hate crimes. Two thirds say that the school's security force is supportive. All of the students feel relatively safe on the campus as gays, lesbians, and bisexuals.

Gay, lesbian, and bisexual students between the ages of 18–22 responded to the survey. Students are sophomores and seniors with SAT scores 900 or higher and grade point averages of 1.99 or higher. Students have majors in the liberal arts and sciences, poultry science, English, and women's studies.

All of the students are openly gay on the campus as well as to some family members. Two thirds are out to their parents. None are considered out-of-state students and most live off campus. One third of the students live in residence halls. All of the students responding came out before attending college, and none said that being gay, lesbian, or bisexual affected their choosing Virginia Tech. However, if information on the climate for gays, lesbians, and bisexuals at Virginia Tech had been available, one third of the respondents would have chosen to go elsewhere.

The respondents are involved in the gay, lesbian, and bisexual student group, which has an average membership of 50 students and sponsors dances, speakers, safe-sex education, and Pride and National Coming Out Day activities. The group receives funding from the student government. In addition, students are active in Our Choice, MAPS, the Poultry Science Association, the Pre-Vet Club, and Greek-letter organizations. The students date other Virginia Tech students and state that their dating activity takes place on the campus. Some students have life partners attending the school. Off campus, students congregate in bars and at local restaurants.

All of the students view coming out as the largest problem at Virginia Tech, with the lack of role models and alcohol abuse following second.

Although gay men's and lesbians' cultural contributions are not a part of regular courses, the school does offer courses on gay, lesbian, and bisexual issues in English, women's studies, and the social sciences. The school does not provide HIV testing, counseling for those who are HIV+ or have AIDS, or condoms. Both the Health Center and the student group provide safe-sex education.

All of the respondents recommend Virginia Tech to other gay, lesbian, and bisexual students "if they become active in the gay community. We have a fairly close group and participate in many activities together."

Washington University, St. Louis • *St. Louis, Missouri*

Of the students responding, two thirds define Washington's position on gay, lesbian, and bisexual issues as noncommittal, while the remaining third view the administration as proactive. Although the university does not have a committee on gay, lesbian, and bisexual issues, sexual orientation is included in its affirmative action statement, and counseling services are available for gay, lesbian, and bisexual students. Housing for cohabitating couples is not available. According to the students, the municipality in which the university is located does not have a civil rights law that includes sexual orientation.

Unanimously, students believe that homophobia is a serious problem on the campus. Those responding report being victims of verbal abuse and harassment. Moreover, all of the students have knowledge of hate crimes committed on the campus. The university maintains hate-crime statistics.

The majority of the students believe that Washington takes action in response to these incidents. All of the students, however, feel strongly that the university's security force is not supportive. One student commented that "a friend was verbally harassed by some males who were presumably fraternity brothers. When he reported the incident to campus police, the officer laughed and wanted to avoid pursuing the matter." Consequently, students feel marginally safe on the Washington campus as gays, lesbians, and bisexuals.

Gay, lesbian, and bisexual students between the ages of 20–23 responded to the survey. Students are sophomores and seniors with SAT scores of 1100 or higher and grade point averages of 2.5 and higher. Students have majors in business administration, finance, and engineering.

All of the students surveyed are openly gay on the campus as well as to family members. A few are not out to their parents. All are considered out-of-state students and live in residence halls. Two thirds of the students responding did not come out before attending university, and said that being gay, lesbian, or bisexual did not affect their choosing Washington. However, if information on the climate for gays, lesbians, and bisexuals at Washington had been available, two thirds of the respondents would have made a different choice.

The respondents are involved in the gay, lesbian, and bisexual student group, which has an average membership of 20–30 students and sponsors speakers, safe-sex education, and Pride and National Coming Out Day activities. The group receives funding from the student government. In addition, students are active in other organizations such as the Business School Alliance, Syzygy, and various service organizations. The students date other Washington students, and some state that their dating activity takes place on the Washington campus. Off campus, students congregate in bars, religious organizations, the bookstore, and in private homes and apartments.

All of the students view coming out as the largest problem at Washington, with the lack of role models and alcohol abuse following second.

Although gay men's and lesbians' cultural contributions are not a part of regular courses, the university does offer courses on gay, lesbian, and bisexual issues in the social sciences and women's studies. The university provides free, confidential HIV testing and counseling for those who are HIV+ or have AIDS. Condoms are not provided free of charge. Both the Health Center and the student group provide safe-sex education.

All of the respondents recommend Washington to other gay, lesbian, and bisexual students, some with reservation.

Wellesley College • *Wellesley, Massachusetts*

Students define Wellesley's position on gay, lesbian, and bisexual issues as noncommittal. Although the college does not have a committee on gay, lesbian, and bisexual issues, sexual orientation is included in its affirmative action policy. In addition, counseling services are available for lesbian and bisexual students; housing for cohabitating couples is not available. Students do not know if the municipality in which the college is located has a civil rights law that includes sexual orientation.

Unanimously, students believe that homophobia is a serious problem on the campus. Those responding report being victims of verbal abuse. Moreover, all of the students have knowledge of various hate crimes committed on the campus, except for assault. The college maintains hate-crime statistics.

Half of students believe that Wellesley takes action in response to hate crimes, and half believe that the administration does nothing in response. However, none of the students feel supported by the college's security force. Three quarters of the students feel safe on the campus as lesbians and bisexuals.

Lesbian and bisexual students between the ages of 21–22 responded to the survey. Students are juniors and seniors with SAT scores of 1100 or higher and grade point averages of 3.5 or higher. Students have majors in biochemistry, women's studies, art, philosophy, and Third World studies.

All of the students are openly gay on the campus and to their families, and at least one is open to her parents. None are considered out-of-state students and all live in residence halls. None of the students responding came out before attending college, and none said that being lesbian or bisexual affected their choosing Wellesley. Furthermore, if information on the climate for lesbians and bisexuals at Wellesley had been available, the respondents' choices would not have been different.

The respondents are involved in the lesbian and bisexual student group, which has an average membership of 50 students and sponsors dances, speakers, safe-sex education, and Pride and National Coming Out Day activities. The group receives funding from the student government. Additionally, students are active in the Feminist Coop. Seventy-five percent of the students date other Wellesley students and 50 percent of those state that their dating activity takes place on the campus. Off campus, students congregate in bars.

All of the students view the lack of student organization as the largest problem at Wellesley, with the lack of role models and coming out following second.

Although gay men's and lesbians' cultural contributions are not a part of regular courses, the college does offer courses on gay, lesbian, and bisexual issues in women's studies. The college provides free, anonymous HIV testing, counseling for those who are HIV+ or have AIDS, and condoms. Both the Health Center and the student group provide safe-sex education.

All of the respondents recommend Wellesley to other lesbian and bisexual students. One student commented that "although not ideal, Wellesley is better than many schools for lesbians and bisexuals." The school has a coordinator for sexuality issues and two professional heads of house who are openly lesbian. The student organization is beginning to meet with gay, lesbian, and bisexual faculty and staff.

Wesleyan University • *Middletown, Connecticut*

Students define Wesleyan's position on gay, lesbian, and bisexual issues as noncommittal, although some say it leans toward being proactive. The university has a committee on gay, lesbian, and bisexual issues, and sexual orientation is included in the university's affirmative action policy. In addition, counseling services are available for gay, lesbian, and bisexual students. Housing for cohabitating couples is not available. According to the students, the municipality in which the university is located has a civil rights law that includes sexual orientation.

Unanimously, students believe that homophobia is a serious problem on the campus. Half of those responding report being victims of verbal abuse. Moreover, all of the students have knowledge of hate crimes committed on the campus, including assault. Students do not know who, if anyone, maintains hate-crime statistics.

Most of the students believe that Wesleyan does nothing in response to hate crimes, but most agree that the university's security force is supportive. Consequently, most of the students usually feel safe on the campus as gays, lesbians, and bisexuals.

Gay, lesbian, and bisexual students between the ages of 19–22 responded to the survey. Students are freshmen, sophomores, and seniors with SAT scores of 1100 or higher and grade point averages of 3.5 or higher. Students have majors in the liberal arts.

All of the students are openly gay on the campus as well as to their parents and families. All are considered out-of-state students and live both in residence halls and off campus. Fifty percent of the students responding came out before attending college, and said that being gay, lesbian, or bisexual affected their choosing Wesleyan. If information on the climate for gays, lesbians, and bisexuals at Wesleyan had been available, the respondents' choices would not have been different.

The respondents are involved in the gay, lesbian, and bisexual student group, which has an average membership of 130–150 students (though the meetings are small) and sponsors dances, speakers, safe-sex education, and Pride and National Coming Out Day activities. The group receives funding from the student government. A small number of students are active in the leather scene. The students date other Wesleyan students and state that their dating activity takes place on the campus. Off campus, students congregate in private homes and apartments.

All of the students view the lack of student organization as the largest problem at Wesleyan, with the lack of role models and coming out following second.

Gay men's and lesbians' cultural contributions are a part of some regular courses (depending on the professor), and the university offers courses on gay, lesbian, and bisexual issues in English, women's studies, history, religion, and the social sciences. The university provides free, confidential HIV testing, and condoms are available for a nominal fee. Counseling for those who are HIV+ or have AIDS is not available. Both the Health Center and the student group provide safe-sex education.

All of the respondents recommend Wesleyan to other gay, lesbian, and bisexual students, with one student commenting that the school is "not perfect but about as good as they get."

West Chester University • *West Chester, Pennsylvania*

Students define West Chester's position on gay, lesbian, and bisexual issues as noncommittal. Although the university does not have a committee on gay, lesbian, and bisexual issues, sexual orientation is included in its affirmative action policy. In addition, counseling services are available for gay, lesbian, and bisexual students. Housing for cohabitating couples is not available. According to the students, the municipality in which the university is located does not have a civil rights law that includes sexual orientation.

Unanimously, students believe that homophobia is a serious problem on the campus. Those responding report being victims of hate mail, vandalism, harassment, and verbal abuse. Moreover, all of the students have knowledge of hate crimes committed on the campus. The student group maintains hate-crime statistics.

All of the students believe that West Chester takes action in response to hate crimes, but none agree that the university's security force is supportive. All feel somewhat safe on the campus as gays, lesbians, and bisexuals.

Gay, lesbian, and bisexual students between the ages of 22–35 responded to the survey. Students are seniors with SAT scores of 1100 or higher and grade point averages of 2.5 or higher. Students have majors in the liberal arts and business administration.

All of the students are openly gay on the campus as well as to their parents and families. None are considered out-of-state students and all live off campus, some with life partners. Few of the students responding came out before attending college, and none said that being gay, lesbian, or bisexual affected their choosing West Chester. However, if information on the climate for gays, lesbians, and bisexuals at West Chester had been available, all of the respondents would have chosen to go elsewhere.

The respondents are involved in the gay, lesbian, and bisexual student group, which has an average membership of 40 students and sponsors dances, safe-sex education, and Pride and National Coming Out Day activities. The group receives funding from the student government. In addition, students are active in the student government. The students date other West Chester students and state that their dating activity takes place on the campus.

All of the students view coming out as the largest problem at West Chester, with the lack of role models and alcohol abuse following second.

Gay men's and lesbians' cultural contributions are not a part of regular courses, nor does the university offer courses on gay, lesbian, and bisexual issues. The university does provide free, anonymous HIV testing, counseling for those who are HIV+ or have AIDS, and condoms free of charge. Both the Health Center and the student group provide safe-sex education.

All of the respondents recommend West Chester to other gay, lesbian, and bisexual students.

Western Michigan University • *Kalamazoo, Michigan*

Students define Western Michigan's position on gay, lesbian, and bisexual issues somewhere between proactive and noncommittal. Although the university does not have a committee on gay, lesbian, and bisexual issues, sexual orientation is included in its affirmative action policy. In addition, counseling services are available for gay, lesbian, and bisexual students. Housing for cohabitating couples is not available. According to the students, the municipality in which the university is located does not have a civil rights law that includes sexual orientation.

Unanimously, students believe that homophobia is not a serious problem on the campus. None of those responding report being victims of hate crimes. However, all of the students have knowledge of hate crimes committed on the campus. No one maintains hate-crime statistics.

All of the students believe that Western Michigan does nothing in response to hate crimes, but all agree that the University's security force is supportive. All of the students feel safe on the campus as gays, lesbians, and bisexuals.

Gay, lesbian, and bisexual students between the ages of 23–27 responded to the survey. Students are juniors, seniors, and graduate students with SAT scores of 1100 or higher and grade point averages of 3.5 or higher. Students have majors in the liberal arts and sciences.

All of the students are openly gay on the campus and most are out to their parents and families. None are considered out-of-state students and all live off campus, some with life partners. The majority of the students responding came out before attending college, and none said that being gays, lesbians, or bisexuals affected their choosing Western Michigan. But if information on the climate for gays, lesbians, and bisexuals at Western Michigan had been available, most of the respondents would have made a different choice.

The respondents are involved in the gay, lesbian, and bisexual student group, which has an average membership of 20–25 students and sponsors dances, speakers, safe-sex education, and Pride and National Coming Out Day activities. The group receives funding from the student government. In addition, students are active in other organizations such as the psychology club, the philosophy club, and the biology and science club. The students date other Western Michigan students and state that their dating activity takes place on the campus. Some have life partners attending the university. Off campus, students congregate in bars, religious organizations, and in private homes and apartments.

All of the students view coming out as the largest problem at Western Michigan, with the lack of role models and student organization following second.

Although gay men's and lesbians' cultural contributions are not a part of regular courses, the university does offer courses on gay, lesbian, and bisexual issues in psychology. The university does not provide free, anonymous HIV testing. Students do not know if counseling is available for those who are HIV+ or have AIDS. Condoms are provided free of charge. Both the Health Center and the student group provide safe-sex education.

All of the respondents recommend Western Michigan to other gay, lesbian, and bisexual students.

Wheaton College • *Norton, Massachusetts*

Students define Wheaton's position on gay, lesbian, and bisexual issues as somewhere between proactive and noncommittal. The college has a committee on gay, lesbian, and bisexual issues, and sexual orientation is included in the college's affirmative action policy. In addition, counseling services are available for gay, lesbian, and bisexual students. Housing for cohabitating couples is not available. According to the students, the municipality in which the college is located has a civil rights law that includes sexual orientation.

Most students believe that homophobia is a serious problem on the campus. Twenty percent of those responding report being victims of vandalism. Moreover, 80 percent of the students have knowledge of hate crimes committed on the campus, including assault. The college maintains hate-crime statistics.

All of the students believe that Wheaton takes action in response to hate crimes. Sixty percent, however, do not agree that the college's security force is supportive. Nearly 60 percent of the students feel safe on the campus as gays, lesbians, and bisexuals.

Gay, lesbian, and bisexual students between the ages of 19–24 responded to the survey. Students are freshmen, sophomores, juniors, and seniors with SAT scores of 900 or higher and grade point averages of 2.5 or higher. Students have majors in psychology, biochemistry, and anthropology.

The majority of the students are openly gay on the campus. Those who are not cite fear of reprisal as the primary reason. The majority, however, are not out to their parents and families. Eighty percent are considered out-of-state students. Students live both in residence halls and off campus. Eighty percent of the students responding came out before attending college, and none said that being gay, lesbian, or bisexual affected their choosing Wheaton. If information on the climate for gays, lesbians, and bisexuals at Wheaton had been available, 60 percent of the respondents would have chosen to go elsewhere.

The respondents are involved in the gay, lesbian, and bisexual student group, which has an average membership of 8–20 students and sponsors speakers, safe-sex education, and Pride and National Coming Out Day activities. The group receives funding from the student government. In addition, students are active in other organizations such as the equestrian team, the Children's Assault Prevention Program, the Asian Student Association, singing groups, and athletics. Most of the students date other Wheaton students and state that their dating activity takes place on the campus.

All of the students view coming out as the largest problem at Wheaton, with the lack of role models and student organization following second.

Gay men's and lesbians' cultural contributions are a part of some regular courses. The college also offers courses on gay, lesbian, and bisexual issues in women's studies and in the social sciences. The college provides free, anonymous HIV testing, but does not provide counseling for those who are HIV+ or have AIDS, nor condoms free of charge. Both the Health Center and the student group provide safe-sex education.

All of the respondents recommend Wheaton to other gay, lesbian, and bisexual students.

Whitman College • *Walla Walla, Washington*

Students define Whitman's position on gay, lesbian, and bisexual issues as noncommittal. The college has a committee on gay, lesbian, and bisexual issues, and sexual orientation is included in the college's affirmative action policy. In addition, counseling services are available for gay, lesbian, and bisexual students. Students do not know if housing for cohabitating couples is available. According to the students, the municipality in which the college is located has a civil rights law that includes sexual orientation.

Unanimously, students believe strongly that homophobia is a serious problem on the campus. None of those responding report being victims of hate crimes. However, all of the students have knowledge of hate crimes committed on the campus. The student group maintains hate-crime statistics.

Students do not know how Whitman reacts to hate crimes. All agree, however, that the college's security force is not supportive, and none of the students feel safe on the campus as gays, lesbians, and bisexuals.

Gay, lesbian, and bisexual students between the ages of 18–20 responded to the survey. Students are freshmen, sophomores, and juniors with SAT scores of 1100 or higher and grade point averages of 3.5 or higher. Students have majors in the liberal arts and theater.

Most of the students are not openly gay on the campus, citing fear of reprisal as the primary reason. None are out to their parents and families. Most are considered out-of-state students and all live off campus. All of the students responding came out before attending college and said that being gay, lesbian, or bisexual affected their choosing Whitman. But if information on the climate for gays, lesbians, and bisexuals at Whitman had been available, most of the respondents would have made a different choice.

The respondents are involved in the gay, lesbian, and bisexual student group, which has an average membership of 15 students and sponsors dances, speakers, safe-sex education, and Pride and National Coming Out Day activities. The group receives no funding from the student government. The students date other Whitman students and state that their dating activity takes place on the campus.

All of the students view coming out as the largest problem at Whitman.

Although gay men's and lesbians' cultural contributions are not a part of regular courses, the college does offer courses on gay, lesbian, and bisexual issues in history, art, education, English, women's studies, and the social sciences. Students do not know if the college provides free, anonymous HIV testing, counseling for those who are HIV+ or have AIDS, or condoms free of charge. Both the Health Center and the student group provide safe-sex education.

None of the respondents recommend Whitman to other gay, lesbian, and bisexual students.

Williams College • *Williamstown, Massachusetts*

Students define Williams's position on gay, lesbian, and bisexual issues as somewhere between proactive and noncommittal. Although the college does not have a committee on gay, lesbian, and bisexual issues, sexual orientation is included in its affirmative action policy. Counseling services are not available for gay, lesbian, and bisexual students, nor is housing available for cohabitating couples. Students do not know if the municipality in which the college is located has a civil rights law that includes sexual orientation.

Unanimously, students believe that homophobia is a serious problem on the campus. The majority of those responding report being victims of verbal abuse and harassment. Moreover, all of the students have knowledge of hate crimes committed on the campus. No one maintains hate-crime statistics.

Although most hate crimes are not reported, the students believe that the college takes action in response to reported incidents. In addition, all of the students feel that the college's security force is supportive. Consequently, all of the students feel safe on the campus as gays, lesbians, and bisexuals.

Gay, lesbian, and bisexual students between the ages of 18–22 responded to the survey. Students are freshmen, sophomores, juniors, and seniors with SAT scores of 1100 or higher and grade point averages of 3.0 or higher. Students have majors in the liberal arts.

The majority of the students are openly gay on the campus and slightly more than half are out to their parents and families. The majority are considered out-of-state students and all live in residence halls. Less than half of the students responding came out before attending college, and none said that being gay, lesbian, or bisexual affected their choosing Williams. Furthermore, if information on the climate for gays, lesbians, and bisexuals at Williams had been available, the respondents' choices would not have been different.

The respondents are involved in at least one of the six gay, lesbian, and bisexual student groups, which have combined average memberships of over 100 students. The groups sponsor dances, speakers, safe-sex education, and Pride and National Coming Out Day activities. Less than 5 percent of the students identify themselves as cross dressers, although the practice is accepted within the community. In addition, students are also active in other student organizations such as student government, minority organizations, women's groups, and in environmental and theater groups. The students date other Williams students and state that their dating activity typically takes place on the campus.

All of the students view coming out as the largest problem at Williams.

Gay men's and lesbians' cultural contributions are a part of regular courses. In addition, the college offers courses on gay, lesbian, and bisexual issues in English, women's studies, political science, and the social sciences. The college provides free, anonymous HIV testing, counseling services for those who are HIV+ or have AIDS, and condoms free of charge. A peer advisory group provides safe-sex education.

The majority of the respondents recommend Williams to other

gay, lesbian, and bisexual students, saying that the school is gay-affirmative. "The community is very active, and gay, lesbian, and bisexual students are becoming increasingly more comfortable on campus as the student population and the school itself continue to change."

Appendix: Student Profiles

I Demographic Information

39% female, 61% male

82% white; 5% African American; 3.5% Hispanic; 2.5% Native American; 1% other

61% have SATS of 1100 or above

72% have GPAS of 3.0 or higher (4-point scale)

11% freshman; 19% sophomores; 22% juniors; 28% seniors; 20% graduate and professional students

83% are openly gay, lesbian, or bisexual (84% of males, 81% of females)

95% of those not open cited fear of reprisal as reason for not being open

59% are open to families and friends; 8% describe themselves as closeted

42% live off campus; 38% live in residence halls; 10% live with partners; 9% live with their families

6.1% belong to fraternities/sororities

5.6% are members of athletic teams

59% were self-acknowledged before college (64% of males, 50% of females)

29.6% sexual orientation influenced choice of college/graduate/professional school

4% describe themselves as cross dressers

5.5% describe themselves as into the leather scene

55% date other students, 46% say activity takes place on campus

28% partners attend same school

II Victimization

Students identified themselves as victims of the following on campus:
11% hate mail
48% verbal abuse
11% physical assault
33% harassment
18% vandalism/property defacement

Students had direct knowledge of victimization of other lesbian, gay, and bisexual students at an even higher rate:
56% hate mail
82% verbal abuse
43% physical assault
76% harassment
63% vandalism/property defacement

40% overall do not feel completely safe on campus:
57% believe school does nothing in response to hate crimes on campus
40% feel police/security force are not supportive
84% believe homophobia to be a serious problem on their campuses

99% have been victims or have direct knowledge of friends on their campuses who have been victimized because of sexual orientation

III Health Issues

26% attempted suicide at least once
8% strong suicide ideation
40% have been tested for HIV infection

2.2% are HIV positive

0% report being symptomatic for AIDS

98% are educated about safe-sex practices

45% cite substance abuse as a major problem facing gays, lesbians, and bisexuals on campus

70% have access to safe-sex education on campus

IV Other Factors

31% left school for one semester or longer

33.4% stopped out/transferred because of coming out/harassment issues prior to coming out

37% report sexual orientation is part of their school's nondiscrimination statement

29% know about campus committees on lesbian, gay, bisexual issues

35% know of curricula specific to or inclusive of bisexual, lesbian, and gay issues

67% report school's position on gay, lesbian, and bisexual issues as negative or noncommittal

62% cite lack of role models as one of the largest problems facing gay, lesbian, and bisexual students on campus

40% state if had information on the climate for gay, lesbian, or bisexual students had been available, their choice of school would have been different

V Recommendations

75% recommend their campuses to other gays, lesbians, and bisexuals with this breakdown for the recommendation:

37% felt more gay, lesbian, or bisexual students would help sensitize their campuses

28% felt their campus was no worse than any other

35% believe their campuses are supportive of gays, lesbians, and bisexuals

35% would not recommend their campuses to other lesbians, gays, or bisexuals

Survey Questionnaire

Make sure that your name does not appear anywhere on this form.

1. Name of School _____
2. Sex   ☐ Male   ☐ Female
3. Age: _____
4. Race: ☐ Asian   ☐ Black   ☐ White
            ☐ Native American   ☐ Other (specify)_____
5. Major: _____
6. Combined SAT score:
   ☐ 1100 or higher   ☐ 900–1099   ☐ 899 or lower
7. What is your student classification?
   ☐ Freshman   ☐ Sophomore   ☐ Junior
   ☐ Senior   ☐ Graduate
8. What is your current grade point average (using a 4-point scale)?
   ☐ 3.5 or higher   ☐ 3.0–3.49   ☐ 2.5–2.99
   ☐ 2.0–2.49
9. Are you open about your sexual orientation on your campus?
   ☐ Yes   ☐ No
10. If not, why?
    ☐ Fear of reprisal   ☐ Knowledge of others' bad experiences
    ☐ Other_____

11. Are you out to your parents and family?
    □ Parents   □ Siblings   □ Other
12. Does your school consider you an out-of-state student?
    □ Yes   □ No
13. Where do you currently live?
    □ Dormitory   □ Fraternity/sorority housing
    □ Athletic dormitory   □ Off campus
    □ Off campus with partner   □ Off campus with family
14. Are you a fraternity or sorority member?   □ Yes   □ No
15. Are you a member of another student group?
    □ Yes   □ No
16. Are you on an intercollegiate athletic team?   □ Yes   □ No
17. Were you a self-acknowledged homosexual before attending college?   □ Yes   □ No
18. Did your sexual orientation affect your choice of schools?
    □ Yes   □ No
19. Had information on the climate for gays, lesbians, and bisexuals at universities and colleges been available to you, would your choice have been different?   □ Yes   □ No
20. Does your school have an active gay, lesbian, and bisexual student group?   □ Yes   □ No
21. Does your group have a formal relationship with the Student Government Association (SGA)?   □ Yes   □ No
22. Does your group receive funding from the SGA?
    □ Yes   □ No
23. How many members are currently in your campus group?_____
24. What activities, if any, have been formally sponsored on your campus? (Check all that apply for gay, lesbian, and bisexual students.)
    □ A dance   □ Speakers coming to campus
    □ A health educator dealing with safe sex and other AIDS-related issues
    □ Activities for Pride and National Coming Out Day
25. Are you a cross dresser?   □ Yes   □ No
26. Are you into the leather scene?   □ Yes   □ No

27. Where do gay, lesbian, and bisexual students congregate off campus?
    ☐ Bar   ☐ Community center
    ☐ Religious organization   ☐ Other_____

28. Do you date students from your school?   ☐ Yes   ☐ No

29. Does your dating activity take place on your campus?
    ☐ Yes   ☐ No

30. If you have a partner does he/she attend the same school?
    ☐ Yes   ☐ No

31. Did you meet him/her at school?   ☐ Yes   ☐ No

32. What is your school administration's position on gay, lesbian, and bisexual issues?
    ☐ Proactive   ☐ Negative   ☐ Noncommittal
    ☐ Don't know

33. Does your school have a committee on gay, lesbian, and bisexual issues?
    ☐ Yes   ☐ No   ☐ Don't know

34. Is sexual orientation included in the antidiscrimination policy?
    ☐ Yes   ☐ No   ☐ Don't know

35. Are counseling services provided for gay and lesbian students?
    ☐ Yes   ☐ No   ☐ Don't know

36. If housing is available on your campus for married or cohabitating couples, may those couples be same-sex?
    ☐ Yes   ☐ No   ☐ Don't know

37. Does the municipality in which your school is located have a civil rights law protecting gays, lesbians, and bisexuals against discrimination?   ☐ Yes   ☐ No   ☐ Don't know

38. In order of largest problem of your gay, lesbian, and bisexual population, rank the following (one being most serious):
    _____ Alcohol abuse
    _____ Other substance abuse
    _____ Coming out
    _____ Lack of role models, i.e. faculty/staff
    _____ Lack of student organization

39. Have you ever attempted suicide? ☐ Yes ☐ No
40. Homophobia is a serious problem at my school.
    ☐ Strongly agree ☐ Agree
    ☐ Disagree ☐ Strongly disagree
41. On your campus, have you ever been the victim of the following hate crimes? (Check all that apply.) ☐ Hate mail
    ☐ Verbal abuse ☐ Physical assault ☐ Harassment
    ☐ Vandalism ☐ Other_____
    ☐ No, I have never been a victim
42. To your knowledge, have any of these occurred on your campus (even if you have not been a victim)? ☐ Hate mail
    ☐ Verbal abuse ☐ Physical assault ☐ Harassment
    ☐ Vandalism ☐ Other_____
    ☐ No, I have never been a victim
43. How does your school administration react to hate crimes?
    ☐ Takes action against perpetrator ☐ Supports victim(s)
    ☐ Makes a stand even if unable to prosecute
    ☐ Nothing ☐ Don't know
44. Who keeps hate-crime statistics on your campus?
    ☐ School ☐ Student group ☐ Both
    ☐ Neither ☐ Don't know
45. Do you, as a gay person, feel safe on your campus?
    ☐Yes ☐No
46. I believe that the police/security at my school are supportive of gay, lesbian, and bisexual students. ☐ Strongly agree
    ☐ Agree ☐ Disagree ☐ Strongly disagree
47. Have you read any books by gay, lesbian, and bisexual authors?
    ☐ Yes ☐ No ☐ Don't know
48. Have you seen movies with gay, lesbian, and bisexual characters and themes? ☐ Yes ☐ No
49. Do you know the history of gays, lesbians, and bisexuals?
    ☐ Yes ☐ No
50. If so, were you self-taught? ☐ Yes ☐ No
51. Does your school offer courses on gay, lesbian, and bisexual issues? ☐ Yes ☐ No

52. In which department?   ☐ English   ☐ History
    ☐ Art   ☐ Women's Studies   ☐ Education
    ☐ Social Sciences   ☐ Other_____

53. Are gay men's cultural contributions part of regular
    courses?   ☐ Yes   ☐ No

54. Are lesbians' cultural contributions part of regular courses?
    ☐ Yes   ☐ No

55. Does your Health Center offer free, anonymous HIV testing?
    ☐ Yes   ☐ No   ☐ Don't know

56. Does your university offer counseling for people who have AIDS
    or who are HIV+?
    ☐ Yes   ☐ No   ☐ Don't know

57. Does your Health Center provide condoms free of charge?
    ☐ Yes   ☐ No   ☐ Don't know

58. Who provides safe-sex education?
    ☐ Health Center   ☐ Student group
    ☐ Both   ☐ Neither   ☐ Don't know

59. Have you ever been tested for HIV?   ☐ Yes   ☐ No

60. Are you positive or negative?   ☐ Positive   ☐ Negative

61. Are you symptomatic?   ☐ Yes   ☐ No

62. Were you tested on campus?   ☐ Yes   ☐ No

63. Have you ever dropped out of college or taken extended time
    off?   ☐ Yes   ☐ No

64. If so, did the reason for this involve:
    ☐ Coming out issues
    ☐ Relationship problems
    ☐ Harassment/victimization by other students
    ☐ Substance abuse
    ☐ Illness

65. Would you recommend your college or university to another gay
    student?   ☐ Yes   ☐ No

Index

Index